Advance praise for the second edition
of *Reciprocal Teaching at Work*

"If you enjoyed Lori's first edition of this book, get ready to love the second! And, if you've never learned about reciprocal teaching, this book is a must-read for you. In this edition, Lori has expanded, refined, and enhanced reciprocal teaching lesson plans and minilessons. With the hundreds of reciprocal teaching lessons Lori has taught over the past decade, her insights and understandings of this research-validated instructional approach have grown significantly. You will find reproducibles and posters for immediate classroom use, student- and teacher-tested ideas and activities for developing students' comprehension in grades K–12, teaching tips, assessment tools, and real-world classroom stories of teachers and students as they explore how to negotiate and understand complex texts. This book has it all."

—MaryEllen Vogt, Past President, International Reading Association,
Associate Professor of Education, California State University,
Long Beach, CA

"In this practical and straightforward book, Lori Oczkus addresses every challenge and answers every question I have ever encountered when working with teachers on reciprocal teaching. She provides teachers with the scaffolding they need to make this powerful approach to comprehension successful with their students. Highly recommended!"

—Kathy Au, Past President, International Reading Association,
Chief Executive Officer, SchoolRise, LLC,
Honolulu, HI

"Lori Oczkus is a master at translating reading research and theory into actual classroom practice. *Reciprocal Teaching at Work* is a very readable volume filled with practical, engaging, and effective comprehension approaches (and examples) that are certain to deepen students' understanding of the texts they read."

—Timothy Rasinski, Professor, Kent State University,
Kent, OH

"Reciprocal teaching is a method of learning for students of any age. Lori's book includes ideas that all elementary, middle, and high school teachers can immediately use to increase student understanding of any content. The engagement and deep understanding that results from the collaborative process makes it a must for all teachers."

—Cathy Bailey, Literacy Consultant,
Lincoln University, PA

"The first edition of this book changed my instruction and, more important, improved my students' learning. I was amazed by how much more I learned from this second edition. This book not only does a great job of answering questions for teachers who haven't used reciprocal teaching but also addresses problems that those who use reciprocal teaching may have encountered. This new edition addresses all grade levels, connects reciprocal teaching to Response to Intervention, and supports student independence through the gradual release of responsibility model. In addition to all this, Lori has included many new lessons and specifically guides principals and coaches on how to use the book for professional development."

—*Kathy Langham, ELL Literacy Coach, National Board Certified Teacher*
Searles Union City, CA

"The second edition of *Reciprocal Teaching at Work* delivers practical ways to utilize this research-based strategy for implementing Response to Intervention with Tier I instruction and Tier II and III interventions. Lori's engaging spin on reciprocal teaching will provide infinite possibilities for instruction and progress monitoring."

—*Mary Jo Fox, K–12 Language Arts Coordinator*
Olathe, KS

"The second edition is chock full of new material, including ideas for working with English-language learners and implementing Response to Intervention. A must-have resource for every classroom teacher, principal, literacy coach, and staff developer trying to close the achievement gap."

—*Audrey Fong, literacy/Intervention/Title I Coordinator*
Milpitas, CA

"Lori's work with students of all ages has produced a multitude of fresh, engaging, and kid-tested lessons! Teachers everywhere will be ecstatic to add these to their strategy toolbox."

—*Mary Jo Barker, Instructional Coach, National Board Certified Teacher*
Fenton, MO

Second Edition

Reciprocal Teaching

at work K–12

Powerful Strategies and Lessons
for Improving Reading Comprehension

Lori D. Oczkus

Foreword by P. David Pearson

INTERNATIONAL
Reading Association
800 BARKSDALE ROAD, PO BOX 8139
NEWARK, DE 19714-8139, USA
www.reading.org

The International Reading Association attempts, through its publications, to provide a forum for a wide spectrum of opinions on reading. This policy permits divergent viewpoints without implying the endorsement of the Association.

Executive Editor, Books   Corinne M. Mooney
Developmental Editor   Charlene M. Nichols
Developmental Editor   Stacey L. Reid
Editorial Production Manager   Shannon T. Fortner
Design and Composition Manager   Anette Schuetz

Project Editors   Charlene M. Nichols and Rebecca A. Stewart

Cover   Design: Lise Holliker Dykes; Photography; Christopher Futcher (left), courtesy of Lori Oczkus (center and right)

The publisher would appreciate notification where errors occur so that they may be corrected in subsequent printings and/or editions.

Library of Congress Cataloging-in-Publication Data

Oczkus, Lori D.

 Reciprocal teaching at work : powerful strategies and lessons for improving reading comprehension / Lori D. Oczkus. -- 2nd ed.

     p. cm.

 Includes bibliographical references and index.

 ISBN 978-0-87207-507-8

 1. Reading comprehension. 2. Reading (Elementary) 3. Cognitive learning. I. Title.

 LB1573.7.O39 2010

 372.47--dc22

                                                                                    2010022812

Suggested APA Reference: Oczkus, L.D. (2010). *Reciprocal teaching at work: Powerful strategies and lessons for improving reading comprehension* (2nd ed.). Newark, DE: International Reading Association.

To all the students and teachers who will benefit from reciprocal teaching, and, as always, with love to my Fab Four—Mark, Bryan, Rachael, and Rebecca

—Lori D. Oczkus

CONTENTS

ABOUT THE AUTHOR ix

FOREWORD xi

ACKNOWLEDGMENTS xiii

MASTER LIST OF LESSONS xv

MASTER LIST OF REPRODUCIBLES xvii

INTRODUCTION 1

CHAPTER 1 15
The Four Reciprocal Teaching Strategies

CHAPTER 2 45
*Getting Started: Introducing and Reinforcing
Reciprocal Teaching*

CHAPTER 3 91
Reciprocal Teaching in Whole-Class Sessions

CHAPTER 4 130
Reciprocal Teaching in Guided Reading Groups

CHAPTER 5   **186**

Reciprocal Teaching in Literature Circles

CONCLUSION   **240**

APPENDIX A   **253**

Informal Assessments

APPENDIX B   **258**

Strengthening Comprehension With Cross-Age Tutors and the Fab Four

APPENDIX C   **265**

Lesson Planning With the Fab Four Menu

APPENDIX D   **269**

Using Reciprocal Teaching With the Internet

APPENDIX E   **272**

Icon and Strategy Posters

REFERENCES   **279**

INDEX   **285**

ABOUT THE AUTHOR

 Lori D. Oczkus is a literacy coach, author, and popular speaker across the United States. Tens of thousands of teachers have attended her motivating, fast-paced workshops and read her practical, research-based professional books. Lori has extensive experience as a bilingual elementary teacher, intervention specialist working with struggling readers, staff developer, and literacy coach. She works regularly with students in classrooms and really knows the challenges that teachers face in teaching students to read! Lori was inducted into the California Reading Hall of Fame by the California Reading Association for her contributions to the field of reading in California and throughout the United States.

This is the second edition of Lori's best-selling book *Reciprocal Teaching at Work*. The *Reciprocal Teaching at Work* DVD (International Reading Association, 2005) won the prestigious Association of Educational Publishers Video of the Year award in 2006.

Lori's other popular titles include *Interactive Think-Aloud Lessons: 25 Surefire Ways to Engage Students and Improve Comprehension* (Scholastic & International Reading Association, 2009); *The Fabulous Four Reading Comprehension Puppets* (Primary Concepts, 2008); *Guided Writing: Practical Lessons, Powerful Results* (Heinemann, 2007); and *Super Six Comprehension Strategies: 35 Lessons and More for Reading Success* (Christopher-Gordon, 2004).

Lori resides in northern California with her husband, Mark, and their three children. She enjoys spending time with her family, traveling anywhere by any means, reading historical fiction, hiking and walking with friends, and occasionally scuba diving.

Author Information for Correspondence and Workshops
For feedback, questions, and information on professional development, you can contact Lori through her website at www .lorioczkus.com.

FOREWORD

A major question about sequels in the movies (*Superman II, Beverly Hills Cop II*, or *Son of Rin Tin Tin*) is whether they measure up to the original. The same could be asked of second editions of really good, really useful books, such as Lori Oczkus's *Reciprocal Teaching at Work: Powerful Strategies and Lessons for Improving Reading Comprehension*. While I did not write the Foreword for the first edition, I did read and use the first edition, and, more important, I have followed Lori's work over the years as a writer and professional developer in an area near and dear to my heart—the development of children's capacity to use comprehension and metacognitive strategies to improve their reading comprehension. In fact, I wrote the Foreword for another of her popular books, *Super Six Comprehension Strategies: 35 Lessons and More for Reading Success*. So, I know a lot about Lori's approach and its utility for and impact on classroom practice. And my judgment about the sequel is simple and straightforward: Lori has managed to accomplish what few Hollywood producers can—to produce a sequel that outshines the original.

How does she manage that achievement? Quite simply by providing an even clearer pathway from research to practice than she did in the original. I have always admired Lori's ability to find a way to make "honest" professionals out of us researchers by finding the unique pathway that permits our research findings to find a home in the ebb and flow of everyday classroom practice. Lori has a way of achieving what I find to be a difficult task—to "curricularize" practices that research documents as effective. It is one thing to conduct an empirical research study, even an instructional research study—as I and numerous colleagues like Annemarie Palincsar, Michael Pressley, Scott Paris, Taffy Raphael, and D. Ray Reutzel have—to validate the efficacy of strategy instruction. It is quite another to figure out how to make it real and regular in classrooms. All kinds of questions arise in curricularizing a great research finding, including the following:

- What's the right dosage? How many times a week should you use it?
- Do you mass (put all your emphasis into one strategy until kids get it under control) or distribute (present a menu of several strategies

and revisit all of them regularly) instruction within and across strategies?

- How do you help kids make a given strategy their own—so that you, as a teacher, don't have to constantly remind them when, why, and how to use it?
- How do they learn which strategy to use when?
- What does that gradual release of responsibility look like in classrooms? When do we as teachers back off? When do we intervene to provide more guidance?
- How does strategy instruction compete with and fit into everything else in the reading curriculum? In the comprehension curriculum?
- What counts as evidence that students are making progress on internalizing and using the strategy?

These are not questions that, as researchers, we are necessarily required to answer when we do a study demonstrating that if you use this strategy or this set of strategies, kids will understand, learn, and remember more from what they read. But they are questions that teachers and, if we are lucky, curriculum designers must answer. And Lori helps us answer them.

I worry a lot about comprehension instruction in our current curricular scene. With all of the emphasis on phonics, phonemic awareness, and fluency stemming from the impact of the National Reading Panel, I get a clear sense that even though comprehension and vocabulary were part of the NRP's "Big Five," they took a back seat to the "Big Three" (phonics, phonemic awareness, and fluency) in the decade of the "aughts" (2000–2009). So when Lori tells these great stories and provides compelling examples of what real teachers are really doing in their classrooms, it gives me hope and faith that not only can this kind of work be done, it IS being done—all over the United States.

As a profession, we are now perched on a ledge in the curricular landscape where a real renaissance in comprehension instruction might actually materialize. And books like this one by Lori Oczkus are just what we need to make that happen. If you are a dedicated teacher who wants to make a difference in the lives and reading dispositions of your students, you'll love this book. And your students (and parents) will thank you for moving them along the pathway to reading independence! Happy reading—and using!

—*P. David Pearson, Dean, Graduate School of Education,*
University of California, Berkeley

ACKNOWLEDGMENTS

On my last day at Stedman Elementary School, the fifth graders handed me thank-you notes for consulting in their school. Grace's heartfelt message is what reciprocal teaching is all about—helping kids improve their reading and enjoy it more.

Dear Mrs. Oczkus,

Thank you for coming to our school. The Fab Four helped me a lot in reading. Now every time that I begin to read a chapter book I predict, question, clarify, summarize, and connect. Thank you very much! It [the Fab Four] makes me want to read more. I like to read more every single day!

Sincerely,

Grace

I feel so fortunate that over the past seven years since the first edition of this book, I've enjoyed the opportunity to share reciprocal teaching with tens of thousands of teachers and students in schools across the United States and even internationally. Between these covers you will find an extension of the thinking and foundations set forth in the first edition. Here you have at your fingertips new additional kid-tested, teacher-approved, research-based lessons that improve reading instruction. I am pleased to have the opportunity to share this practical and proven material with you!

Comprehension strategy instruction that is well done (not overdone) and that emphasizes reading and meaning is alive and well! When we as educators wisely model and guide strategy instruction and then spend the majority of our class time providing time for students to read and apply the strategies, they end up like Grace—as students who enjoy reading and have improved comprehension and test scores (Allington, 2001; Routman, 2003). Reciprocal teaching is a wonderful technique for engaging students in more practice reading, because it is based on the gradual release of responsibility model of instruction (Pearson & Fielding, 1991). Thanks belong to researchers Anne Brown and Anne Palincsar, who in 1984 first brought us this wonderful multiple-strategy technique called reciprocal teaching. I am also grateful to the many other researchers listed in the references in this book who work on teachers' behalf to "prove" which teaching methods actually work. Some of my favorites include P. David Pearson, Richard Allington, Cathy Collins Block, D. Ray Reutzel, and Tim Rasinski.

I'd also like to extend a heartfelt thanks to my wonderful team of reviewers who read and quickly responded to my manuscript as I wrote it. They helped with everything from plowing through the lessons at midnight or 6 a.m. to voting on a subtitle for the book (which, by the way, is much like naming a baby). I handpicked this group for their deep knowledge of reciprocal teaching, years of experience teaching the Fab Four, and their brutal honesty. I knew they'd be picky and that way ultimately you, the reader, would end up with a more useful book! Thanks to my literacy sisters who span the country—Audrey Fong, Carol Wilcox, Mary Jo Barker, Kathy Langham, and Cathy Bailey. Thanks also to Mary Jo Fox and Ellen Osmundson who weighed in on the Response to Intervention piece. Special thanks to the editorial team at IRA led by Corinne Mooney and Charlene Nichols: I especially appreciate your trust, enthusiasm, and unwavering support for my work with teachers.

Most of all, thanks to my wonderful family for their unending support and love. My deepest appreciation goes to my husband of 25 years, Mark, and our three treasures, Bryan, Rachael, and Rebecca.

MASTER LIST OF LESSONS

Chapter 2

Lesson 1: Using a Read-Aloud to Introduce/Reinforce the Fab Four 64

Lesson 2: Using the Fab Four Bookmark 70

Lesson 3: Introducing the Reciprocal Teaching Team—The Fab Four. 75

Minilesson: Roll Your Prediction! 84

Minilesson: Pop the Questions 85

Minilesson: Pause and Clarify It! 87

Minilesson: A "Clear" Summary 89

Chapter 3

Lesson 1: Cooperative Table Groups and the Fab Four 102

Lesson 2: The Four Door Chart: Discussion Guide and Assessment Tool . . .106

Lesson 3: Which One Do We Need? Name That Strategy! 113

Lesson 4: Pass the Mat 119

Minilesson: Prediction Stroll Line 124

Minilesson: Post Your Question 125

Minilesson: Clarify and Underline a Word or Idea 126

Minilesson: Cooperative Group Summaries 128

Chapter 4

Lesson 1: A Guided Reading "Generic" Plan for Fiction or Nonfiction 148

Lesson 2: Using Graphic Organizers During Guided Reading. 155

Lesson 3: Coaching and Meeting Individual Needs During
Guided Reading 164

Lesson 4: Watch Your Qs and Cs During Reading! 169

Lesson 5: Fast Fab Four 174

Minilesson: Word Pop Prediction 178

Minilesson: Question Starters 180

Minilesson: Clarify Bookmark 181

Minilesson: Draw or Dramatize Summaries 184

Chapter 5

Lesson 1: Fishbowl: It's Your Role!. 206

Lesson 2: Jigsaw Expert Huddles. 217

Lesson 3: Rotating Roles. 220

Lesson 4: Using What I Know and What I Wonder Strips 222

Lesson 5: The Do All Four Challenge!. 225

Lesson 6: Practicing Reciprocal Teaching Strategies With the Reciprocal
Teaching Spinner 227

Lesson 7: Fab Four Free-for-All!. 231

Minilesson: I Predict That I Will Learn.... 235

Minilesson: Pick a Question. 236

Minilesson: Clarify It: Picture It! 237

Minilesson: Limited-Word Summary Challenge!. 238

MASTER LIST OF REPRODUCIBLES

Chapter 2
Fab Four Bookmark 74

Chapter 3
Instructions for Making a Four Door Chart .110
Four Door Chart 112
Fab Four Mat. 123

Chapter 4
Basic Comprehension Chart for Guided Reading Groups 153
Reciprocal Teaching Guided Reading Lesson Plan Guide 154
Fab Four Chart 160
Story Map Prediction Chart 161
Fab Four Combo Chart: Story Map/Fiction 162
Fab Four Combo Chart: Nonfiction/Compare–Contrast 163
Reciprocal Teaching Observation Chart for Guided Reading 168
Watch Your Qs and Cs Record Sheet 173
Fab Four Dial 177
Clarifying Words Bookmark 183
Clarifying Ideas Bookmark 183

Chapter 5
Reciprocal Teaching Observation Sheet 203
Self-Assessment Form for Reciprocal Teaching Literature Circles 204
Literature Discussion Sheet for Reciprocal Teaching 205
Role Sheets 211
Reciprocal Teaching Spinner 230

Appendix A

Rubric for the Reciprocal Teaching Strategies 254
Predicting 255
Questioning 255
Clarifying 256
Summarizing 256
Using the Reciprocal Teaching Team When I Read 257

Appendix B

Assessment Tool to Assess How Your Little Buddy Is Doing 263
Focused Strategy Lessons to Use With Your Little Buddy 264

Appendix C

Fab Four Lesson Plan Menu 267
Fab Four Strategy Starters 268

Appendix E

Icon Poster: Predict 273
Icon Poster: Question 273
Icon Poster: Clarify 274
Icon Poster: Summarize 274
Strategy Poster: Predict 275
Strategy Poster: Question 276
Strategy Poster: Clarify 277
Strategy Poster: Summarize 278

INTRODUCTION

I t is no wonder that reading comprehension continues to hold a prominent place on the list of "very hot" topics in the 14th annual "What's Hot" in literacy research survey conducted by Cassidy and Cassidy (2010). Teachers across the United States continue to report that students have difficulty comprehending what they read. In recent years, an alarming 69% of fourth graders and 70% of eighth graders read below the proficient reading level on the National Assessment of Educational Progress (National Center for Education Statistics, 2009). Some students can decode words, but have difficulty understanding what they read. As a staff developer and literacy coach, I have experienced this phenomenon firsthand: In the schools where I work, which range from urban to suburban schools, many students have trouble summarizing or pulling main ideas from their reading. The students may complete a reading assignment and not even realize that they had problems understanding the text. Sometimes while focusing on decoding, primary students lose comprehension as they learn to read. Second-language learners often find the vocabulary load overwhelming, and most students struggle when reading nonfiction texts. Likewise, in my own bilingual, fifth-grade classroom, the students experienced difficulty reading and understanding the grade-level social studies text and literature anthology.

Teachers often complain that students cannot remember what they read and are not really engaged with the text. Recent reading research suggests that an urgent need exists for educators to teach comprehension strategies at all grade levels from primary to secondary grades (Block, Parris, & Whiteley, 2008; Kincade & Beach, 1996; Pearson & Duke, 2002).

Students at all grade levels need strategies for clarifying unknown words and ideas that they encounter while they read. Many students need modeling and guided instruction in answering and asking comprehension questions and in making better predictions. Summarizing feels like a daunting task to many students as they struggle to sort out main ideas and order events in a text. What tested strategies can teachers use to improve their students' reading comprehension?

Reciprocal teaching is a scaffolded discussion technique that is built on four strategies that good readers use to comprehend text:

predicting, questioning, clarifying, and summarizing (Palincsar & Brown, 1984). Although reciprocal teaching was introduced in reading journals in the 1980s, this research-proven technique for teaching multiple comprehension strategies is now becoming more widely recognized and used. Students who engage in reciprocal teaching not only improve in their reading level but also retain more of the material covered in the text (Reutzel, Smith, & Fawson, 2005). Research also points to using cooperative or collaborative learning with multiple strategies and highly recommends reciprocal teaching as an effective practice that improves students' reading comprehension (National Institute of Child Health and Human Development [NICHD], 2000; Pearson & Duke, 2002; Pressley, 2002; Reutzel et al., 2005). During reciprocal teaching lessons, students assist one another in applying the four reciprocal teaching strategies.

Originally, reciprocal teaching was designed as a paragraph-by-paragraph discussion technique in which the teacher would model each of the four strategies in a think-aloud, demonstrating the use of the strategies by talking through his or her thoughts while reading. Then, students would take turns "being the teacher" and using a think-aloud with each strategy. Since the original model was developed, however, the creators (Palincsar & Brown, 1984) and others (Cooper, Boschken, McWilliams, & Pistochini, 2000; Eggleton, 1996; Lubliner, 2001) have field-tested other models and teaching ideas that build on the original intent of reciprocal teaching. Regardless of the classroom setting, which may include teacher-led or peer-led groups, the original goal of reciprocal teaching—to improve students' reading comprehension—is maintained. This teaching model allows the teacher and students to scaffold and construct meaning in a social setting by using modeling, think-alouds, and discussion.

The goals of reciprocal teaching (Harvey & Goudvis, 2007; Keene & Zimmermann, 2007; McLaughlin & Allen, 2002; Oczkus, 2004; Pearson, Roehler, Dole, & Duffy, 1992) are the following:

- To improve students' reading comprehension using four comprehension strategies: predicting, questioning, clarifying, and summarizing
- To scaffold the four strategies by modeling, guiding, and applying the strategies while reading
- To guide students to become metacognitive and reflective in their strategy use

- To help students monitor their reading comprehension using the four strategies
- To use the social nature of learning to improve and scaffold reading comprehension
- To strengthen instruction in a variety of classroom settings— whole-class sessions, guided reading groups, and literature circles
- To be part of the broader framework of comprehension strategies that comprises previewing, self-questioning, making connections, visualizing, knowing how words work, monitoring, summarizing, and evaluating

What the Research Says About Reciprocal Teaching

Palincsar and Brown (1986), known as the creators of reciprocal teaching, found that when reciprocal teaching was used with a group of students for just 15–20 days, the students' reading on a comprehension assessment increased from 30% previously to 70–80%. According to a study by Palincsar and Klenk (1991), students not only improved their comprehension skills almost immediately but also maintained their improved comprehension skills when tested a year later. This powerful teaching technique is especially effective when incorporated as an intervention for struggling readers (Cooper et al., 2000) and when used with low-performing students in urban settings (Carter, 1997). Although originally designed for small-group instruction with struggling middle school students, reciprocal teaching has proved to yield positive and consistent results with primary and upper grade elementary students who are taught in large-group, teacher-led settings and in peer groups (Coley, DePinto, Craig, & Gardner, 1993; Cooper et al., 2000; Kelly, Moore, & Tuck, 1994; Myers, 2005; Palincsar & Brown, 1984, 1986; Palincsar & Klenk, 1991, 1992). Rosenshine and Meister (1994) reviewed 16 studies of reciprocal teaching and concluded that reciprocal teaching is a technique that improves reading comprehension.

Lubliner (2001) pointed out that reciprocal teaching is an effective teaching technique that can improve on the kind of reading comprehension that is necessary not only for improved test scores but also for life in the Information Age. A growing need exists for students to learn sophisticated reading skills that they can employ in the workforce and in a world that is bursting with print materials and data. Students should be prepared to comprehend and evaluate a wide variety of complicated texts, from books to electronic sources, and reciprocal teaching strategies can help them achieve that goal.

How Reciprocal Teaching Fits Into the Rest of the Reading Program

Even though reciprocal teaching is a powerful research-based teaching technique, it is not comprehensive enough to stand alone as a method for teaching reading comprehension. Reading is a complex process that has many facets, and reciprocal teaching was designed to focus on just four important strategies that good readers use to comprehend text (predicting, questioning, clarifying, and summarizing). McLaughlin and Allen (2002) and others (Harvey & Goudvis, 2007; Keene & Zimmermann, 2007; Oczkus, 2004) provide a broad framework for teaching comprehension that comprises the following eight strategies necessary for teaching students to understand what they read:

1. *Previewing*—Activating prior knowledge, predicting, and setting a purpose
2. *Self-questioning*—Generating questions to guide reading
3. *Making connections*—Relating reading to self, text, and world
4. *Visualizing*—Creating mental pictures
5. *Knowing how words work*—Understanding words through strategic vocabulary development, including the use of graphophonic, syntactic, and semantic cueing systems
6. *Monitoring*—Asking whether a text makes sense and clarifying by adapting strategic processes
7. *Summarizing*—Synthesizing important ideas
8. *Evaluating*—Making judgments

Some additional resources that will give you the big picture for teaching reading comprehension appear in Table 1.

Think of reciprocal teaching as a reading vitamin that ensures reading success and strengthens overall comprehension instruction. The reading program provides a healthy diet of comprehension, but when students also partake in at least two weekly doses of reciprocal teaching, their reading improves and they become stronger. Reciprocal teaching

Table 1
Resources on Teaching Reading Comprehension

Block, C.C., & Parris, S.R. (2008). *Comprehension instruction: Research-based best practices* (2nd ed.). New York: Guilford.

Duffy, G.G. (2009). *Explaining reading: A resource for teaching concepts, skills, and strategies.* New York: Guilford.

Duke, N.K., & Pearson, P.D. (2002). Effective practices for developing reading comprehension. In A.E. Farstrup & S.J. Samuels (Eds.), *What research has to say about reading instruction* (3rd ed., pp. 205–242). Newark, DE: International Reading Association.

Harvey, S., & Goudvis, A. (2007). *Strategies that work: Teaching comprehension for understanding and engagement* (2nd ed.). York, ME: Stenhouse.

Hoyt, L. (2002). *Make it real: Strategies for success with informational texts.* Portsmouth, NH: Heinemann.

Keene, E.O., & Zimmermann, S. (2007). *Mosaic of thought: The power of comprehension strategy instruction* (2nd ed.). Portsmouth, NH: Heinemann.

McLaughlin, M., & Allen, M.B. (2009). *Guided comprehension in grades 3–8* (combined 2nd ed.). Newark, DE: International Reading Association.

McLaughlin, M., & Vogt, M.E. (Eds.). (2000). *Creativity and innovation in content area teaching.* Norwood, MA: Christopher-Gordon.

Miller, D. (2002). *Reading with meaning: Teaching comprehension in the primary grades.* Portland, ME: Stenhouse.

Oczkus, L.D. (2004). *Super six comprehension strategies: 35 lessons and more for reading success.* Norwood, MA: Christopher-Gordon.

Oczkus, L.D. (2009). *Interactive think aloud lessons: 25 surefire ways to engage students and improve comprehension.* New York: Scholastic; Newark, DE: International Reading Association.

Pearson, P.D. (1985). Changing the face of reading comprehension instruction. *The Reading Teacher, 38*(8), 724–738.

Pressley, M. (2002). *Reading instruction that works: The case for balanced teaching* (2nd ed.). New York: Guilford.

complements core reading instruction. In the schools in which I consult, reciprocal teaching is taught side by side with the other comprehension strategies.

We teach one of the comprehension strategies from the broader list each week, focusing on that strategy during whole-class and small-group instruction. We call this the "focus strategy of the week." Then, the teachers select a regular time for students to employ the four reciprocal teaching strategies so they can experience the power of multiple-strategy instruction. The kid-friendly term I use for the broader list is the "Super Six," which are making connections, predicting/inferring, questioning, monitoring/clarifying, summarizing/synthesizing, and evaluating (Oczkus, 2004), and the term I use for the reciprocal teaching strategies is the "Fab Four."

For example, in Kathy Langham's fifth-grade room, she posts the Super Six in a list and teaches one strategy each week with her basal reader and social studies text. The Fab Four is posted right next to the Super Six, arranged in a circle. Kathy's students use the Fab Four during literature circles with novels twice during the week. A first-grade teacher, Mr. Romero, displays the strategies in the same way, with the Super Six on one poster and the Fab Four in a circle on another. He uses a character for each of the reciprocal teaching strategies and displays props to represent and prompt each one (props will be explained in more detail later in the book). His class of 6-year-olds understands that when it is time to read with the Fab Four they will employ all four strategies in the same lesson, usually during a read-aloud or partner reading. Students benefit from ongoing instruction in all of the comprehension strategies as well as the Fab Four. Chapter 2 provides more detail about introducing reciprocal teaching in any classroom.

My Experiences With Reciprocal Teaching

What do you know about reciprocal teaching? I like to survey teachers and ask them to categorize themselves on their level of knowledge about reciprocal teaching using an exercise metaphor. See where you fit into the survey. Are you a bystander? You've heard about reciprocal teaching but haven't tried it. Or are you a walker? You've just dabbled in using the four reciprocal teaching strategies. Maybe you are a jogger, and you've actually used reciprocal teaching full force for some time. Or perhaps you are a runner or someone who has years of experience using reciprocal teaching (or RT, the unofficial nickname among fans).

When I speak to an audience of teachers and ask them if they have heard of or tried reciprocal teaching, depending on where I am in the United States, the experience level varies. Once I define the strategy, more heads nod with familiarity, but many teachers admit to having little experience with reciprocal teaching. I, too, had heard about reciprocal teaching and its effectiveness early in my teaching career, but with a busy schedule, I placed this strategy on my to-do list and only dabbled in it a bit with my students. If I had known the incredible impact that reciprocal teaching can have on reading comprehension, I certainly would have incorporated it into my teaching much sooner. Reciprocal teaching has revolutionized my teaching, and writing books on the topic has given me the opportunity to help thousands of teachers dramatically improve comprehension in their classrooms.

My interest in reciprocal teaching was awakened while I was serving as a literacy coach and consultant in an inner-city school in Berkeley, California, USA, where the staff and I used reciprocal teaching as part of an intervention for struggling readers (Cooper, Boschken, McWilliams, & Pistochini, 1999). Many of the intermediate students in our intervention read two or three years below grade level and, although they could decode words, were severely lacking in reading comprehension skills. After just three months of using the reciprocal teaching strategies with these students three times per week, we witnessed dramatic results. Many of the struggling students had jumped one or two grade levels in reading ability. We also saw their attitudes change from reluctant and negative to more confident and assured. We witnessed students who had struggled now learning to love reading.

I asked myself, if reciprocal teaching yields such promising longitudinal results in an intervention group, why not weave this strategy into the fabric of classroom reading instruction so all students could benefit from it? So began my journey. As a literacy consultant and coach in many schools in the San Francisco Bay area and around the United States, I have shared reciprocal teaching with thousands of teachers in myriad classrooms and at a variety of grade levels. As I continued using reciprocal teaching with struggling readers in various schools and settings, their teachers noticed that within a few weeks the below-level readers became more confident and motivated readers. After more results revealed that the students had improved by one to two grade levels, I began to wonder if reciprocal teaching could be applied to other teaching contexts.

I found research to support student growth in reading comprehension in a variety of settings, not just with struggling readers (e.g., Carter, 1997; Palincsar & Brown, 1984, 1986; Palincsar, Brown, & Campione, 1989; Palincsar & Klenk, 1991, 1992). Then, I began to experiment with reciprocal teaching in my own teaching during whole-class sessions, guided reading groups, and literature circles. Although it took time to introduce, model, and reinforce the reciprocal teaching strategies, the lessons were worth the effort, as my students improved their use of reading comprehension strategies and their understanding.

Because most of the students had some experience with predicting, questioning, clarifying, and summarizing, I built on their knowledge by presenting the four strategies as a package. My students enjoyed the engaging lessons and benefited from using reciprocal teaching throughout the day, because we applied the strategies in content area reading.

I have used reciprocal teaching in every way possible to strengthen students' comprehension. I have taught the reciprocal teaching strategies—predicting, questioning, clarifying, and summarizing—to the whole class by using Big Books and short newspaper and magazine articles. Reciprocal teaching provides me with a simple, consistent lesson format to use with any grade level during guided reading (see Chapter 4). We give struggling readers an extra dose of reading comprehension instruction by using reciprocal teaching in special intervention groups (see Cooper et al., 1999). During literature circles, students take on the roles of the predictor, questioner, clarifier, and summarizer as they construct together the meaning of a text while deepening their understanding of the four strategies. We also train cross-age buddies to focus on reciprocal teaching strategies as they read and discuss picture books together. By employing these strategies in a variety of settings, you can provide your students with many opportunities to use the strategies to improve their reading comprehension.

What Is New in the Second Edition?

Writing a second edition is not an easy task, especially when the first edition has been well received in the field. I still believe in the principles I wrote about in the first edition of this text. The research on reciprocal teaching remains consistent and solid. However, in the past seven years since I first wrote about reciprocal teaching, I've taught hundreds of lessons and gained new insights from many K–12 teachers across the United States and internationally. (*Reciprocal Teaching at Work* has been translated into French!) So, the main goal this time around is to share new, exciting, and easy-to-implement lessons and ideas to make your reciprocal teaching even more effective.

The second edition has the following features:

- Updated, creative, exciting lessons and tips for using reciprocal teaching in whole-class settings, guided reading groups, and literature circles

- New insights on the implementation of reciprocal teaching and easy options for getting started at any grade level
- More explicit support materials and visuals, including reproducibles and posters, to use when guiding students in the use of the four reciprocal strategies
- Ideas and lessons in every chapter that will help you differentiate instruction for all readers, including struggling readers and English-language learners (ELLs)
- Expanded specific suggestions for K–5 and adolescent literacy in grades 6–12
- Suggestions for using reciprocal teaching as a Response to Intervention (RTI)
- Additional assessment options to guide your instruction
- More ideas for helping students become independent in their use of the strategies
- Extra support materials in the appendixes, including practical ideas for using reciprocal teaching with your core district program, ways to incorporate reciprocal teaching when using the Internet, and a flexible lesson plan menu for easily creating dozens of fresh lessons for your grade level

This book is designed to equip you with all of the tools you need so that ultimately you can use reciprocal teaching to improve your students' reading comprehension skills and attitudes toward reading.

Online Staff Development Guide

In addition, I created a staff development guide that provides a detailed outline for staff development or self-study of reciprocal teaching. This guide can be found on IRA's website at www.reading.org/general/publications/books/bk507.aspx. Principals, literacy coaches, and study teams will find the suggestions helpful as they design and lead meetings.

The staff development guide includes the following:

- Proven suggestions for conducting better discussions and meetings—that is, how to get beyond "I liked...."
- Ideas for incorporating *Reciprocal Teaching Strategies at Work*, the award-winning DVD companion to the book (available at www

.reading.org), and informal free clips of reciprocal teaching in action in real classrooms (available at www.reading.org/general/publications/books/bk507.aspx)

- The Reciprocal Teaching Lesson Observation Form to use in coaching

The online guide includes the following outline of study for each chapter in the book:

1. Read and Discuss—Questions and points to consider before, during, and after reading
2. Try Reciprocal Teaching in Your Room—Lessons to try prior to meeting with colleagues
3. Professional Development Discussion Breakout Groups— Teachers choose topics and divide into teams to discuss and report back to the entire group
4. Teacher as Reader—Optional reading at the adult level to practice reciprocal teaching strategies firsthand
5. Before the Next Meeting—Suggestions for teaching and observing others

Organization of the Second Edition

The chapters of this book are organized around classroom settings and can be read in any order to suit the needs of your students and teaching style. However, I recommend reading Chapter 1 first, because it covers the rationale and important understandings central to reciprocal teaching, outlines the four reciprocal teaching strategies, and explains options for getting started. Whether you implement reciprocal teaching during whole-class lessons, guided reading groups, or literature circles, the principles of this multiple-strategy approach are the same. However, the teaching method varies slightly in each of these different settings, and you will need to make adjustments for your grade level as well (see Table 2).

Chapter 1 includes many foundational ideas to help you begin using reciprocal teaching with your class and keep it going all year long. Each of the four strategies—predicting, questioning, clarifying, and summarizing—is described in detail, with ideas for prompting students to use the language unique to it. Because teachers sometimes encounter obstacles when implementing reciprocal teaching, the chapter includes

Table 2
Reciprocal Teaching in Different Classroom Settings

Classroom Setting	Why Use Reciprocal Teaching in This Setting?
Whole-class session	• To introduce the class to reciprocal teaching strategies • To continually model the four strategies for students in teacher think-alouds • To establish common language and terms • To provide reinforcement in core required reading and content area reading throughout the school day
Guided reading group	• To reinforce or introduce reciprocal teaching strategies in a teacher-led, small-group setting • To provide extra support or intervention to students who struggle or to English-language learners • To differentiate instruction based on informal assessments and students' needs • To provide a Response to Intervention
Literature circles	• To release responsibility to students for reciprocal teaching strategies • To reinforce and strengthen student use of reciprocal teaching strategies

practical ways to overcome such difficulties and information about the four critical foundations necessary for getting the most from reciprocal teaching: scaffolding, thinking aloud, thinking metacognitively, and learning cooperatively. Models for using reciprocal teaching as an RTI plan are outlined with suggestions for using reciprocal teaching during each tier of instruction. Suggestions for incorporating reciprocal teaching into a broader list of comprehension strategies are outlined.

Chapter 2 is loaded with practical ways to introduce reciprocal teaching in your classroom. You might also try a variety of these lessons throughout the year to continue deepening your students' understanding of the strategies. Introductory lesson ideas include sharing the Fab Four using read-alouds and poetry, incorporating characters to represent each strategy, and using hand gestures to cue the strategies. Icons, posters, and bookmarks provide supports for students as they work in pairs and teams to practice the strategies. A discussion of texts and materials to use during reciprocal teaching lessons is provided.

Chapter 3 offers engaging lessons to introduce the whole class to the four reciprocal teaching strategies via depicting each strategy as a character, modeling the use of a variety of resources, and scaffolding with collaborative and partner activities. The Four Door Chart (see page 110), popular with students as well as teachers, serves as a useful discussion guide and progress-monitoring assessment too. Practical lessons assist students in remembering and internalizing reciprocal teaching strategies for eventual independent use.

Many new ideas for leading students in reciprocal teaching discussions in guided reading groups are given in Chapter 4. Lessons for use with fiction and nonfiction are outlined. These teacher-led, small-group lessons can be the training ground for students' transfer to literature circles. The chapter includes a variety of suggestions for using graphic organizers, learning cooperatively, and teaching word analysis. In addition, intervention lesson ideas for struggling students are provided, along with suggestions for the effective use of coaching prompts during guided reading. Practical ideas for keeping the rest of the class busy during guided reading are outlined.

Chapter 5 explores reciprocal teaching in literature circles, which is an excellent way to continue to provide students with opportunities to strengthen their use of reciprocal teaching strategies as they become more independent. Lessons for introducing the roles of predictor, questioner, clarifier, and summarizer are provided. The chapter also outlines a special discussion director role that rounds out the literature circle with prompts for connecting students' background knowledge and questions to the text. Many innovative tools, such as role sheets, a discussion spinner, and minilessons on each of the four strategies, are included. Easy options for getting started with literature circles are included as well as suggestions for teaching students literature circle social skills. Finally, the chapter offers literature circle assessment tools for students and teachers.

The Conclusion summarizes the main points about reciprocal teaching as an effective method for teaching reading comprehension and offers a quick reference for readers who have a specific question about how or why reciprocal teaching should be part of their classroom agenda. In the Conclusion, teachers' common questions about reciprocal teaching are addressed in a practical question and answer format.

The appendixes include the following useful tools to support reciprocal teaching in the classroom:

- Appendix A: Informal Assessments
- Appendix B: Strengthening Comprehension With Cross-Age Tutors and the Fab Four
- Appendix C: Lesson Planning With the Fab Four Menu
- Appendix D: Using Reciprocal Teaching With the Internet
- Appendix E: Icon and Strategy Posters

Special Features in This Book

The lessons in Chapters 2 through 5 all follow a similar format (see box).

Background and Description	• Thoughts and reflections on and experiences from using the lesson • Brief description of the lesson • Reciprocal teaching strategies emphasized and what else may be needed
Materials	• Supplies needed for the lesson
Teacher Modeling	• Providing scaffolded instruction; modeling the strategies for students in a think-aloud
Student Participation	• Releasing to students the responsibility for using the strategies first in partners and collaborative teams, then independently
Assessment Tips	• Assessing students after the lesson

Minilessons that focus on individual reciprocal teaching strategies are found near the end of each chapter and can be used when students need reinforcement for a particular strategy. The minilessons follow the same format with similar headings as the longer lessons in each chapter. Keep in mind that reciprocal teaching strategies should be taught in concert with one another, so if you focus on only one strategy during a minilesson, let your students know how that strategy fits back into the larger framework of all four reciprocal teaching strategies used to comprehend text. Remind your students that readers rarely use one strategy at a time while reading; instead, they use the four strategies together as they make their way through a text.

Throughout this book you will find the "Classroom Story" feature, which includes detailed accounts of reciprocal teaching lessons taken from classrooms around the United States. Some of these stories focus on the strategies specifically, and others help show you what the strategies look like at a variety of grade levels. You will also find many classroom examples throughout each chapter to give you a better look at how reciprocal teaching looks at a variety of grade levels. I include a combination of actual student and teacher names as well as pseudonyms, because some of the lessons are retold exactly as they happened and others are combinations of lessons I've taught or observed. So as you read, you'll find dozens of classroom examples sprinkled throughout the book to provide you with a variety of examples of reciprocal teaching in action!

This book extends the successful research of those who have so generously shared their reciprocal teaching ideas. The chapters are organized in a practical manner to make it easy for you to implement this instructional method in your own classroom. In addition to the many chapter features previously described, each chapter contains ready-to-use reproducible forms that will help students understand the reciprocal teaching strategies and the texts that they are reading. The goal of this book is to provide you with the practical, motivating tools that you need to improve the reading comprehension of all students by using reciprocal teaching strategies.

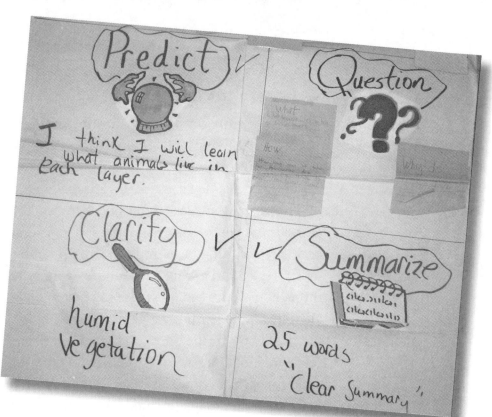

CHAPTER 1

The Four
RECIPROCAL
TEACHING
Strategies

Prediction is when you say what you think is going to happen in the book and you look at all the clues like the cover, pictures, and chapter headings.

—Rachael, grade 4

Reciprocal teaching is a scaffolded discussion technique that incorporates four main strategies—predicting, questioning, clarifying, and summarizing—that good readers use together to comprehend text. Think about how you use these strategies in your own reading as an adult. For example, when you read an article in a newspaper, magazine, or on the Internet, first you look at visuals and skim as you predict what it is about. Then as you read, you alternate between clarifying ideas and words by rereading and using other fix-up strategies and asking questions or wondering. You summarize throughout your reading and predict what will come next. All readers do all of this quite naturally every time they read. I like to call the strategies the "Fab Four" or the "Be the Teacher" strategies, because students can relate to and understand these terms. I often model them for students and even explain how I use these four strategies in my own reading to make the point that all readers use these as they work through text. The idea with reciprocal teaching is to name the strategies as we use them to bring them to a more explicit level for our students.

Reciprocal teaching fits with any grade-level lesson using fiction or nonfiction. Following are just a few examples of how all four strategies can be used in lessons at a variety of grade levels ranging from K to 12.

- First graders gather on the rug as Mrs. Chang reads aloud the Big Book *Funky Fish* by Jill Eggleton. She stops periodically throughout the reading to ask the students to make hand motions that represent each of the strategies—predict, question, clarify, and summarize. The students turn to partners to share their thoughts aloud as they use each of the strategies. The class makes a list of words to clarify and strategies for figuring them out.

- Down the hall, the fifth graders in Mr. Erickson's room sit in literature circles and each take on a different role as they work their way through a nonfiction text on volcanoes using the reciprocal teaching strategies. The discussion director leads the group members in a lively exchange as they predict, question, clarify, and summarize the reading material. After they read, they make a poster with a 25-word summary and a drawing to share with the class.

- Across town at the high school, ninth graders form discussion circles with other students who've read the same stories by Edgar Allan Poe. They each jot down a quick-write prior to the discussion and then share their brief predictions, questions, words and ideas to clarify, and summaries. They each share a "Why do you think..." discussion starter and informally run through the reciprocal teaching strategies.

Each reciprocal teaching strategy plays an important role in the overall reading comprehension process. As I mentioned earlier, the four strategies are part of a larger reading comprehension program that is based on all the strategies that good readers use, such as previewing, self-questioning, visualizing, making connections, monitoring, knowing how words work, summarizing, and evaluating (McLaughlin & Allen, 2002; Oczkus, 2004). However, when we use reciprocal teaching we focus solely on four key reading strategies—predict, question, clarify, and summarize—as we use them in a package rather than separately. The order in which the reciprocal teaching strategies are used is not fixed; it depends on the text and the reader. For example, sometimes when I am reading a mystery with students, we naturally pause between chapters, bursting with predictions for what will happen next before we summarize, ask questions, and clarify the clues that we have so far. Other times, however, it may be more natural to summarize and clarify before making predictions and asking further questions.

This chapter offers a description of each reciprocal teaching strategy, along with prompts and tools to encourage students to use the language of a given strategy. The prompts provide students with the necessary support to become independent in the strategies, and, when combined with constant modeling of the strategies, they also help students deepen their reading comprehension and ability to apply the reciprocal teaching strategies. This chapter also covers ways to overcome common obstacles your students may encounter when using the four strategies, as well as suggestions for materials to use and ways to group students during reciprocal teaching. Ideas for using reciprocal teaching as a schoolwide RTI strategy are also included.

Predicting

Many students have been exposed to this popular strategy. Students often define predicting as a form of guessing, and they seem to enjoy making predictions. Predicting goes beyond guessing and involves previewing the text to anticipate what may happen next. Readers can

Table 3	
Predicting With Fiction and Nonfiction	
Predicting With Fiction	**Predicting With Nonfiction**
Preview cover, title, and illustrations.	Preview headings, illustrations, and text features, such as maps, captions, and tables.
Preview text structure looking for clues using story structure: setting, characters, problem, resolution, events, and a theme or lesson.	Look for clues to predict.
Use the frame: I think this is about...because....	Preview text structure and decide if it is compare–contrast, sequence, main idea and details, cause–effect.
	Use the frame: I think I will learn...because....

use information from the text along with their prior knowledge to make logical predictions before and during reading. Predicting differs when reading fiction or nonfiction. Refer to Table 3 to note the differences.

For both fiction and nonfiction, stop periodically during the reading and ask students to gather clues from the text read up to that point and to look ahead to make predictions for the next portion of the text. In addition to discussing predictions you can use a graphic organizer, such as a story map or Venn diagram, which fits the text type. Giving students the opportunity to preview what they read by discussing text features and using graphic organizers provides them with visual clues for predicting.

The language that students may use with predicting includes the following phrases (Mowery, 1995; Oczkus, 2009):

I think....

I'll bet....

I wonder if....

I imagine....

I suppose....

I predict....

I think I will learn...because....

I think...will happen because....

Predicting is a strategy that assists students in setting a purpose for reading and in monitoring their reading comprehension. It allows students to interact more with the text, making them more likely to become interested in the reading material while improving their understanding (Fielding, Anderson, & Pearson, 1990; Hansen, 1981). In my experience, students seem to enjoy predicting and do so with exuberance.

Questioning

I teach students to ask several types of questions during reciprocal teaching. I often bring in a toy microphone as a prop to help me make metaphors about questioning as we read. I tell students that before and during reading, good readers ask wonder questions. During reading we ask quiz questions or questions that are answered or inferred from the text. I tell students that quiz questions are like the type asked on the popular television program *Are You Smarter Than a 5th Grader?* Many students begin by asking questions about unimportant details. However, as I continue to model question formulation and students share their questions with the class, the quality and depth of their questions increase. I also model how to ask questions based on inferences and main points in a text. Finally, I model how to ask thinking or discussion-type questions, such as "Why do you think...?" One fourth grader asked his literature circle, "Why do you think the *Titanic* was so important?" Questioning motivates students to interview, quiz, and challenge one another to think deeply about the text.

Younger students and adolescents naturally wonder and ask questions about the world around them. When students are encouraged and taught to ask questions as they read, their comprehension deepens (Armbruster, Lehr, & Osborn, 2001; Keene & Zimmermann, 1997). Good readers ask questions throughout the reading process (Cooper, 1993; Palincsar & Brown, 1986), but formulating questions is a difficult and complex task. When students know prior to reading that they each need to think of a question about the text, they read with an awareness of the text's important ideas. They automatically increase their reading comprehension when they read the text and generate a question (Lubliner, 2001). During reciprocal teaching discussions, students can be asked to "be the teacher" as they create questions to ask one another that are based on important points in the reading.

Most students enjoy asking questions and being the teacher during reciprocal teaching discussions. For example, during guided reading sessions, try giving each student a sticky note to mark the portion of text that he or she wants to turn into a question. Then have students share their questions with one another. Students of all grade levels seem to have difficulty waiting to ask their questions, and they prefer to ask questions before they summarize, clarify, or predict the next portion of text. I have learned that it is best to take advantage of the students' enthusiasm, and I allow students to share questions with the group first. If we are short on class time, I will pair students and have them ask their partners questions, or I will have the students individually write down their questions.

Questioning is an important strategy for good readers. In reciprocal teaching lessons, students learn to generate questions about a text's main idea and important details, and about textual inferences, thereby improving their reading comprehension skills. In addition, questioning often becomes the favored strategy of many students.

Clarifying

Clarifying or monitoring comprehension includes more than just figuring out difficult words in a text. A broader definition of clarifying includes keeping track of one's comprehension of the text and knowing fix-up strategies to maintain meaning during reading. I once observed a creative second-grade teacher use a toy car and tool belt to help explain to her students this concept. The teacher placed the toy car under a text while reading a Big Book. Then, from time to time, she would pretend that the car was stuck and at the same time stop at a difficult word or sentence to clarify. She wore a toy tool belt and pulled out her gadgets to help her clarify, which included a pointer or rereader to read over confusing parts or words; a different pointer for a read-on tool to read ahead for clues to figure out words; a word chopper for breaking words into known parts, including beginning and ending sounds, familiar word parts, and syllables; and a glittery pair of "visualizing" glasses to help make pictures in the readers' heads. What a great metaphor for what it means to clarify while reading!

Clarifying helps students monitor their own comprehension as they identify problems they are having in comprehending portions of text or figuring out difficult words. Clarifying is a complex strategy that involves two basic steps: (1) identifying or admitting that one is stuck on a word or idea, and then (2) figuring out how to remedy the situation. Most students can easily begin by identifying words that they need help deciphering. I often model how to figure out a difficult word and call on volunteers to share such words and describe how they figured them out. We also may work through a word together by discussing known word chunks and sounds and the context around the word. If your students are reluctant to admit that any vocabulary or larger portions of text have caused them problems, a good strategy is to ask them to find a word (or part of the text) that they figured out but that might be difficult for a younger student. Then, ask them to tell the class how they would teach the word to the younger student. Sometimes, this technique increases student participation when a class is first starting to learn about clarifying.

Although students can be taught to identify difficult words readily and work through them, it is far more difficult for some students to recognize unclear sentences, passages, or chapters. Perhaps the difficulties occur because even though students can read every word in a given portion of text, they still do not understand the main idea of the reading. During this step of reciprocal teaching, the teacher and students have the opportunity to share fix-up strategies to construct meaning. I find it extremely helpful to model clarifying using the strategy frame "I didn't get the sentence...so I...." I then select an entire sentence and put a larger sticky note under it directly on the book or text and model how to reread, read on, and figure out an unclear sentence. Next, I ask the students to find another sentence that is tricky and mark it using a sticky note. Using the prompt encourages students and gives struggling readers and ELLs language they can rely on.

The language of clarifying may include the following prompts:

Identifying the problem

- I didn't get [the word, sentence, part, visual, chapter] so I [used fix-up strategies, reread, read on, broke the word into parts, skipped it, asked a friend, thought about my connections]
- I didn't understand the part where....
- This [sentence, paragraph, page, chapter] is not clear. This doesn't make sense.
- I can't figure out....
- This is a tricky word, because....

Clarifying strategies

To clarify an idea

- I reread the parts that I don't understand.
- I read on to look for clues.
- I think about what I know.
- I talk to a friend.

To clarify a word

- I reread.
- I look for word parts that I know.
- I try to blend the sounds together.
- I think of another word that looks like this word.
- I read on to find clues.
- I try another word that makes sense.

The clarifying step of reciprocal teaching makes problem solving during reading more explicit for students. When they learn to identify and clarify difficult words or confusing portions of text, students become more strategic readers.

Summarizing

Teaching students to summarize is a research-based, effective way to improve overall comprehension (Duke & Pearson, 2002). Reciprocal teaching provides students with many opportunities to exercise their summarizing muscle as they formulate frequent verbal summaries throughout the reading of a text. Summarizing is a complex process that requires the orchestration of various skills and strategies, including recalling important events or details, ordering points, and using synonyms or selecting vocabulary. The summary organization is based on the type of text—either narrative or expository (Lipson, 1996). When summarizing a story, students may use the setting, characters, problem, events, and resolution to guide their summaries. A nonfiction text requires students to determine important points or categories of information and arrange them in a logical order. It is no wonder students often moan and groan (and teachers, too!) when we say, "Time to summarize," because summarizing is a challenging strategy.

There are many creative ways you can engage students in summarizing. To provide more practice and improve students' abilities to summarize, try stopping throughout a text to allow students to give verbal summaries or dramatize text rather than requiring them to always write summaries of longer pieces of text. You might ask each student to select a favorite part of a chapter in a novel or book and sketch on a sticky note a quick drawing to represent that scene (Oczkus, 2009). Then, other students in the group can share their favorite parts, and the group can place the parts in order and practice a group verbal summary. Or, students can write down five key points from a nonfiction text and make up hand motions for each word or phrase for a hand motion summary (Oczkus, 2009). Summary practice can be fun as we guide students to select and order main points in any text.

During reciprocal teaching, the teacher and students take turns modeling summarizing throughout a text. Students may use the following prompts to guide their summaries:

- The most important ideas in this text are....

- This part was mostly about....

- This book was about....

- First,....

- Next,....

- Then,....

- Finally,....

- The story takes place....

- The main characters are....

- A problem occurs when....

Summarizing is extremely important because strong evidence exists that practice in summarizing improves students' reading comprehension of fiction and nonfiction alike, helping them construct an overall understanding of a text, story, chapter, or article (Rinehart, Stahl, & Erickson, 1986; Taylor, 1982). In reciprocal teaching lessons, students are provided with frequent opportunities to witness others' summarizing and to participate in creating their own summaries, which helps them become more proficient readers.

Overcoming Obstacles When Implementing Reciprocal Teaching

Although study results indicate that students benefit from instruction using reciprocal teaching (see Introduction for examples), teachers may encounter some common problems when implementing the strategies in their classrooms. Table 4 lists some of these problems—such as students' struggling to use the strategies, creating a noisy classroom, and becoming bored with the strategies—and their possible solutions. Teachers also can anticipate difficulties with a specific reciprocal teaching strategy and overcome them with the suggestions provided in Table 5.

Table 4
Problems That Teachers May Encounter With Reciprocal Teaching and Suggested Solutions

Problem	Solution
Your students are not able to employ all four reciprocal teaching strategies easily.	• Use teacher modeling to introduce reciprocal teaching. Frequent teacher modeling is necessary. • You and your students can participate in think-alouds during which students explain how and why each strategy is helping them read.
Your students are having trouble using the four strategies in longer texts.	• Start by using small chunks of text, such as a few paragraphs, and try gradually increasing the chunks used during reciprocal teaching lessons to pages, lessons, and eventually entire chapters.
You are not sure how to assess your students' progress.	• Observe your students' verbal responses. • Ask students to write brief individual responses for each strategy, or have a group collaborate on a response. • To assess individual progress, call on any student in the group to share, or collect written responses. (See Four Door Chart, page 110.)
Even with teacher modeling, your students still are not employing the strategies on their own.	• Scaffold students' progress through teacher or peer models, and have students take turns using the strategies. Allow for this constant turn-taking for the strategy to work well. • Ask students to verbalize why each strategy is important. Metacognition will aid them in using the strategies when they read on their own. • At the start of a lesson, ask students to share examples of how they used the Fab Four in their reading at home or on their own. Encourage specific examples. • Bring in your reading material from home and demonstrate a think-aloud using a brief excerpt from a newspaper or magazine article. Tell how you use the Fab Four.

(continued)

Table 4 (*continued*)
Problems That Teachers May Encounter With Reciprocal Teaching and Suggested Solutions

Problem	Solution
The classroom sometimes is noisy during reciprocal teaching lessons.	• Reciprocal teaching does require discussion and a certain amount of noise, but instruct students on how to work together quietly. Encourage six-inch voices whereby students whisper so a person sitting six inches away can hear them but no farther away. • Circulate around the room to observe and listen in on groups. Call on groups to perform for the class and model quiet discussions.
You feel that you do not have enough time for reciprocal teaching strategies.	• Have students talk through the four strategies (as opposed to writing them). • Find time by weaving the strategies throughout the day into your core reading and content area lessons. Once students are familiar with the four strategies, you can fit them into lessons you are already teaching. • Only use reciprocal teaching in discussions without any writing to save time and provide more practice. • Once students are familiar with all four strategies, select just one or two per lesson to model in a think-aloud. • Use reciprocal teaching at least two or three times per week in any combination of settings in order to see results.
Your struggling readers are having trouble using reciprocal teaching strategies with peers in grade-level material.	• Try meeting with struggling readers once a week to practice the strategies. Meet as an intervention group twice a week all year if possible. • Keep modeling each of the strategies! • Use reciprocal teaching as a Tier II Response to Intervention plan for struggling readers. Be sure to monitor and assess weekly. Teach minilessons when needed or move students into Tier III lessons with fewer students in the group and even easier text.
Reciprocal teaching has become boring for the students or the teacher.	• Do not use teacher-led lessons all the time. Let students select reading material, and group by interest. • Use the lesson ideas for each strategy found in the chapters of this book. Try something fun with one of the four strategies in each lesson. • Include in your lessons other reading comprehension strategies such as making connections to prior knowledge and responding to literature.

Reciprocal Teaching at Work: Powerful Strategies and Lessons for Improving Reading Comprehension (second edition) by Lori D. Oczkus. © 2010. Newark, DE: International Reading Association. This table adapted from Hacker, D.J., & Tenent, A. (2002). Implementing reciprocal teaching in the classroom: Overcoming obstacles and making modifications. *Journal of Educational Psychology, 94*(4), 699–718. May be copied for classroom use.

Table 5
Overcoming the Difficulties That Students Experience With Reciprocal Teaching Strategies

For Common Problems Students Have With...	Try...
Predicting • Making imaginative predictions that are not based on textual clues • Making wild predictions that don't relate to the text • Making simple, surface-level predictions • Not returning to predictions after reading to check their accuracy • Not predicting using prior events in fiction • Predicting awkwardly with expository text • Not using text features to predict in nonfiction	• Modeling predictions by using think-alouds and textual clues • Teacher modeling of surface-level predictions and below-the-surface predictions (e.g., lessons to be learned) • Inviting the discussion director of small reciprocal teaching groups (see Chapter 4) to return to predictions after reading to check accuracy • Periodically stopping and summarizing what has happened so far and adding, "Now I think...because...." • Asking students to preview illustrations and headings and think about what they believe they will learn from an expository text
Questioning • Asking only literal or superficial questions • Asking silly, trivia-type questions • Not asking any inferential questions • Younger students not understanding what a question is • Needing more practice in asking questions	• Modeling how to formulate different types of questions • Continually modeling higher level questions that require using textual clues and prior knowledge • Asking students to reflect: How does this question help us understand the text? • Providing question starters, such as "Why do you think...?" • Giving students three-word question starters such as "How did the...?"—use a toy microphone to prompt questioning • Asking students to read the material and write several questions before meeting with a group • Asking partners to alternate roles—one student reads aloud and the other asks a question • Having students first read the material silently while hunting for questions, then read the material aloud before writing questions to answer and discuss
Clarifying • Skipping the clarifying step altogether because they think there is nothing to clarify • Clarifying words, not ideas • Letting the teacher do all the clarifying • Confusing clarifying and questioning	• Modeling words and ideas to clarify • Using the prompt "I didn't get the [word, idea, chapter] so I...." • Requiring that every student provide an example (tell them, if they have nothing to clarify, to select a word or idea a younger student might have trouble reading) • Having students hunt for places in the text where they visualized or had difficulty visualizing and reread • Using the Clarifying Bookmarks (see page 183)

(continued)

Table 5 (continued) Overcoming the Difficulties That Students Experience With Reciprocal Teaching Strategies	
For Common Problems Students Have With...	**Try...**
Clarifying (continued)	• Providing copies of one page of a text and having students underline words to clarify in one color and sentences to clarify in another • Asking students to circle or write words or sentences to clarify • Using this prompt to get at clarifying misconceptions and strategies for solving—"I didn't get the.... so I...." • Modeling the difference between questioning and clarifying • If using the characters, discussing the difference between Clara Clarifier's job and Quincy Questioner's job
Summarizing • Giving summaries that are word-by-word retellings of the text • Providing summaries that miss main points or that are too long • Rarely including main themes in summaries • Disliking summarizing because it is difficult for them	• Having students work in groups on other strategies but as a class to contribute to a teacher-guided summary • Asking groups to write a summary to share with the class for comments and ideas for revision, then having them rewrite and share again on large posters or transparencies or the document camera • Having groups write and share summaries, and asking the class to vote for the strongest summary • Getting at deeper themes by asking students to write letters to you or a classmate telling what they learned from the book • Trying the "clear" summary minilesson in Chapter 2 (page 89) • Making the summarizer task fun by having a student be a reporter, and using a toy microphone or drawing a quick sketch on a whiteboard or sheet of paper

Reciprocal Teaching at Work: Powerful Strategies and Lessons for Improving Reading Comprehension (second edition) by Lori D. Oczkus. © 2010. Newark, DE: International Reading Association. This table adapted from Hacker, D.J., & Tenent, A. (2002). Implementing reciprocal teaching in the classroom: Overcoming obstacles and making modifications. *Journal of Educational Psychology, 94*(4), 699–718. May be copied for classroom use.

The Essential Lesson Foundations

In addition to being aware of the problems that students may encounter when using each strategy, successful reciprocal teaching instruction includes the following four instructional foundations: scaffolding, think-alouds, metacognition, and cooperative learning.

Scaffolding	• Are there opportunities for students to witness a strong model done by a teacher or other student?
	• Is there supported guided practice with peers?
	• Are visual and other supports (gestures, posters, strategy starters) available to cue students to use the strategies?
Think-alouds	• Did the teacher conduct one or more think-alouds by reading aloud from the text and demonstrating his or her thinking?
	• Did the teacher truly model and not just assign the strategies?
Metacognition	• Did the lesson open with a quick review of the strategies and their definitions?
	• Did the lesson end with a discussion of how the strategies helped with the text that day?
	• During reading, did the teacher and students discuss the "how to" steps for each of the strategies?
Cooperative learning	• Did students work in pairs or groups to discuss the Fab Four?

Keep these building blocks in mind when introducing and extending reciprocal teaching lessons in any setting, from whole-class groupings to literature circles.

The four foundations work together in the following ways to make lessons successful:

- The teacher models using constant think-alouds.

- Students work in cooperative pairs or teams to practice on their own cooperatively.

- The teacher expertly provides the right amount of scaffolding, which might include a language frame or prompt such as "I didn't get...so I...."

- The lesson also includes lots of metacognition as students and the teacher discuss the steps to using each strategy and at the end of the lesson know which one was most helpful.

When I demonstrate and coach lessons in classrooms, I ask teachers to watch carefully for each of the following foundations that support students as they employ reciprocal teaching strategies. Please note that for each of the four foundations I've included a classroom example to show how the foundations enhance the reciprocal teaching lessons and ultimately comprehension.

Scaffolding

Scaffolding reading instruction is similar to teaching a child how to ride a bicycle. First, the child watches people riding bicycles to get the idea and motivation for his or her own riding skills. Then, the parent holds on to the bicycle's seat and guides the child for a time. Eventually, the parent lets go of the seat but remains nearby (possibly even running next to the bicycle) in case support is needed. Finally, the child pedals away on his or her own.

During reciprocal teaching, the instruction is scaffolded, or supported. The students can see models of the four strategies, experience some "seat holding" as they try out reciprocal teaching in a supported environment, and, finally, work independently as they read while using reciprocal teaching strategies to help them comprehend the text. Every time students are engaged in reciprocal teaching, each has the opportunity to participate in scaffolded instruction, because modeling and support are integral steps of the reciprocal teaching model (see Figure 1). Therefore, students are propelled to the next reading level as the support that they receive guides them through more difficult texts and reading tasks. This support is often called the gradual release of responsibility, as students move through the steps from observing the teacher to performing the task on their own (Pearson & Fielding, 1991). I like the simplicity of the steps—I do, we do, you do—to show the progression of scaffolding.

Other scaffolds that support students as they try out the strategies include using characters, props, or hand motions to represent each strategy. Visual scaffolds include icons, bookmarks, and posters with the language of the strategies clearly displayed so students can refer to them as they use the strategies with peers and on their own. These tools also provide you with ways to prompt students as they practice the reciprocal teaching strategies in a variety of texts.

Classroom Example   Mrs. Valentino reads aloud from a second-grade basal text to her class and stops to model her predictions after reading the first page. She uses the strategy frame "I think...because..." and bases her prediction on the events that just occurred in the text. She explains

Figure 1
Teacher Providing Support to Students

the rationale for her prediction by rereading a portion of the text. Then, she asks students to turn to a partner and also use the frame. She continues modeling using the strategy frames for clarifying, questioning, and summarizing. When partners work together to practice the strategies they use their bookmarks and a classroom poster with icons and strategy frames to guide their discussions. (These materials will be discussed in Chapter 2.)

Think-Alouds

Reciprocal teaching is not a pencil-and-paper activity. It was designed as a discussion technique in which think-alouds play an integral part. During a reciprocal teaching think-aloud, the reader talks aloud about each of the four strategies. Think-alouds show students what a good reader is thinking while reading, which again provides scaffolding toward developing good reading comprehension.

The steps to reading comprehension are less tangible than, say, the steps to a math problem, so this type of instruction may be new to teachers and students alike. Successful reciprocal teaching gives students ongoing opportunities to witness and conduct think-alouds using the four strategies. The teacher should not introduce reciprocal teaching and then abandon the modeling. Instead, some teacher modeling in the form of think-alouds should occur every time students engage in reciprocal teaching lessons and should be conducted by the teacher and the students, who can take turns verbalizing the use of the reciprocal teaching strategies. This method allows students to see more clearly the steps to creating understanding while reading.

The steps to a good think-aloud include the following (Oczkus, 2009):

1. Introduce the strategy	• Ask students what they know about it. • Define the strategy (e.g., "Questioning is when..."). • Options include using a prop, such as a toy microphone for questioning.
2. Model each strategy through a think-aloud	• Think aloud using an example from the reading material: "When I read this, I [predict, question, clarify, summarize]"
3. Provide support and guided practice	• Pairs or teams of students turn and talk, and find examples.
4. Provide independent practice	• Students look for examples to share later with their pairs or groups.
5. Wrap up	• Ask students what they learned about the reading and which strategy helped them the most as they read, predicted, questioned, summarized, and clarified.

Classroom Example   The fifth graders pull out their weekly news magazines and prepare to read about earthquakes. Mr. Clark reads aloud the first column of the page-long article and pauses to model his thinking. After asking the students what they know about summarizing, he rereads the text, tells how he selects the important key points, summarizes, and asks students to turn and share the summary with a partner. Mr. Clark continues alternating between modeling aloud and allowing partners to turn and chat about the remaining three strategies: predict, question, and clarify. The students read the rest of the article independently and share with their partners questions, words, or sentences to clarify, and their updated summaries. To end the lesson, Mr. Clark asks students to reflect on which strategy helped them the most in understanding earthquakes.

Metacognition

Metacognition is the awareness of one's own thinking processes. The think-aloud process goes hand in hand with metacognition, as students talk about their thinking and how they are using predictions, questions, clarifications, and summaries. As the teacher, you can lead your students by sharing how the strategies have helped you comprehend a given text. Think of comprehension lessons as "metacognitive sandwiches," because you begin the lesson with the objective, such as a minilesson on predicting, and you end the lesson with a review by students of how the strategy helped them. I find that most students can name the strategy that helped them the most during the lesson but find it difficult to describe how or why. When you first ask students to tell how the strategies helped them, you will need to provide explanations and assistance. For example, when a student replies that predicting helped him most today but can't explain why, you might add, "Predicting helps us stay interested in the text and to keep on reading to see what happens next." Most likely you will get head nods for your modeling. Eventually students will begin to explain their strategy use without as much prompting. Another technique I really like to use, especially with primary students, is to ask, "Which strategy did you like using the most today?" Primary students (and sometimes intermediate students, too) answer this one with zeal. For example, one first grader told me she liked questioning because we used the toy microphone, it was fun, and it made her feel smart. What could be better than that?

A discussion rich with metacognitive thinking will include student comments such as the following:

> Prediction helped me the most today because it got me interested in the reading.

Clarifying helped me figure out the word *citizen*, because I thought of the word *city*, and I reread the sentence to see what made sense.

Summarizing helped me remember all the important events in the story.

I had to reread the book to get the main idea, so I could ask a question.

Metacognition is an integral component in reciprocal teaching, because students learn to consciously think about and reflect on their strategy use. Ultimately, all students are trained to employ the same strategies that good readers use when monitoring their reading comprehension, and, therefore, students improve their own comprehension.

Classroom Example   The students in Mrs. Carr's fourth-grade class finish reading the social studies lesson on the California Gold Rush. She asks the students to reflect on how the Fab Four helped them understand the text. Sammy says that summarizing several times throughout the reading helped him remember the main points. Kadeem felt that clarifying using the frame "I didn't get the sentence, so I..." helped him reread to make sure he understood the hardest concepts. Questioning was fun for Sara as she stumped her group and they were forced to reread and infer to answer her question. Kendra enjoyed scanning the text and studying the pictures and captions before reading to make predictions.

Cooperative Learning

The National Reading Panel (Armbruster et al., 2001) recommends cooperative learning for improved reading comprehension, especially in content area texts. Because reciprocal teaching is intended to be a discussion technique, cooperative learning is integral to it. Reciprocal teaching builds on the cooperative nature of learning that causes one's reading comprehension to be deepened through social interactions. Cooperative learning provides opportunities for struggling readers and ELLs to participate in the lessons through discussions, even when the text may be above their reading level. The cooperative learning may include constant "turn and talk" with partners, triads, and table groups (see Figure 2). Although in this book I show you how to make quick-write tools, such as a Four Door Chart (discussed in Chapter 3), keep in mind that *all* of the positive research results were achieved with reciprocal teaching as an oral discussion technique not a writing assignment. If you wish to achieve positive growth in your students' comprehension, provide time for cooperative discussions using

Figure 2
Students Engaged in Cooperative Learning

reciprocal teaching. Keep the writing at a minimum with the purpose of prompting the discussions.

The cooperative nature of reciprocal teaching is an important part of the scaffolded instruction, think-alouds, and metacognition inherent to reciprocal teaching lessons. Even when I teach whole-class lessons, I incorporate quick activities throughout the lesson that require students to turn to a partner in order to engage the students in more cooperative learning practices. Cooperative learning also occurs when students and teachers think aloud during discussions and their metacognition is made public. According to Kagan (1989), cooperative learning needs to encompass positive interdependence, individual accountability, equal participation, and simultaneous interaction. When students participate in reciprocal teaching lessons, they are held accountable for their role and have ample opportunities to participate.

The following are some examples of cooperative learning in various classroom settings: If the class is reading a social studies text, I may model a summary of a portion of it and ask partners to work together to create a summary for the next section. When reading a novel as a class, groups of students each may be assigned a strategy to report on to the class. Even during guided reading group sessions, I might have pairs ask each other their questions after reading. Cooperative learning is, of course, already in place during literature circles, in which students may work together to construct a recording sheet that includes their group members' collaborative efforts for a prediction, question, clarification, and summary.

Classroom Example   After each two-page spread of the sixth-grade science text, Mrs. Fox pauses to model the use of the Fab Four. She selects one of the four strategies to model with a think-aloud and then asks students to turn and talk to partners as they work their way in pairs through a verbal summary, quiz questions, words and ideas to clarify, and a quick look to predict what the next pages will cover. Mrs. Fox rotates around the room to assist and prompt each group as they work cooperatively. Each student records a question, a word to clarify, a prediction, and a one-sentence summary on a Four Door Chart (a reproducible version can be found in Chapter 3).

What Reciprocal Teaching Does Not Accomplish

Recently, a sixth-grade teacher made an alarming comment to me: "Since my students are so needy and read well below grade level, I am abandoning everything else and only focusing on the Fab Four." This teacher understood the research on reciprocal teaching and figured it was the lifeline his students so desperately needed; however, he missed the point. Reciprocal teaching and its promise of improving students' reading levels hold true. However, this technique has its place as part of the reading curriculum several times per week or even daily. It is important to remember that it is not a complete reading curriculum in itself.

Although reciprocal teaching touches on four important strategies that students will use almost every time they read, students also need instruction in interacting with the text through personal connections, connections to other books, and connections to the broader world around them (Keene & Zimmermann, 1997). Depending on the text selection, the teacher may activate the students' prior knowledge or may need to supply some background information before reading to help them understand the text better. Many texts also require and invite the reader to make an aesthetic response to reading (Rosenblatt, 1978). Rich classroom discussions—in which students have opportunities to react personally and emotionally to the reading, to express their opinions of the text, and to evaluate the text—are extremely valuable in teaching reading. Discussions of the author's craft, the theme of the piece, or controversial issues addressed in texts are all critical for helping students comprehend text. If reading instruction were to focus only on the four reciprocal teaching strategies, teachers would miss out on important opportunities to build students' reading comprehension based on many of the humorous, interesting, and emotional responses that students have to what they read. It is through these types of aesthetic responses that teachers often are able to motivate students to love reading.

Table 6 offers a list of professional books and classroom materials on reciprocal teaching and lessons for teaching it. Table 1 (see page 5 in the Introduction) includes a general list of books on comprehension.

Table 6
Books on Reciprocal Teaching or With Lessons That Strengthen Reciprocal Teaching

Cooper, J.D., Boschken, I., McWilliams, J., & Pistochini, L. (2001). *Soar to success: The intermediate intervention program*. Boston: Houghton Mifflin.

Eggleton, J. (2006). *Connectors: Improve comprehension skills through reciprocal reading using nonfiction text series of leveled text*. Huntington Beach, CA: Pacific Learning.

Lubliner, S. (2001). *A practical guide to reciprocal teaching*. Bothell, WA: Wright Group.

Oczkus, L.D. (2008). *The fabulous four: Reading comprehension puppets*. Berkeley, CA: Primary Concepts.

Reciprocal Teaching at Work: Powerful Strategies and Lessons for Improving Reading Comprehension (second edition) by Lori D. Oczkus. © 2010. Newark, DE: International Reading Association. May be copied for classroom use.

Reciprocal Teaching as Part of an RTI Plan

RTI is "a process of implementing high-quality, scientifically validated instructional practices based on learner needs, monitoring student progress, and adjusting instruction based on the student's response" (Bender & Shores, 2007, p. 7). The goal of RTI is to help struggling students catch up and avoid special education by providing intense, research-based levels of assessment, instruction, and interventions (Howard, 2009). The idea is to try as many interventions as possible before the student is labeled as learning disabled.

Typically, RTI is organized around three tiers of quality instruction in reading. In many ways, RTI is what good teachers have always done as they adjust instruction to meet the needs of struggling students. In RTI, all students are exposed to quality literature, varied grouping formats, and assessments, including an initial screening in Tier I. Students who do not respond to this well-designed instruction are assessed further and placed in Tier II small-group instruction with just three or four students. The reading specialist or classroom teacher delivers Tier II lessons and continually assesses struggling students. If the target students do not respond to this intensive small-group model, a Tier III plan is administered that includes lessons delivered in an even smaller group or one on one. Constant assessments inform instruction throughout all tiers (Cooper, Kiger, & Robinson, 2011).

Reciprocal teaching strategies can be incorporated as the basis of instruction in all three tiers of an RTI plan. In my extensive work in schools, I've witnessed many strong models using reciprocal teaching as an intervention for struggling students. In every instance, whether as an in-class model or an after-school small-group intervention, students have shown improvement in comprehension due to the extra dose of strategies.

The following are some examples of successful intervention models with reciprocal teaching:

- The intermediate teachers at Randall School, a diverse site, taught whole-class and literature circle reciprocal teaching lessons with core district-mandated texts. The teachers assessed and identified struggling readers and met with them briefly during class at least three times per week in small guided reading groups to provide more intensive reciprocal teaching instruction. The teachers monitored the target students' progress using informal weekly observations, running records, and administration of the Qualitative Reading Inventory (QRI; 2010) three times over the year.

- At Washington School, an inner-city site, we documented dramatic growth on the Developmental Reading Assessment (DRA; 2001) by teaching an after-school intervention using leveled texts and reciprocal teaching three times per week. In class, students employed the same strategies during whole-group and cooperative lessons as well as in a cross-age tutoring program. Most of our students read on or near grade level after just three months of instruction. The fourth graders went up two grade levels in just three months, from a second-grade reading level to fourth-grade!

- Cypress School, a rural site, designed an innovative intervention for primary students using nonfiction texts and reciprocal teaching during guided reading for improved comprehension and reading scores.
- Cooper et al. (2000) found that in just 76 days of instruction, students in the research group performed significantly better than the control group on measures of retelling, question answering, and reading comprehension. The students in the research group also read at a higher level. Since this initial study, many schools across the United States use Cooper and colleagues' (2001) method and materials as an intervention (this program is called Soar to Success).

Because reciprocal teaching is a strong, research-based classroom technique that also consistently yields results when used as an intervention, schools might consider reciprocal teaching as a solid option for an RTI plan.

Although there are other comprehension strategies that are important to teaching students to read, researcher Barbara Taylor (2008) suggests that because instructional time is limited, teachers implementing RTI may focus on the strategies that many studies support and that the National Reading Panel recommended (NICHD, 2000). The most effective strategies include the following:

- Predicting by using graphic organizers with fiction and nonfiction
- Question answering and question generating
- Comprehension monitoring
- Summarizing

According to studies (Fuchs, Fuchs, & Vaughn, 2008), these strategies improve student comprehension when taught explicitly. Also, researchers suggest that teachers incorporate cooperative learning, a foundation of reciprocal teaching, to improve student comprehension. Most important, Taylor (2008) suggests that we pay attention to the National Reading Panel's recommendation to teach students to use multiple strategies in small-group discussions and other natural contexts (NICHD, 2000; Pressley, 2006). Because reciprocal teaching is a multiple-strategy approach that invites students to use all four recommended strategies using cooperative learning, it is a solid and effective option for providing research-based instruction to students in all three tiers of an RTI plan.

When reinforced in all three tiers, students receive the same powerful strategies with varying levels of intensity. In Table 7, you will find an outline of ideas for using reciprocal teaching in each of the tiers, along with assessments to monitor student progress. Following is a detailed description of the RTI tiers of instruction and possible ways to use reciprocal teaching in each.

Table 7 Reciprocal Teaching as a Response to Intervention (RTI)		
RTI Tiers	Ideas for Using Reciprocal Teaching as an RTI Strategy	Ongoing Assessment Tools
Tier I Excellent quality instruction for all students • Exposure to rich and varied reading materials • A variety of groupings for differentiating instruction in whole-class, small-group, and independent structures (e.g., workshop model) • Mix of heterogeneous and homogeneous groupings, flexible groupings	• Teach all four reciprocal teaching strategies together as a multiple-strategy package: predict, question, clarify, summarize. • Use tools to model reciprocal teaching strategies: teacher think-alouds, posters, bookmarks, spinners (resources throughout this book). • Incorporate reciprocal teaching in a variety of grouping formats (whole group, small groups, teacher led) based on need; student-led literature circles or pairs (workshop model, partnerships, independent reading).	• Administer overall screening device several times per school year (e.g., Fountas & Pinnell, 2007a, 2007b). • Provide frequent informal ongoing assessment for all students (retelling, running records, observations rubric page). • Ask students to give predictions, words or points to clarify, questions, and summaries (record observations). • Administer more frequent assessments for struggling students (1 time per week or more). • Use a Four Door Chart (page 110) for students to record their responses.

(continued)

Table 7 (continued)
Reciprocal Teaching as a Response to Intervention (RTI)

RTI Tiers	Ideas for Using Reciprocal Teaching as an RTI Strategy	Ongoing Assessment Tools
Tier I *(continued)*	• Provide targeted instruction through minilessons on predicting, questioning, clarifying, and summarizing. • Use reciprocal teaching with reading materials at instructional and independent reading levels for both fiction and nonfiction. • Incorporate reciprocal teaching in read-alouds, shared reading, small groups, partner reading, and independent reading.	• Ensure quality instruction and fidelity by making sure all lessons are built on the four foundations of reciprocal teaching: modeling and think-alouds, cooperative learning, metacognition, and scaffolding (see online study guide for Reciprocal Teaching Lesson Observation Form).
Tier II Targeted small-group instruction • Smaller groups of 3–6 students • Meets daily or several times per week • Taught by classroom teacher or specialist • More frequent assessment	• Meet with target students and provide small-group instruction using all four reciprocal teaching strategies and texts at the group's instructional reading level. • Teach quick minilessons based on student needs and the four strategies: predict, question, clarify, summarize. • Provide extra word work and support in phonics and phonemic awareness after reading texts using the Fab Four.	• Coach students daily during guided reading and record observations (see Chapter 4 for prompts and observations). • Give frequent running records and retelling assessments (once per week).
Tier III Intensive one-on-one or small-group instruction • Meets daily with classroom teacher or reading specialist • One on one or small group of three • Daily assessments/ observations	• Provide more direct instruction in books at the student's instructional level using all four reciprocal teaching strategies. • Continue to provide the specific word work needed based on observations. • Provide minilessons on each of the strategies when needed.	• Coach each student daily during guided reading using all four strategies and provide prompts. • Give daily running records and retelling assessments. • Provide necessary additional word work to target specific needs.

Tier I

Tier I revolves around excellent regular classroom teaching using proven research-based methods and rich literature with all students. During Tier I instruction, teachers vary the grouping methods and materials to differentiate instruction for all learners. After an initial screening, such as the Benchmark Assessment System (Fountas & Pinnell, 2007a, 2007b), the teacher continues to assess student progress during instruction to determine which students need more instruction or intervention. Throughout Tier I, students are exposed to a variety of rich literature and explicit teacher modeling. Allington (2009) suggests that we provide all students with easy access to a wide range of interesting texts that they enjoy reading. He tells us that the single most important factor that determines the success of an intervention for struggling readers is matching the students to texts they can read fluently, accurately, and with comprehension.

Implications for Using Reciprocal Teaching During Tier I   Tier I includes strong whole-group instruction and guided reading groups with reciprocal teaching. Literature circles and cross-age tutoring with "little buddies" might also be part of Tier I instruction with the Fab Four strategies. Students can be grouped heterogeneously or homogeneously based on need. Targeted minilessons on each of the four strategies (predict, question, clarify, summarize) may be taught to strengthen their use. Informal observations as well as written responses (e.g., the Four Door Chart, page 110) provide glimpses into student thinking. It is especially important that instruction in reciprocal teaching be grounded in scaffolding, think-alouds, metacognition, and cooperative learning to promote maximum gains and success (see earlier section in this chapter, "The Essential Lesson Foundations"). Teachers may want to observe one another or work with a literacy specialist to ensure that they are teaching all four strategies using the foundations throughout all lessons, including in Tier I.

Tier II

Second-level, or Tier II, instruction also takes place in the regular classroom and usually involves providing small-group instruction with students of similar needs grouped together. Either the classroom teacher or the reading specialist may provide this extra dose of targeted instruction. Studies have shown that the schools using the most small-group instruction consistently make more gains in reading (Taylor, 2008). The teacher uses frequent, usually weekly or even daily, assessments to document the struggling students' progress and needs. Please note that small-group instruction is also part of Tier I. However, this tier involves targeting the struggling students and placing them in even smaller groups that meet daily if possible. It is ideal to meet with just three or four students for a stronger level of intervention.

Implications for Using Reciprocal Teaching During Tier II   In Tier II students work with reciprocal teaching again using all four strategies, but in a smaller group of only three to six students. The students meet daily or several times a week for an additional dose of reciprocal teaching that is delivered by either the reading specialist or classroom teacher, using easier to read texts. Constant assessment in the form of running records and retellings or commercial assessments provides valuable information on the students' progress. Minilessons in each of the four strategies may be delivered when students show the need for targeted instruction in predicting, questioning, clarifying, or summarizing. Intensive word work around phonic and phonemic elements found in the texts read may follow the reciprocal teaching comprehension lessons. If the student does not respond with enough growth to this intensive small-group version of reciprocal teaching, a Tier III intervention may be necessary.

Tier III

If a student still struggles after Tier II instruction, then it may be determined that the student needs a Tier III intervention or an even more intensive dose of instruction, this time in a small group of students. The classroom teacher or reading specialist may deliver this daily instruction along with constant assessments.

Implications for Using Reciprocal Teaching During Tier III   Tier III using reciprocal teaching includes working with a small group of just three or four students, or even one on one. It is best if this instruction is provided daily with either the teacher or another trained individual. Again, reciprocal teaching strategies and books at the student's instructional level provide intensive intervention. Daily assessments and observations are necessary to guide instruction at this level.

When reciprocal teaching is used across all three tiers of instruction, students benefit from the consistent but varied exposure to the comprehension strategies that will make the biggest difference in their achievement.

Assessment Options for Reciprocal Teaching

Assessment tools for reciprocal teaching include the observation of students during discussions and some occasional, brief, written responses using the four reciprocal teaching strategies.

What to look for (see Rubric for the Reciprocal Teaching Strategies in Appendix A)

- Student use of each strategy
- Orchestrated use of all four strategies
- Ability to define each strategy and explain how it helps with reading comprehension

How to help students

- Teach the single-strategy minilessons at the end of each chapter to small groups or the whole class to strengthen the use of a particular strategy.

CHAPTER SUMMARY

- Reciprocal teaching is a scaffolded discussion technique based on the four strategies all good readers use: predicting, questioning, clarifying, and summarizing. The strategies are used flexibly and in any order.

- Reciprocal teaching can be used with any reading material, fiction or nonfiction, in grades K–12 or even with adults.

- Good readers use text structure, other clues from the text, and their own experiences to make logical predictions. Questioning is important because good readers self-question before, during, and after reading. Clarifying assists students in identifying problems or areas of confusion as they read and offers ways to solve the problems. Summarizing is a complex skill that requires students to select and arrange in order only the most important points from the text.

- When attempting to implement reciprocal teaching, teachers and students may face common obstacles and difficulties (see Table 4, pages 24–25, and Table 5, pages 26–27).

- The essential foundations, or building blocks, to successful reciprocal teaching instruction are scaffolded instruction, think-alouds, metacognition, and cooperative learning.

- The four strategies are part of a larger comprehensive reading program that is based on all the strategies that good readers use, such as previewing, self-questioning, visualizing, making connections, monitoring, knowing how words work, summarizing, and evaluating.

- Reciprocal teaching makes for an effective, research-based strategy to incorporate into all three tiers of an effective RTI plan.

- When assessing students as they use the strategies, use the assessment tools in Appendix A.

CHAPTER 2

Getting Started: Introducing and Reinforcing
RECIPROCAL TEACHING

It depends on the level of the kid, how hard I make the question.

—Stephani, grade 4, bilingual student

How to Begin Using Reciprocal Teaching
With Your Students

One of the burning questions teachers often pose is, Should I teach all four strategies before I put them together in a reciprocal teaching lesson? This is a natural concern, as most students are not yet proficient in any of the strategies, and it seems daunting to expect them to use all four at once. However, studies suggest that teachers may introduce all four as quickly as possible to benefit from the power and research behind multiple-strategy instruction (NICHD, 2000; Reutzel et al., 2005). Therefore, you do not have to wait until students are completely competent or familiar with each of the four reciprocal teaching strategies before you jump in and begin using them in lessons together. In one urban school in which I worked, we introduced the strategies for just a few days each and then taught guided reading groups using the Fab Four. After three months, the struggling fourth graders moved from reading at a second-grade level to their own grade level.

This chapter contains many examples of easy and effective ways to begin using reciprocal teaching in your classroom. Although there is no right way to introduce reciprocal teaching to your class, you should quickly teach or review each of the strategies and jump as quickly as possible into using all four, even with primary-grade children. You can always back up and teach a focused minilesson on one of the strategies to strengthen its use if need be. Reciprocal teaching can be introduced in either whole-group or guided reading lessons. If you wish to run literature circles, then try training your students in the strategies during whole-group or guided reading lessons first. This chapter specifically includes ideas for introducing your class to reciprocal teaching using read-alouds, mentor text, characters and props, and hand motions or gestures for each of the strategies. Print supports include posters, bookmarks, and ideas for supporting the strategies, such as using strategy dice or a Fab Four Dial. The hands-on lessons range from using a folding Four Door Chart for recording responses for discussions to ideas for shared reading and reciprocal teaching. Suggestions for reading materials that work best when introducing the Fab Four are also included.

If you teach middle and high school students, you may wish to bring in short, high-interest news or Internet articles with topics that will grab your students' attention as you model the four strategies for the first time and then ask students to work in groups to practice the Fab Four. Elementary teachers may prefer using mentor texts, picture books that target a particular strategy (see page 52), or even short articles or poetry. For example, Mary Jo Barker, a literacy coach, likes to use the short poem "The Little Blue Engine" by Shel Silverstein with elementary grades because of its brevity, humor, and surprise ending. The natural pauses between stanzas provide opportunities for students to participate in summaries and to predict. Students can clarify vocabulary such as *chug*. Students make up questions for one another after Mrs. Barker models hers: "Why do you think the engine thought he could make it up the hill?"

Following are some effective ways to introduce your class to the Fab Four.

Practical Ways to Introduce Reciprocal Teaching Strategies to Your Class

Read-Alouds

You can introduce and reinforce reciprocal teaching through read-alouds at any grade level. The key is to make sure you are modeling all four strategies in the same lesson. Also, it is important to alternate between providing teacher modeling for each strategy and allowing students to talk in pairs throughout the lesson. Select any fiction or nonfiction read-aloud for your grade level to use as you introduce reciprocal teaching to your students (see Lesson 1 in this chapter, page 64). A read-aloud is a great way to continue to reinforce reciprocal teaching all year long.

Use short pieces from newspapers, picture books, comics, and the Internet for just a few moments a day to model the flexible use of the strategies in any reading material. Try bringing in a recipe, map, travel guide, article, or even a novel you're reading and read aloud examples to show students how you use the strategies, too. The best part about reading aloud with the Fab Four is that there is no preparation involved. Just jump in and do it! By sharing your own reading, students can see that the Fab Four strategies are not only "school" strategies but also flexible tools that good readers use all their lives.

Shared Reading of Poetry

Poetry makes for very effective, rich reading material to model reciprocal teaching strategies. Plus, you can conduct a quick reciprocal teaching lesson using any poem appropriate for your grade level. First, make predictions based on the title and artwork, and skim and scan the text for key vocabulary. Then, enjoy the poem by reading it aloud or inviting the class to read along in a shared reading. For shorter poems, predict first, then read the entire poem. After reading, model how to clarify tricky words or parts, ask questions, and summarize. Invite the students to take turns with partners to clarify more words or parts, ask questions, and try out their own summaries. If the poem is longer, read only a stanza or two, pause, and model all four strategies, inviting partners to practice the strategies before moving on. Pause several times during the poem and run through all four strategies by modeling and allowing partners to discuss. Poetry is especially great for identifying not just words to clarify but entire phrases and metaphors that might be hard to understand. You can also ask students to clarify what they are visualizing or to pose questions they'd like to ask the poet.

**Figure 3
Sample Four Door Chart**

Four Door Chart

The Four Door Chart (Oczkus, 2006) is a popular, hands-on way to introduce your students to the four strategies and to assess their progress in the use of the strategies. Teachers from all grade levels send me glowing feedback on this super-simple paper-folding activity that serves as a quick assessment tool during reciprocal teaching discussions (see pages 110–112 for directions for folding a Four Door Chart and a Four Door pattern). For younger children, you might want to fold and cut the four doors prior to the lesson. Older students from upper elementary to high school enjoy making and personalizing their own Four Door Charts for recording their Fab Four discussions (see Figure 3).

During a Four Door lesson, the teacher alternates modeling each strategy, inviting students to sketch or write a response for each strategy behind the corresponding door, and then providing opportunities throughout the lesson for students to share responses with partners. It is best not to overuse the Four Door, though, as reciprocal teaching is a discussion technique and the Four Door slows down the discussion. Eventually wean your class off of the Four Door Chart as they become more proficient in their use of strategies and focus on oral discussions. You can occasionally use a Four Door as an informal assessment to see how the students are growing in their use of the strategies (see Rubric for the Reciprocal Teaching Strategies, page 254). During minilessons that focus on a particular strategy, try having students write the same strategy on every door. For example, in a lesson on asking thoughtful questions during reading, students write "I wonder..." on all four doors, then as they read the text they fill in the doors with their questions.

Fab Four Characters and Props

In the schools in which I teach, we find that students remember and internalize the reciprocal teaching strategies when you introduce them using the Fab Four characters (Oczkus, 2004). Rick Wormeli (2009), in *Metaphors and Analogies: Power Tools for Teaching Any Subject*, says that "whether your students are six or sixteen, they can learn to identify and use metaphors to deepen comprehension of any subject" (p. 9). The characters introduced in this chapter provide a concrete way to help students understand reading strategies. The metaphors for each strategy work with any grade level and make the reading strategies come alive as students read the text with the Powerful Predictor, Quincy the Questioner, Clara the Clarifier, and Sammy the Summarizer (see Lesson 3 in Chapter 3, page 113, for a description of the characters). If you like to act a bit silly when the classroom door closes, you might dress up and use a different voice and prop for each character as you conduct think-alouds. If you'd rather leave that to someone else, then a simple alternative is to bring in props to hold up during your think-alouds. You might use a snow globe for a crystal ball to predict, a toy microphone to model questioning, a pair of glasses to wear when you clarify, and an old camera to represent summarizing (see Figure 4 for examples). If a prop is not available, then at a minimum, show a picture of one of the props or use one of the icons on the pages in this book.

Figure 4
Fab Four Props

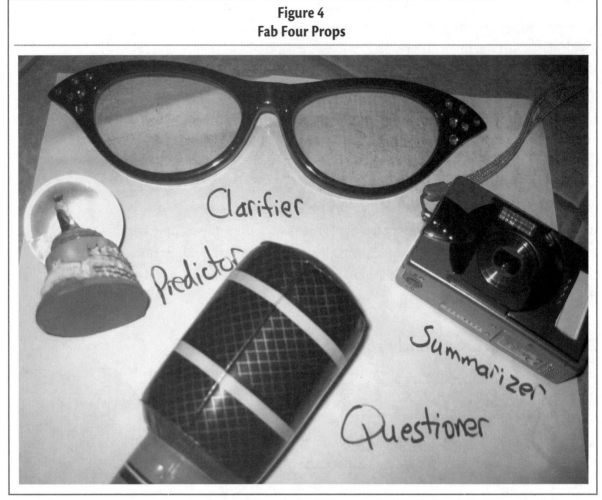

You can use the characters in this book or even create your own that fit your grade level (Oczkus, 2009). One middle school in which I worked created a set of characters based on reality television characters. Another tried using rap musicians selected by the students. One kindergarten chose familiar cartoon characters such as SpongeBob SquarePants and Handy Manny to teach the Fab Four. Primary teachers sometimes enjoy using puppets to represent the characters (Myers, 2005; see Figure 5). You can see the reading comprehension puppets I created, available at www.primaryconcepts.com/rdgcomp/Comprehension-Puppets.asp.

Figure 5
Fab Four Puppets

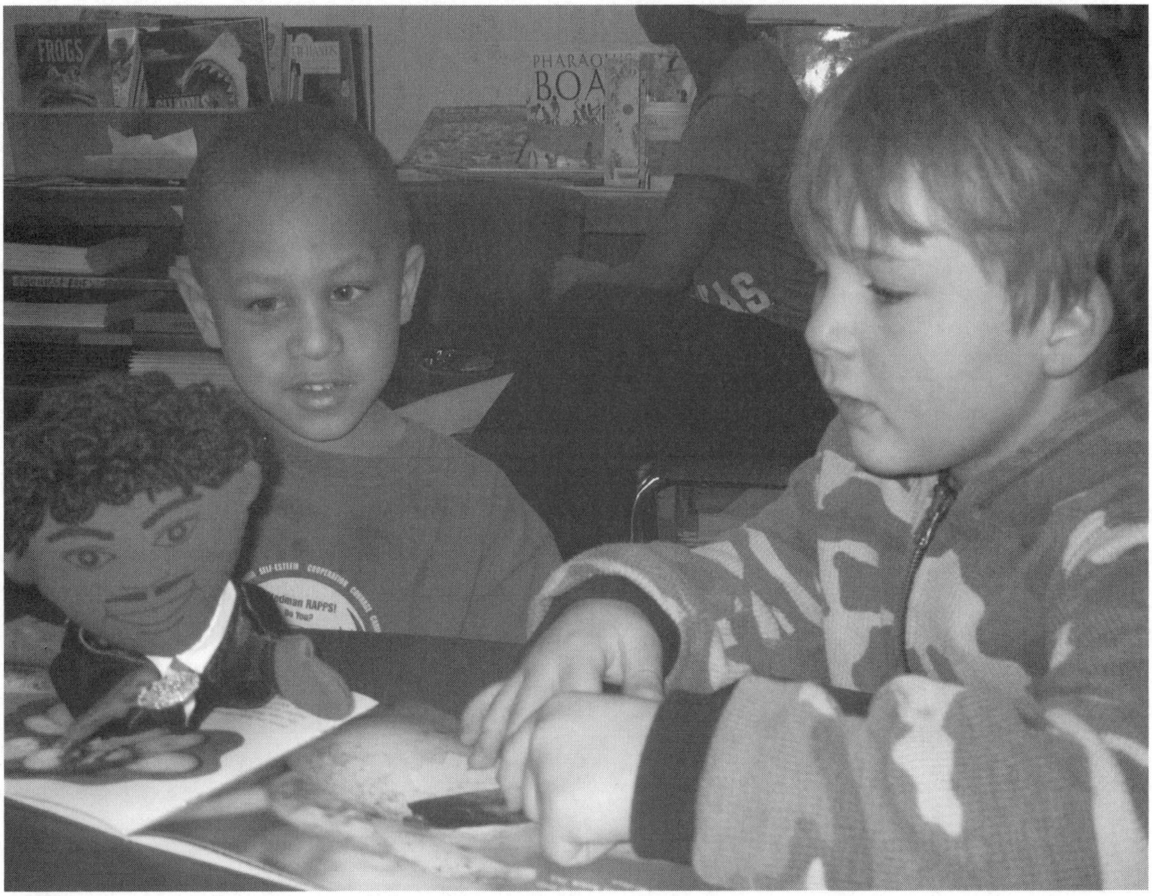

Reciprocal Teaching at Work: Powerful Strategies and Lessons for Improving Reading Comprehension (second edition) by Lori D. Oczkus. © 2010. Newark, DE: International Reading Association. Fabulous Four Reading Comprehension Puppets used by permission. © Primary Concepts. www.primaryconcepts.com. May be copied for classroom use.

Mentor Texts for Each Strategy

Another effective method for introducing all four strategies is to spend a few days or even as much as a week on each of the Fab Four strategies by reading aloud mentor texts. Mentor texts are special, memorable books you return to over and over for different purposes. In selecting a mentor text to help teach one of the reading strategies, teachers look for a reading experience that naturally calls for the strategy we wish to teach (Oczkus, 2009). Mentor texts also can be used during minilessons to help support and reinforce a strategy with which students are struggling, such as summarizing. Teachers can select a mentor text in the form of a

Table 8 Mentor Text Recommendations	
Strategy	**Books**
Predict	• *What Do You Do With a Tail Like This?* by Steve Jenkins and Robin Page • *Tree of Birds* by Susan Meddaugh
Question	• *The Stranger* by Chris Van Allsburg • *Charlie Anderson* by Barbara Abercombie • *The Three Questions* by Jon J Muth
Clarify	• *Gleam and Glow* by Eve Bunting • Chet Gecko Mystery series by Bruce Hale • *Owl Moon* by Jane Yolen
Summarize	• *Animals Nobody Loves* by Seymour Simon • *Listen to the Wind: The Story of Dr. Greg and* Three Cups of Tea by Greg Mortenson and Susan L. Roth

picture book that invites the students to use a particular strategy. Perhaps you select a mystery to predict, an interesting animal article for questioning, a short story for summarizing, or a book with descriptive passages for clarifying. When you introduce the Fab Four with a series of picture books, students can focus on learning about the strategies rather than struggling with challenging text. Then, you can show students how to unlock comprehension using the Fab Four in more difficult grade-level reading materials. Use any picture books appropriate to your grade level or that you have on hand in your classroom. You do not need to purchase any special titles; however, Table 8 provides a list of some teacher and student favorite mentor texts for each of the strategies.

Supports and Practical Tools to Reinforce Reciprocal Teaching Strategies

This book contains many supports for helping scaffold reciprocal teaching strategies for your students. There are a variety of multisensory ways you can support your students when teaching with the Fab Four, including using hand gestures or motions to cue the strategies and a selection of visual supports, such as icons for charts, bookmarks, and classroom posters with discussion prompts. (See Appendix E for icon and strategy posters.)

Fab Four Gestures

Many students are kinesthetic learners and respond well when teachers use gestures and other hand movements during lessons. Researchers have discovered that using hand gestures or motions to represent comprehension processes yields strong results in grades K–3 (Block et al., 2008). I have also found that hand motions work to make learning more concrete for students in grades K–6 and for struggling readers and

ELLs (Oczkus, 2009). Middle school and high school students respond with positive results to more active lessons as well. High school teacher Brian Grimm, from Tulsa, Oklahoma, finds that his students' scores in English improve when he incorporates kinesthetic learning as students clap their hands overhead for topic sentences and stomp their feet for details (Plummer, 2009). My own high school–age daughter often reviews her Spanish vocabulary with me before a test, and we create hand motions to represent the words.

Even our strongest readers respond well to using hand motions for the strategies. Research (National Center for Education Statistics, 2006) indicates that the number of kinesthetic learners in our classrooms is increasing, so using gestures is a natural means of learning for many students! The purpose of using the gestures is to cue the strategies—that is, when students see the hand motion, they recall what the strategy is, why and when we employ it, and how to use it when reading (Oczkus, 2009). Picture these scenarios using gestures during Fab Four lessons:

- First graders are gathered around on a rug to listen to a Big Book read-aloud. The teacher asks the students to make the gesture for predicting, and all the students pretend to hold a crystal ball and rub their hands on it as they share predictions. Throughout the reading, the teacher stops to have the students use predict, question, clarify, and summarize hand motions when they turn to partners to share their thoughts. Even the wiggliest little ones are fully engaged in the lesson.

- Instead of raising their hands during small-group discussions, a class of fifth graders has learned the hand gestures for each reciprocal teaching strategy. The students meet in their literature circles and know they can signal when they have a thought about one of the strategies by using the hand motion for that strategy. The discussion director in one group notices a group member is making the signal for clarify and invites that student to share his or her idea. Several students piggyback on the point the student wants to clarify and offer ideas. Later during the reading, four group members are signaling at the same time. One is making the signal for question, one to clarify, and two others for prediction. The rich lively discussion is interrupted by the recess bell.

- When working their way through the novel *To Kill a Mockingbird* by Harper Lee, the eighth graders engage in very lively class discussions. A hush falls over the class as Mrs. Jimenez reads aloud a few pages from last night's reading assignment. As she reads, she encourages students to use the hand signal for clarify whenever they hear a word or idea they'd like to clarify. Throughout the reading, the students subtly motion the pause sign for clarify. After a few minutes, Mrs. Jimenez invites students to turn to their table group members to discuss the points they wish to clarify in the text she just read. Jaime's group discusses the word *umbrage* and the possible meanings of the phrase "family's mental hygiene." Each group creates a hand motion to go with one of the words or phrases they clarified to help them remember its meaning.

Following are descriptions of the simple hand motions that we use for each of the Fab Four strategies. Figure 6 shows students using each gesture.

Figure 6
Fab Four Gestures

Predict

Clarify

Question

Summarize

Predict   To evoke a fortune teller, move both hands around a pretend crystal ball. As you move your hands around the invisible ball, talk about text clues and any picture clues. Use the language of predicting, such as, "I predict this is about...because...."

If you wish to use a different metaphor or character and hand motion with students, the weight lifter is also well received. Tell students that when we predict we use visual clues like pictures as well as text clues to make predictions. Form a fist with each hand and pretend to lift a weight as you bend your arm. Tell the students that each hand represents clues from either the text or the visuals.

Question   Make a fist and use it as a pretend microphone as you make up questions about the reading. Encourage students to use the prompt, "I wonder..." or the question starters why, what, how, when, where, and who. Also, invite students to ask "Why do you think..." questions as well as questions that require inferential thinking to answer.

Clarify   Clarify is an important complex strategy that requires multiple hand signals to assist students in understanding, which is the hallmark of a good reader (Paris, Wasik, & Turner, 1991). These hand signals include making glasses and making a pause symbol similar to that on a remote control.

For glasses, form circles with your index fingers and thumbs and place them over your eyes to represent eyeglasses that help you clarify words and ideas and visualize as you read. The pause gesture is a sophisticated signal that students of all ages are willing to use. Remote controls have pause buttons, and there probably isn't a student in your classroom who doesn't know that a pause control is represented by two parallel lines. Bend your arms at the elbows and form two parallel lines. Explain to students that when they clarify, it is like pushing a pause button for a moment to think and figure out difficult words before reading on or even rereading. Use your hands to point to the right or left to indicate a reread (rewind) button and a read on (fast forward) button.

Summarize   Summarize has a couple fun hand motions that help make this difficult strategy come alive, such as using a lasso to rein in main ideas and taking a picture of only the important parts.

For the lasso, pretend to "rope up" the main ideas in the text and create a summary. Tell students that sometimes we create a longer summary or a shorter one. Pretend to twirl a lasso over your head as you talk about your summary.

My friend Kathy Langham, a fifth-grade teacher and staff developer, prefers to use the metaphor of a tourist taking a zillion pictures. When I use this metaphor, I tell the students that on my recent family vacation at the beach I took 500 photos and ask if they'd like to see them. They chuckle, nod, and chime in on a resounding "No!" So, I ask them how many photos I should show my friends and how I should select them. The students usually tell me to select around 15–20 photos of only the highlights. Then, we pretend to take snapshots of main points from the text by holding up a pretend camera and making a clicking noise as we shoot a summary. High school and middle school students especially relate to this metaphor for choosing highlights in a text.

Print Supports for Reciprocal Teaching Lessons

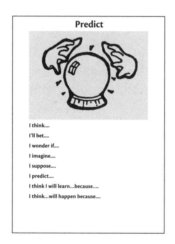

Posters The strategy posters provide students with an icon to help them remember the metaphor for the strategy, such as the crystal ball for predicting or the glasses for clarifying. The strategy discussion starters or prompts give students language they can depend on as they talk throughout the lesson to a partner or the group. All students, especially ELLs, benefit from the discussion starters, as these frames provide helpful scaffolds for using academic language. When these posters are displayed in the room in a spot where students can refer to them, discussions improve and the students are more likely to use the strategies as they read throughout the day. (See Appendix E for these materials.)

Bookmarks The Fab Four Bookmark is a wonderful personal reference tool for the strategies (see page 74). You may wish to give every student a laminated one. Bookmarks are useful discussion guides during whole-class lessons, so when students turn to a partner they have the language of the strategies right in front of them. If you keep a set at the guided reading table you can pass them out during small-group instruction. Sometimes students refer to the bookmarks during literature circles. Bookmarks make helpful discussion guides for students to use in a partner reading center in the classroom or as a tool when reading to a cross-age buddy or younger child (see Appendix B for a lesson to use with cross-age buddies). The bookmark possibilities are endless!

Icons for the Dry-Erase Board or Posters   The icons are flexible tools that you can utilize in a variety of ways to teach and display the strategies in your classroom (see Appendix E). You may wish to laminate these and put magnetic tape on the back of each to use them on the dry-erase board or interactive whiteboard for a quick way to record student responses during discussions.

I also like to have a stack of the icons ready and duplicated on paper in the room so I can make quick posters on chart paper. I simply tape a copy of each icon on my quick poster for a visual reminder of the strategy as students and I record their responses during our discussions (see Figure 7).

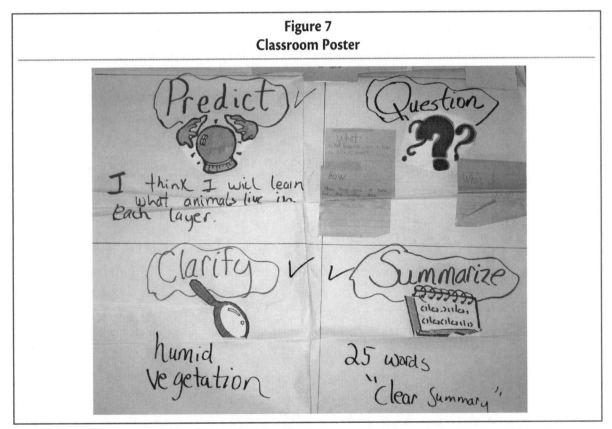

Figure 7
Classroom Poster

Strategy Dice   When students roll strategy dice, they use strategy prompts to guide their partner and literature circle discussions. Dice can be used with the whole class, in guided reading groups, for literature circles, or even at centers. They work like this: Provide one set of dice for students in a pair or group. Create a quick list of six prompts you want your students to use and number them to correspond with the sides of the dice. (See Appendix E for a list of prompts for each strategy.) When the students roll their dice they see which strategy they've landed on and then use that prompt. The following list provides some examples:

1. Predict: I think...will happen because....
2. Question: I wonder....
3. Clarify: I didn't get the word...so I....
4. Summarize: This was mostly about....
5. Free choice: Any strategy
6. Free choice: Any strategy

Dice are helpful when introducing a strategy, because you can include multiple prompts for the same strategy, such as six starters for just summarizing or clarifying. When students become more familiar with the strategies, the dice may be used with four strategies plus two free-choice sides. For example, if a student rolls the dice and it lands on clarify, then that student leads the group in clarifying something in the text. The next student may roll the dice and land on question and ask a discussion question or quiz question of the group.

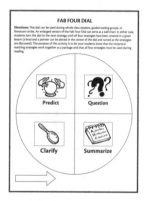

Fab Four Dial   When I first began using this print support, I used a paper plate, a brad, and a pointer to create a Fab Four Dial that I would turn to indicate which strategy we were "on" as we moved our way through all four strategies during any given lesson. Now I use tag board and the Dial with the names of the strategies on it (see Chapter 4, page 177). The Dial is helpful to show students that we use all four strategies flexibly and in any order. I like to sit down with a group, show them the Dial, and move it to the strategy we are using at the moment (see Figure 8).

The Fab Four Dial contributes to the metacognition or awareness of the strategies and serves a different purpose than the Reciprocal Teaching Spinner (discussed in Chapter 5, page 230). I use the Dial as a teacher tool to demonstrate metacognition during lessons to represent the strategy we are working on. However, the Spinner is a game-like tool that we use to spin and land on a strategy and then use it. So, in essence, we use the Dial to show our thinking and the Spinner to dictate where the lesson goes next!

Reading Materials to Use During Fab Four Lessons

During staff development workshops, teachers often ask me what type of reading material works best for reciprocal teaching lessons. The answer is straightforward: Any and all reading material is suitable for reciprocal teaching. The strategies work naturally and are easily employed with any type of fiction or nonfiction text of any length. You can use everything from Big Books to novels to your class's social studies text, and reciprocal teaching will continue to enhance your students' reading comprehension, so you do not need to purchase any special materials for the lessons.

Figure 8
Fab Four Dial

Reciprocal Teaching at Work: Powerful Strategies and Lessons for Improving Reading Comprehension (second edition) by Lori D. Oczkus. © 2010. Newark, DE: International Reading Association. May be copied for classroom use.

You might use easy-to-read, high-interest material that is below your students' grade level when introducing reciprocal teaching strategies, then move quickly into grade-level reading choices. Although reciprocal teaching can accelerate students' reading levels (Cooper et al., 1999), grade-level texts are preferable in reciprocal teaching lessons, because students can be taught to cope with the demands of those texts in a scaffolded or supported manner. During guided reading, you can use reciprocal teaching with leveled texts that fit students' reading level and increase in difficulty over time. The ultimate goal of reciprocal teaching is to give students the tools to build reading comprehension skills for challenging texts.

For reciprocal teaching with any given text, the strategies should be used with workable text chunks. When introducing reciprocal teaching to a class, use paragraphs or pages as stopping points for you and your students to employ the reciprocal teaching strategies. You also can use lessons in textbooks, chapters in fiction books, and entire short articles as appropriate text chunks for instruction. It is easier to scaffold and support students in reciprocal teaching strategies when the text chunks are small enough for them to absorb.

Assess your students' use of the reciprocal teaching strategies with a variety of reading materials, so you can monitor and adjust your lessons to fit students' needs.

- Are your students' predictions based on clues from the text or its illustrations?

- Are your students' questions literal or inferential, and are they based on the text?

- Are your students able to identify troublesome words and at least two strategies for deciphering them? Are any students identifying difficult ideas and ways to clarify them?

- Are your students able to tell you which strategy was the easiest for them to use and which was the hardest? How competent are the students with the strategies that they say are the hardest?

- Are your students' summaries succinct, including only the important points in the proper order? Do your students use language from the text in their summaries? Are their summaries getting at the text's major themes?

In Table 9 you will find a variety of suggested reading materials, helpful tips for using each type of material with reciprocal teaching, and ideas for teacher modeling and assessment of student progress.

Table 9
Using Reciprocal Teaching With a Variety of Reading Materials

Reading Material	Considerations and Reciprocal Teaching Tips	Teacher Modeling	Student Participation	Assessment Tips
Novels/chapter books (fiction or nonfiction)	• Use with whole class or small group. • These may not have visual supports.	• Model skimming and scanning to predict (and review to clarify, question, and summarize).	• Groups or pairs use the strategies after each chapter. • Mark text with sticky notes during reading to show strategy use.	• Observe and record student responses. • Students fill in a Four Door Chart after chapters. • Model more often, every few pages, for struggling readers.
Picture books	• Use for modeling and introducing or reinforcing the strategies as a mentor text at any grade level.	• Model during a read-aloud pausing several times to run through all four strategies. • Use as a mentor text; may focus on one particular strategy.	• Students work in teams after the teacher models using the bookmark.	• Use a Four Door Chart to record responses. • Have students use gestures to indicate strategy use.
Content area textbooks (e.g., science, social studies)	• Use natural breaks headings, lessons for Fab Four lessons • Use the text features, such as maps, charts, graphs, and captions.	• Model with one heading or portion of text. • Model strategies for clarifying difficult words and rereading for concepts.	• Pairs or groups work in teams using the Fab Four Bookmark. • Assign one strategy to each table to share with the class.	• Students record strategy use on a Four Door Chart or discussion sheet.
Basal or anthology	• Use illustrations and other text features to reinforce reciprocal teaching.	• Model during whole-class or small-group lessons. • Run through all four strategies, but select a focus strategy of the day to model thoroughly.	• Pairs or table groups work in teams to discuss portions of text. • During reading, students may use sticky notes to mark strategy use in text.	• Observe student responses. • Students fill in a Four Door Chart or discussion sheet. • Have students use gestures in whole-class discussions or in table groups.

(continued)

		Table 9 (continued)		
	Using Reciprocal Teaching With a Variety of Reading Material			
Reading Material	**Considerations and Reciprocal Teaching Tips**	**Teacher Modeling**	**Student Participation**	**Assessment Tips**
Big Books (fiction or nonfiction)	• All students can see the text.	• Model using props and characters. • Model after every page or two-page spread.	• Students use gestures with partners. • Turn and talk to partners throughout the lesson.	• Observe student responses and gestures.
Leveled or decodable books (fiction or nonfiction)	• Use in small-group instruction. • Use illustrations and text features.	• Model all four strategies at the beginning of the lesson. • Emphasize a strategy with which students have trouble	• Students read silently and mark with sticky notes the tricky words and places to ask questions. • Partners read and discuss Fab Four.	• Record student responses on the Fab Four Chart (see page 160). • Coach individuals during guided reading (see page 143). • Record strategy coaching and use the Reciprocal Teaching Observation Chart (page 168).

After the Introduction to Reciprocal Teaching: Next Steps

Once you've introduced your class to the four strategies and taught a number of lessons during whole-group or guided reading, consider the following next steps for maximum success:

- Select a time, at least twice per week, to conduct reciprocal teaching lessons so your students may benefit from the power of multiple-strategy instruction.

- Continually model using think-alouds for each of the strategies.

- Encourage all students to discuss the strategies throughout Fab Four lessons with partners or in groups.

- Model and invite students to reflect on how the strategies help them as they read.

- Continually assess students to decide which strategies the students need and the minilessons or focus strategy lessons to teach.

- Try the reciprocal teaching model in small-group instruction (see Chapter 4).

- Try returning to quick oral lessons using read-alouds to reinforce the strategies all year long.

The remaining lessons in this chapter outline in greater detail ways to introduce and enhance reciprocal teaching using read-alouds, the Fab Four Bookmark, metaphors, characters and props, and the Four Door Chart. Minilessons at the end of the chapter give you options for strengthening the use of any given individual strategy.

The remaining chapters in this book provide you with lesson choices for whole-class instruction, guided reading groups, and literature circles with reciprocal teaching. If you use the Fab Four consistently in your classroom you will see a difference in just a few weeks and more significant progress in just a few months. Your students will not only grow in their comprehension and reading levels, but also they will become more independent readers. Enjoy the journey!

Lesson 1: Using a Read-Aloud to Introduce/Reinforce the Fab Four

One of my favorite no-fuss ways to jump in and quickly introduce the reciprocal teaching strategies is through a read-aloud. Whether you teach ninth grade or kindergarten, this lesson is for you! Although the lesson examples here show how to introduce the four strategies, a read-aloud is a great way to reinforce the Fab Four all year long. You can read aloud from *any* appropriate material while modeling the four strategies and invite your students to join you in trying them out. You don't need any special materials, and you can turn any read-aloud into a lesson without any preparation! Just grab a good book and begin.

You can use any texts, including newspaper articles, basal anthology pieces, chapter books, Big Books, or picture books. When introducing the strategies, you may want to read aloud from an easy level of text, so students can focus on the strategies, not difficult concepts or challenging reading material. Students don't need to have a copy of the material. The entire lesson should be conducted orally and students should not be required to write any responses. This oral practice provides students the opportunity to use the Fab Four the way good readers do, quite naturally during the reading process. I like to incorporate some sort of visual, such as the posters, icons, or Fab Four Dial to help students internalize the names of the strategies and maybe even the strategy starters we use as the language for each. At a minimum, I write "predict, question, clarify, summarize" on the chalkboard so that as I model each strategy, we name them.

MATERIALS

- Any appropriate reading material you wish to read aloud to your class

- Optional: An overhead projector, document camera, or interactive white board to show the reading material to the class, and props such as a lasso or camera, microphone, glasses, and snow globe for a crystal ball or weights for the weight lifter

1. When introducing reciprocal teaching strategies to your students, ask them to tell you what good readers do. Students turn and share more ideas with partners.

2. Share the objective of the lesson. Tell students that you are going to model four of the strategies that good readers use to understand or comprehend what they read: predict, question, clarify, and summarize. Optional ideas include the following:

    • Write the four strategies and if you wish the starters on a board or chart.

    • Use the posters, icons, or Reciprocal Teaching Dial (see Appendix E and Chapter 4, page 177).

    • Use a prop for each strategy (see page 49–50).

3. Before reading aloud from the text, tell the students you are going to show them how to predict. Preview the title, book cover, and a few illustrations or headings from inside the reading. Model a prediction. For fiction, say, "I think this is about...because...," or "I think...will happen because...." For nonfiction, say, "I think I will learn... because...." Invite students to try making their own predictions with a partner or in their groups.

4. Begin reading aloud a few pages in a longer text or just a few paragraphs in a shorter one. Pause and tell students you are going to let them know what you are thinking. Tell them you are going to run through all four strategies for the portion of text you just read aloud. (If using a visual such as the posters or a chart you've made listing the strategies, refer to it.)

• *Question:* Model how to ask a question about the text you've read so far. Tell students you are asking either a wonder that starts with "I wonder..." or a quiz question, one that a teacher or game show host might ask. Or, model a discussion or thinking question that starts with "Why do you think...?"

    Invite students to ask partners a question immediately following your question. It is fine if some students repeat your question.

• *Clarify:* Find a word or entire sentence in the text to clarify and model how to figure it out using a variety of fix-up strategies. Use this frame to model clarifying: "I didn't get the [word, sentence, part], so I [reread,

read on, chopped the word into smaller parts, thought of what would make sense, etc.]."

Immediately after you model how to clarify a word or sentence, invite students to turn to partners to find another example to clarify and then tell how they figured it out. If students say they have nothing to clarify, remind them they can select something with which a younger student might have trouble.

- *Summarize:* Model how to reread and skim text to gather points to summarize. Give a quick summary of the material read so far. Begin with one of these frames: "So far..." or "This is mostly about...."

  Have students turn to partners and give a summary of the reading so far. It is fine if they repeat your model. Encourage students to verbalize the summary using the frame you chose.

- *Predict:* Show students how to predict again for the next portion of text. Tell them reasons for your predictions that might be based on what you've read so far, your preview of the next few pages, or your own background experience with the topic. Use one of the appropriate frames: "I think...will happen because...." or for nonfiction, "I think I will learn...because...." When using nonfiction, model for students how to look ahead at headings and illustrations and how to skim the words in the text to make powerful predictions.

  Have students turn to partners and repeat the frame to share their predictions for the read-aloud text.

GUIDED PRACTICE/ STUDENT PARTICIPATION

1. Continue reading aloud, pausing after every few pages, and modeling all four strategies for each segment of text you read. After each of your think-alouds, invite students to share with their table groups or partners their own strategy use. Encourage them to repeat the language frames to start their discussions. Then have students share their responses with the entire class. This kind of small-group interaction encourages all students to try the strategies in a supportive environment.

2. Use partner practice in another text. Have student pairs work together through a text to try the strategies aloud.

3. After your think-aloud or even throughout the lesson, ask your students to reflect on strategy use. Ask them, "How did I use each reciprocal teaching strategy to help me read this text, and which strategy did you think was the most helpful?"

The following tips may help you assess your students when using the Fab Four during read-aloud lessons:

- Listen to your students' discussions. Are students using the strategy frames to share their responses?

- Informally evaluate students' use of the strategies by listening to pairs of students as they share and as they contribute to the discussion:

  - Are students using text clues and background knowledge to make logical predictions?

  - Are students asking questions that can be answered in the text or inferred?

  - Do students give examples of clarifying words and ideas and ways to clarify?

  - Do students summarize the text and include important points and even select vocabulary?

Introducing the Fab Four

Primary   Throughout a read-aloud, Mrs. Lopez invites her class to first watch her use each of the four strategies and then try them with a partner. She selects a first-grade favorite, *Mr. Gumpy's Outing* by John Burningham, a lively tale about too many barnyard animals crowding onto a boat. She explains that good readers use four important strategies as they read and holds up the Fab Four Dial as she names each strategy. "Visualize turning the dials in your head to each strategy as I show you how to use them and then ask you to try the strategies out with your partners," she explains. The little readers are game as she begins by asking them to turn the dial to predict, so they can think about what the story will be about. While previewing the cover and a few of the first pages, Mrs. Lopez models a prediction using the frame "I think...because...." The students turn to their partners and use the same language to each share a prediction. The read-aloud begins and naturally turns into a shared reading as the repetitive, cumulative story unfolds. She invites a few students up to dramatize a few of the story events. After four pages she stops to ask students to turn the dial in their heads to each of the four strategies as she provides a model for a quick summary, a question to ask Mr. Gumpy or one of the animals, and a word to clarify. The pairs try each of the strategies immediately following Mrs. Lopez's model using the same strategy starters: "So far...," "I didn't get the word...so I...," "Mr. Gumpy [or an animal], why did you...?," and "I think...will happen next." The students chime in to finish the reading and, at the end of the book, Mrs. Lopez models the four strategies again and allows pairs to try them after each model. Students return to their desks to draw their favorite parts of the story.

Intermediate   The fifth graders in Mrs. Langham's class pull out their basal anthologies and open to Gary Soto's short story, "La Bamba," a tale about an embarrassing moment in a school talent show. Mrs. Langham asks students what good readers do. Students offer a mix of comprehension strategies like predicting or summarizing, and behaviors, such as "Good readers read a lot." Mrs. Langham begins the lesson by explaining that today students will use four strategies good readers use, then writes them on the board. The Fab Four posters are prominently displayed alongside the dry-erase board, and she refers to them throughout the lesson. She invites the students to watch as she previews the first few pages of text and makes a prediction. The students turn to a partner and do the same. She then reads aloud two pages of the text and pauses to model all four strategies. After each think-aloud, she invites the students to try the strategies with a partner. Each time, students use the strategy starters found on the posters. During the questioning step, the students try role-playing the main character, Manuel, as other students ask him questions about the story and his feelings. Mrs. Langham reads aloud from the text and pauses to model and allow pairs to use the strategies four times during the class period. Before the bell rings, she asks the students to reflect on their strategy use and to think about which one they thought was most helpful today and why. Juan shares, "I like predicting because it kept me interested." Petra concludes, "Questioning was fun. It is like being on a game show."

Secondary   The ninth graders in Mr. Green's English class file into the classroom and settle into their desks in late January. He asks the students if they've followed the introduction of Apple's latest product launch, the iPad. Almost all hands go up. Using the interactive whiteboard and his computer, he shows a marketing piece from Apple Computers from the Internet. He explains that as he reads the information, he will demonstrate the Fab Four strategies that all good readers use to process the text and even the promotional DVD online clip. Mr. Green begins by asking students to discuss at their tables what they already know about the iPad. Then, he continues by inviting students to share their responses.

"Every January, Apple announces a new technology product or product line."

"We don't have an Apple, but we have a PC."

"The iPad is based on touch technology."

"I want one because it looks so cool for downloading music and photos."

Mr. Green then skims the headings and demonstrates his predictions. He shares that he thinks the text will explain the features of the new technology because that is the purpose of a marketing text. He invites students to skim the article and then chat at their tables about what they think the reading will be about. After quickly sharing predictions, Mr. Green reads four paragraphs and stops to think out loud and model his questions, which mostly center around wonders, such as, "I wonder why I need this tool. I wonder how this technology fits in to my life if I already have a cell phone with the same applications, a computerized reader device, and an MP3 player." He invites students to share what they are wondering, and a lively discussion ensues. Then, Mr. Green continues by modeling points he wants to clarify, more predictions, and a quick summary of the reading so far. He provides a few minutes for the students to run through the same strategies at their tables before he continues reading the article. After he is through, Mr. Green models a summary, more questions, and ideas and vocabulary that he wants to clarify. He asks the students to rank from 1 to 4 which of the strategies were most useful in reading the article. A lively debate ensues as students chime in with the merits of each of the four.

"Skimming the text to predict helped me the most, as it helped me think about what I know before reading."

"I liked asking wonders before we read each section, because that kept my interest."

"Summarizing was the most helpful, because we did it in small chunks not for the entire article."

"I like discussing our parts to clarify and not having to write anything."

The students practice the Fab Four strategies by choosing to read either a news article from the *New York Times* reporting on the iPad launch or a *PC World* article comparing the iPad and the Amazon Kindle for educational classroom use. The students use all four strategies but focus on comparing and contrasting as part of their summaries. Throughout the rest of the week, students bring in cartoons, articles, and editorials on the iPad to discuss using the Fab Four.

Lesson 2: Using the Fab Four Bookmark

BACKGROUND AND DESCRIPTION

The Fab Four Bookmark (see page 74) provides prompts for each reciprocal teaching strategy and aids students as they work their way through texts and reciprocal teaching discussions. It is a useful tool in introductory lessons with reciprocal teaching and also serves as a guide every time you use reciprocal teaching strategies throughout the school year. You can apply this flexible teaching aid in a variety of settings, including whole-class sessions, partner interactions, guided reading groups, and literature circles. If you choose, print the bookmark and laminate it for durability. One second-grade teacher I know stores the laminated bookmarks in plastic bins at the center of each cluster of desks. A middle school teacher copies the bookmark for all of his students to use in literature circles. When the bookmarks are easily accessible, you can ask students to grab them anytime and weave reciprocal teaching strategies into a read-aloud, shared reading, or social studies lesson. Students quickly turn to a partner, using the bookmark as a discussion guide during whole-class lessons or at a center or workstation.

This lesson requires multiple-strategy use—understanding that good readers use more than one strategy during a given reading—and emphasizes think-alouds as an integral part of reciprocal teaching. Remind your students that there are other strategies that good readers use, such as previewing, making connections, and visualizing (Keene & Zimmermann, 1997; McLaughlin & Allen, 2002; Pearson et al., 1992).

MATERIALS

- A Big Book or multiple copies of the reading material
- A copy of the Fab Four Bookmark (laminated, optional) for each student (see page 74)
- An overhead projector, interactive whiteboard, or document camera to show the reading material to the class

1. When introducing reciprocal teaching strategies to your students, ask them to tell you what good readers do and list those ideas on a chart that the whole class can see.

2. Pass out the Fab Four Bookmarks and tell your students that you will model four strategies that good readers use to comprehend text effectively. Tell your students that the strategies will help them better understand and remember what they read and that they will have the opportunity to think aloud and take turns "being the teacher" after watching you demonstrate.

3. Use a Big Book or hand out multiple copies of the chosen text, so all of your students can see it. For effective modeling, you might use an overhead projector copy of the same text that the students have in their hands. Or, you could use a document camera to show the text as you model. You may want to put the bookmark on the overhead or document camera projector as well.

4. Model for your students the use of all the prompts. First, predict by previewing the text's title, covers, headings, and illustrations. Next, read aloud a paragraph or two from the text. After reading, model a think-aloud using the other prompts on the reciprocal teaching bookmark—question, clarify, and summarize. You might end the think-aloud by predicting again what might happen in the next portion of the text.

5. Use the bookmark continually to model all four reciprocal teaching strategies during think-alouds. Over time, your students will become familiar with the language of the strategies and the multiple-strategy use of reciprocal teaching.

6. After your students understand that reciprocal teaching strategies work together as tools for comprehending a text, you may want to focus on one strategy at a time while using the bookmark prompts and modeling a think-aloud. This modeling can be done in a whole-class, guided reading, or literature circle setting.

1. After your think-aloud or even throughout the lesson, ask your students to reflect on strategy use. Ask them, "How did I use each reciprocal teaching strategy to help me read this text, and which strategy was the most helpful?"

2. Guide the use of one strategy with partners or table groups. Rather than expecting your students to produce all four strategies at once, model a think-aloud for one of the strategies, then use the following guided practice steps:

- Guide the class in coming up with an example of the chosen strategy (e.g., if you modeled a prediction, have your students help you generate another one).
- Allow time for your students to try generating examples of the strategy by working in pairs or table groups (see Figure 9). Then, have them share with the entire class. This kind of small-group interaction encourages all students to try the strategies in a supportive environment.

Figure 9
Two Fifth-Grade Students Using the Fab Four Bookmark

Reciprocal Teaching at Work: Powerful Strategies and Lessons for Improving Reading Comprehension (second edition) by Lori D. Oczkus. © 2010. Newark, DE: International Reading Association. May be copied for classroom use.

3. Use partner practice. Have student pairs work through a text together to try the strategies aloud. Use one of the following scenarios:

- Each student takes a turn reading the text aloud and trying all four strategies.

- Each student reads the text aloud, and the listening partner tries all four strategies.

- Each partner alternates reading aloud and helping the other with all four strategies.

- Each partner alternates reading aloud, and each chooses two reciprocal teaching strategies to try.

The following tips may help you assess your students when using the Fab Four Bookmark to scaffold and practice reciprocal teaching strategies:

- Circulate around the classroom and listen to your students' discussions. Are they referring to the bookmark's prompts as they work their way through the text?

- Note with which strategies your students are most and least proficient.

- Observe whether your students' predictions are supported by clues from the text.

- Note whether your students are just restating the text or giving a concise summary.

- Note whether your students ask only literal questions and whether the questions are from the text.

- Note whether your students recognize several techniques for clarifying unknown words.

- Provide additional support for students struggling with the strategies by using the bookmark while meeting with small, guided reading groups.

- Use the minilessons found at the end of Chapters 2–5 to reinforce each individual strategy. Teach these lessons in small groups or to the entire class. (See Table 5, pages 26–27, for further suggestions about what to do when your students have problems using the strategies.)

Fab Four Bookmark	**Fab Four Bookmark**

 Predict

Use clues from the text or illustrations to predict what will happen next.

I think...because...
I'll bet...because...
I suppose...because...
I think I will learn...because...

 Question

Ask questions as you read. Some are answered in the book, and others are inferred.

I wonder....
Who? What? When? Where? Why? How?
Why do you think?

 Clarify

How can you figure out tricky or hard words and ideas?

I didn't get the [word, part, idea] so I:
• Reread   • Ask if it makes sense
• Read on   • Talk to a friend
• Sound words out

 Summarize

Using your *own* words, tell the main ideas from the text in order.

This text is about....   Next,....
This part is about....   Then,....
First,....   Finally,....

 Predict

Use clues from the text or illustrations to predict what will happen next.

I think...because...
I'll bet...because...
I suppose...because...
I think I will learn...because...

 Question

Ask questions as you read. Some are answered in the book, and others are inferred.

I wonder....
Who? What? When? Where? Why? How?
Why do you think?

 Clarify

How can you figure out tricky or hard words and ideas?

I didn't get the [word, part, idea] so I:
• Reread   • Ask if it makes sense
• Read on   • Talk to a friend
• Sound words out

 Summarize

Using your *own* words, tell the main ideas from the text in order.

This text is about....   Next,....
This part is about....   Then,....
First,....   Finally,....

Lesson 3: Introducing the Reciprocal Teaching Team—The Fab Four

Sometimes as educators, we do some pretty crazy things to help our students learn. Once the classroom door closes, we often use puppets, character voices, humor, and songs to keep learning fun and memorable. Every so often when we cut loose, the students beg us for more! I've used the Fab Four character ideas in literally hundreds of lessons with great success. Students of all ages enjoy the characters that bring the comprehension strategies to life. Teachers share many interesting and fun adaptations to this idea as well.

This lesson is useful for introducing all four reciprocal teaching strategies in an entertaining manner that has a lasting impact. The lesson shows students how reciprocal teaching strategies work together and separately while someone is reading a text.

The goal of the lesson is to introduce students to all four strategies by watching the strategies in use during a teacher think-aloud. If you are a bit shy, use either the characters' voices or the props; otherwise, use both simultaneously. After this initial lesson, you might not use the characters again, but you might refer to them as you continue modeling the strategies during think-alouds. Mrs. Jimenez, a fifth-grade teacher, continually refers to the characters and displays the props, even though she only acted them out a few times. She often asks the students, "WWCD, or what would Clara the Clarifier do in this instance? What is her job?" or "WWQD, what would Quincy the Questioner do?" The students are hooked with the metaphor and the humor. How far you take the reciprocal teaching characters depends on your students and their interest in the characters. I suggest you decide what you are comfortable with on the scale of kookiness and try the lesson with your students.

The following are some options to consider for your think-alouds:

- Use these characters or create your own.
- Decide how far to take the metaphor. You might dress up and use the props, use just the props, have a student dress up, use puppets, or simply use an icon or photo.

- A fourth-grade teacher came up with a surfer dude to represent the clarifier. This comical choice allowed him to use a Southern California accent and say, "I don't really get it, dude."

- Ask high school or middle school students to select their own metaphors by thinking of actors or musicians (including rappers!) to go with each of the jobs of the strategies.

- A literacy consultant, Julie Wise, adapted my metaphor and character idea in her work with middle school and high school students by developing three separate sets of Readers Theatre lessons incorporating real-world settings that include mystery, sports, and medical characters. My favorite are her sports characters because the pitcher predicts, the coach clarifies, the quarterback questions, and the sports reporter summarizes. The class reads a short nonfiction piece or story (e.g, from *Chicken Soup for the Teenage Soul: 101 Stories of Life, Love and Learning* by Jack Canfield, Mark Victor Hansen, and Kimberly Kirberger). Then, during reading, Wise asks for four volunteers to read aloud from a Readers Theatre script as they role-play characters that represent the four strategies. The rest of the class observes the actors and discusses the role the strategies play in helping comprehend the text. Students work in groups to try out the strategies as they read and discuss the remaining text.

- Intermediate specialist Jennifer Grillo employs a really creative take on the Fab Four. Instead of acting them out herself, she selects a student to surprise the class by knocking on the door and entering the classroom dressed as one of the characters. She plays a song on her MP3 player (e.g., "The Pink Panther Theme" by Henry Mancini for predicting) to accompany the grand entrance (for a list of songs, see Oczkus, 2009, page 90). The student then poses as the strategy character and explains what his or her job is during reading. What could be a more memorable hook for a think-aloud lesson on a reading strategy?

- I've received feedback from teachers in at least half a dozen schools across the United States who have sent me e-mails to share that staff members dressed up as the Fab Four characters and put on a skit for their grade-level students or sometimes even the entire school! Everyone giggles and remembers such a playful exposure to the reciprocal reading strategies.

- Sometimes primary teachers prefer using puppets for the characters (Myers, 2005). You can select any puppets you already have to use as the four strategy characters. I created the Fab Four Reading Comprehension puppets to go with these lessons (see www.primaryconcepts.com

- If the character thing is just not for you, feel free to hold up just the prop, such as the microphone to represent questioning or a camera for summarizing, during your think-aloud lesson.

A brief description of the characters follows.

Peter (or Madam) the Powerful Predictor

Two different characters can be used for the role of the Powerful Predictor—either a weightlifter with an Arnold Schwarzenegger–like voice or a fortuneteller. You should choose whichever character better suits your students' interests. The weightlifter character, Peter the Powerful Predictor, needs small hand weights as props. For the fortuneteller, Madam the Powerful Predictor, use a flowing scarf and colorful, beaded necklaces as props.

Quincy the Quizzical Questioner

Quincy is a fast-talking game show host who sports a necktie, sports coat, and plastic microphone, preferably the kind that echoes. He usually begins his part of the lesson by shouting out, "Who, what, when, where, why, how, and what if? I am Quincy the Quizzical Questioner! I ask questions before, during, and after reading."

Clara the Careful Clarifier

Clara is a sophisticated lady who wears white gloves, wacky reading glasses, and a feather boa, and carries a pointer. She uses phrases such as "Yes, darling" and "That would be quite lovely" throughout the lesson. She often holds the reading material very close to her face as she tries to clarify a word or reread a portion of text for understanding.

Sammy the Super Summarizer

There are two choices for the summarizer character. Sammy can be either a cowboy with a cowboy hat and a lasso, rounding up the main idea—"I am Sammy the Super Summarizer, and I round up the main ideas and summarize anything I read"—or a tacky tourist who totes a camera and shoots photo after photo but then stops to contemplate which ones to send to a friend or put online.

The Fab Four can be used in many different classroom settings and grade levels to introduce reciprocal teaching strategies to students in a creative way. Good readers sample, rotate, and make constant use of all four strategies to construct meaning from a text (Palincsar & Brown, 1984). Your goal is to help your students feel the flow of using all four strategies together. In the classes that I have taught, students seem to more easily remember the reciprocal teaching strategies and how they help readers when I use this rather comical lesson plan. (The Classroom Story on page 81 shows this lesson plan in action.)

MATERIALS

- Any text—a newspaper article, Big Book, or a fiction or nonfiction selection from a reading series—will work as long as students can see the text. Use a document camera, interactive whiteboard, or overhead projector if necessary.

- Props for each character:

  Peter (or Madam) the Powerful Predictor: hand weights, or a flowing scarf and colorful, beaded necklaces, respectively

  Quincy the Quizzical Questioner: a necktie, sports coat, and a plastic microphone (that echoes, if possible)

  Clara the Careful Clarifier: glasses, white gloves, or a feather boa

  Sammy the Super Summarizer: a rope lasso and a cowboy hat, or sunglasses, tourist hat, and camera

TEACHER MODELING

1. Brainstorm and chart strategies that good readers use. Ask your students what good readers do to understand what they read. Have pairs or table groups brainstorm ideas and then list their responses on a piece of butcher paper or a dry-erase board.

2. Share the objective of the lesson. Tell your students that today you will focus on four strategies that good readers use to comprehend text as they read and that you are going to introduce them to the strategies as characters who will think aloud.

3. Introduce each character. Tell your students that each character will help you read the chosen text effectively and that you will be thinking

aloud to model what a good reader thinks while trying to make meaning from a text.

4. Your students will need to see the reading material you are using, so use either a Big Book or an article on an overhead projector or document camera, or make sure your students have copies of the text. Throughout the lesson, model the reciprocal teaching strategies after reading small bits of text, such as paragraphs or pages.

- *Predictor*: Using either the Peter the weight lifter or the fortuneteller character, preview the text by looking at the title, author, covers, and several illustrations within the book. Model how to use clues from the text to make predictions. Use language such as "I previewed the title, cover, and illustrations, and using these clues, I predict that...."

- *Questioner*: Use a plastic microphone as you model how to ask questions throughout the reading process. Show students how to ask questions before reading by previewing the text and wondering aloud what it is about. During the reading, stop periodically and say, "Here is a great spot where a teacher might ask a question. Let me reread the paragraph. I think a great question for this text might start with the question word *how*." Continue to pause and ask questions that check your understanding of the text. Also, model how to answer questions as you read.

- *Clarifier*: Role-playing as Clara the Careful Clarifier using a pair of silly glasses (think party store!), choose a long or difficult word and pause to think aloud about how to decipher it based on chunks, sounds, meaning, and context. You also might choose an entire sentence or passage and think aloud about how to reread (one of Clara's most useful strategies) to gather meaning.

- *Summarizer*: Choose which summarizer character you prefer—either the cowboy or the tourist—to summarize the page or paragraph that you have read aloud. Demonstrate the value in rereading several times and thinking about the main ideas to shrink material into a concise summary.

STUDENT PARTICIPATION

1. Reflect on the strategies. After your first reading and strategy modeling, ask your students what they noticed about each character. Ask questions such as, "How did each character help me understand the reading?" "What did each character do or say?" and "How could we

use these strategies to help us understand what we read?" List your students' responses on a piece of butcher paper or a dry-erase board.

2. Guide your students to use the strategies themselves. Lead a guided discussion by asking your students which character they would like to see go first. You might even allow students to vote for the strategy to go first on the next segment of text to show the flexibility of the strategies. Read aloud another segment of the text as you role-play. After each character models his or her think-aloud, have your students work in pairs to come up with additional predictions, questions, points or words to clarify, or summaries.

3. Have individual students or pairs draw the Fab Four characters. Instruct students to sketch what they think the characters look like and maybe even write a line or two about their jobs. Students should write or discuss a reflection on how each strategy helps them comprehend what they read. They may refer to the list that the class has already created on the butcher paper or dry-erase board. Discuss, share, and then display on the classroom wall the reciprocal teaching characters that your students draw. (See Figure 10 for an example.)

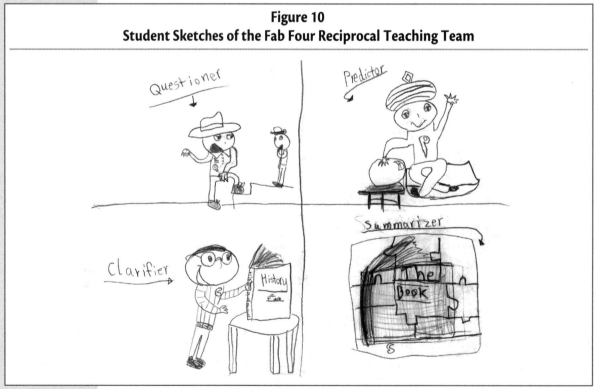

Figure 10
Student Sketches of the Fab Four Reciprocal Teaching Team

Circulate around the classroom and listen to pairs of students during the guided activity after your students have heard a model for a reciprocal teaching strategy. Do the pairs copy the model? Students may offer the same summary as yours. Copying is OK at this early stage if the students understood the model. The following points will help you determine whether your students understood.

- Do your students come up with a sensible but new prediction, question, point or word to clarify (or way to clarify the word that you modeled), or summary?
- Do the students' drawings reflect the character who uses the strategy during reading?
- Can your students verbalize to one another the jobs of each reciprocal teaching team member?

If your students are having difficulty verbalizing the jobs, drawing the characters, or giving their own examples for each strategy, consider teaching the minilessons that separately reinforce each of the reciprocal teaching strategies. Also, use the suggestions found in Table 5, Overcoming the Difficulties That Students Experience With Reciprocal Teaching Strategies (see pages 26–27), when your students have problems using any of the four strategies.

Introducing the Reciprocal Teaching Team—The Fab Four— to Grade 2 Using Nonfiction Text

As I wait for the second graders to arrive after lunch, I check my goodie bag to see if I have all the props for my reciprocal teaching characters lesson. I always feel a little silly using voices and props to dramatize the strategy characters (especially in front of the teachers who watch me), but the effort is worth it! In the classrooms where I teach this lesson, the students catch on to the strategies a bit faster. In this particular second-grade class, today is the first time that these students will be introduced to the reciprocal teaching model, even though their teacher has introduced some of the good reader strategies—previewing, self-questioning, making connections, visualizing, knowing how words work, monitoring, summarizing, and evaluating (Keene & Zimmermann, 1997; McLaughlin & Allen, 2002; Pearson et al., 1992). These students most likely will have some familiarity with the four reciprocal teaching strategies: predicting, questioning, clarifying, and summarizing.

Predicting   As the students gather at my feet on the rug next to my chair, I begin the lesson by telling them that they are about to meet four characters that help them read every day. The book I have chosen to model from is the nonfiction text *Antarctica: Land of* *the Penguins* by Jonathan and Angela Scott (2005). I ask the students to think about what they already know about penguins and to share that with a partner using the frame "I think I already know..." (Oczkus, 2004). The lively partner chats include such comments as, "I saw that movie *March of the Penguins*" and "They live in the cold." I tell the students that this information they already know will help them make predictions as they read.

I then say, "Boys and girls, I'd like you to meet my friend Peter the Powerful Predictor." The students wait with great anticipation as I dig around in my mystery bag, pull out some small hand weights, and begin lifting one in each hand as I talk about making powerful predictions. I try to use an Arnold Schwarzenegger–like voice, which is difficult to maintain throughout the entire lesson, but all the kids know who he is and love it when I try. The students giggle as they watch in earnest to see what this "crazy lady" will do next.

Then, I show the book's cover and talk about the powerful predictions that I can make by using the book's captions and pictures. I conduct a brief preview of the first few pages by studying illustrations and headings to make predictions: "I predict for the first part of the book that I will learn about Antarctica where the penguins live and about different types of penguins, yaaah" (I model in my Austrian accent). Then, I ask the students to work with a partner to give at least two additional predictions, and we share our predictions in a whole-class setting.

Questioning   Next, I ask the students to close their eyes, so I can introduce them to another character from the reciprocal teaching team—Quincy the Quizzical Questioner. I unzip my mystery bag and dig around to reveal a plastic microphone that echoes as I use an announcer voice for Quincy. "I am Quincy the Quizzical Questioner, and I have some questions as I read," I boom into the microphone. Then, I read aloud just four pages of the text as myself, and as I read, I stop to be interrupted by Quincy: "Hey, how can penguins survive in the coldest place on earth? I wonder why the authors chose to write about mostly Antarctica in the first nine pages. Maybe because they wanted us to really understand how difficult it is to survive there and how penguins do it. I wonder if any humans have ever tried to live there for very long."

I ask the students to pair up again to look over the first four pages of the book, choose a page, and make up a question to ask the group. I tell them that they can ask a question that is answered in the text or one that is not. The pairs are eager to share their questions:

"How many kinds of penguins live in Antarctica?"

"How much does an emperor penguin weigh?"

"What is an iceberg?"

Clarifying   When I am finished alternating between reading and questioning for several pages, I stop and tell the students that there is another character they should meet— Clara the Careful Clarifier. For Clara's props, I reach into my bag and pull out a pair of large glasses and a pointer. I choose a sophisticated accent and say, "Hello, children. I'm Clara the Careful Clarifier, and I am here to see if there are any words or parts in the story that I don't understand, darlings."

I look on page 5 and read, "'The area of the Antarctic nearly doubles in size in winter.' I didn't get how the Antarctic can be bigger in the winter, so I reread the sentence, looked at the map, and saw that the gray area expands due to ice that surrounds it in winter. Then it melts in the summer, and the area gets smaller. I thought about what I know about ice, yes darlings, I did." Then, I continue in my Clara voice to reread the sentence and tell the students that it makes sense now. Next, I model how to clarify a word by figuring out the word *enormous*. I show the students how to break the word into syllables and how to read on for context clues. Once again, I ask pairs of students to work together, this time to find a word that may need to be clarified. Pairs share their words and explain to the class how they deciphered them.

Summarizing   Finally, I tell the students that it is time for Sammy the Super Summarizer to pay them a visit. For this part, I wear my cowboy hat and use a jump rope as a lasso that I twirl above my head.

Playing the cowboy, I say, "I'm rounding up the main idea, class. Watch this, I'm gonna reread the pages to myself quickly to get the information fresh in my head, then I will be ready to sum up the main idea!" I page through the text, mumbling various main points to myself. The students giggle as I thumb through the book hunting for important points. Then, I model a summary of the 11 pages of the book read so far. As I give my verbal summary, I point to the pictures in the book to reinforce the vocabulary I am using in my summary.

"Antarctica is at the south end of the world and is the coldest, windiest place on earth with the biggest ocean waves surrounding it. Antarctica is covered with snow and ice and includes islands, a mainland, glaciers, icebergs, and no trees. No humans live there, but seven kinds of penguins, including the large emperor penguin, make Antarctica their home!"

Because summarizing can be so challenging, I invite the students to skim the same pages that I just summarized and then summarize them with a partner. I tell them that it is OK to copy my summary. This is great practice for them to recall the text.

After all that modeling, I have the children go back to their desks and, using the Fab Four Bookmark, work with a partner through the next four pages of the book, stopping to predict, question, clarify, and summarize.

Reflection and Next Steps   After I circulate around the room to listen to the student pairs, I conduct a whole-class discussion, asking students to review the four strategies and tell me what each character does to help us read. In the weeks to come, the classroom teacher and I will use a variety of techniques with reciprocal teaching and will model the strategies while using Big Books, articles, and short stories.

Minilesson: Roll Your Prediction!

Description and Comprehension Strategies

This lesson focuses on the language of predicting. After modeling each of the strategy starters for predicting in a series of think-alouds, ask students to roll strategy dice at their desks with partners and in groups to practice using the language of the strategies.

Materials

- Strategy dice; or write the prediction starters on the dry-erase board in front of the classroom or on a chart and number them to correspond with the dice numbers as follows:

    1. I think I will learn...because....

    2. Maybe...because....

    3. I think...will happen because....

    4. Next, I think...because I know....

    5. and 6. I'll bet...because....

Teacher Modeling

1. Ask students to help you list ways to start predictions. Chart responses.

2. Number the responses and model in a think-aloud each one for students using a text that they can all see (i.e., projected, multiple copies, Big Book).

3. Roll the dice and, whichever number comes up, model how to use that strategy starter. Repeat once more and model the strategy starter that corresponds with the dice number you roll.

Student Participation

1. After you model each starter for predicting, invite students to turn to partners or their table teams to repeat the starter and make another prediction.

2. Continue asking students to try each starter right after you model it.

Assessment Tips

- Listen and observe conversations. Are students making strong predictions? Are they using text clues and their background experiences to formulate their rationale for their predictions? Can they verbally fill in the "because..." portion of the frame with logical reasons?

- Ask students to reflect: "Which starter helped you most in predicting with this text today? Why?"

- Use what you learn from your observations to model new think-alouds.

Minilesson: Pop the Questions

Description and Comprehension Strategies

Students often experience difficulty creating meaningful questions about texts. By using a microphone prop, students role-play and ask three kinds of questions about the text to deepen their comprehension.

Materials

- Microphone prop (inflatable, toy, or real microphone)
- Four Door Chart for recording questions (see page 110)

Teacher Modeling

1. Select a text to model one of the types of questioning with any of the following:

   - *Wonders*—Good readers wonder before and during reading by pausing and asking, "I wonder...?" about the text.

   - *Quiz Questions*—These questions that begin with *who, what, when, where, why,* and *how* and require students to go back to the text and find an answer directly or infer an answer using text clues and background knowledge.

   - *Thinking Questions*—These begin with "Why do you think...?" or "How did you...?" and require the student to use inferences to answer.

2. As you think aloud, pause and tell students how you are constructing your question based on the text: "I think I will ask...here, because I am thinking...."

3. Teach a series of lessons on questions to help students learn the different types of questions that good readers ask as they read. Use a variety of texts from fiction to nonfiction. Model in whole-group and guided reading lessons.

Student Participation

1. After you model one type of question listed above, invite students to create their own questions based on the text and questions that require inferential thinking. Ask them to work in pairs and use either toy microphones or their fists as pretend ones. Share the best questions with the class.

2. Students take turns role-playing as characters from the text and use microphones to ask the characters questions. They work in groups or pairs to create interview questions.

3. Encourage students to record their questions on a Four Door Chart.

(continued)

Minilesson: Pop the Questions (continued)

Assessment Tips

- Listen and observe conversations. Are students asking logical questions? Are they asking only literal questions?

- Ask students to reflect: "Which questions helped you most in understanding this text today? Why?"

- Use what you learn from your observations to model new think-alouds on questioning.

- Collect the Four Door Charts and note problems students are having with asking questions.

Minilesson: Pause and Clarify It!

Description and Comprehension Strategies

Students need to recognize difficulties in their reading and know when to apply fix-up strategies to clarify. Teach a series of lessons that focus on different problems readers may encounter when they read and the strategies they need to clarify those problems.

Materials

- Clara's glasses (optional)
- Chart paper
- Text displayed for students to see

Teacher Modeling

1. Select a text to model. Use the hand motion for pause (see page XX for a description of this gesture) and ask students to follow along as you model the following ways to clarify. You can do all of these in the course of one lesson or separate them out into different lessons.

    - Pause to clarify a word: "I didn't get the word...so I [reread, read on, thought of a synonym that makes sense, chopped the word into parts (beginning sound, ending sound, parts I know, syllables), sounded it out]."

    - Pause to clarify a sentence: "I didn't get the sentence where it says...so I [reread, read on, said it in my own words, thought about what I know, visualized, asked a friend]."

    - Pause to clarify a part, paragraph, or chapter: "I didn't get the [paragraph, chapter, part] where it says...so I [reread, read on, visualized, thought about what I know, asked a friend]."

2. Read another chunk of text and model again selecting either a word, sentence, or part to clarify. Make a list on a chart of all the strategies for clarifying.

Student Participation

1. After each example, ask students to turn to their partners or table groups to find new examples. Encourage students to use the frame "I didn't get...so I [select from fix-up strategies]."

2. Have students fold and cut a Four Door Chart (see page 110) and then write an example on each door. On the inside, they can describe which strategies helped them get beyond the places where they paused to clarify.

(continued)

Minilesson: Pause and Clarify It! (continued)

Assessment Tips

- Listen and observe conversations. Are students using a variety of strategies to clarify? Are they able to identify entire sentences and parts of the text that are difficult? If students say they get everything, ask them to select something a younger student might not understand as an example.

- Collect the Four Door Charts and see if students are identifying words and ideas to clarify and how they are using a variety of strategies to do so. Reteach and model clarifying often!

- Use what you learn from your observations to model new think-alouds on clarifying.

Minilesson: A "Clear" Summary

Description and Comprehension Strategies

Each cooperative group or pair writes a summary on an overhead transparency, or on regular paper to project with a document camera, to share with the class. Students write summaries for fiction or nonfiction texts or both. Comprehension strategies include writing a concise, clear summary and choosing main points to order in the summary.

Materials

- A copy of the text for each student
- One overhead transparency or paper per pair or group, or paper to show on the document camera
- Transparency pens or markers for each group
- Summarizing character prop of a camera or cowboy's rope (optional)

Teacher Modeling

1. Choose a text that is familiar to the class. Model writing a summary with the overhead projector and decorate it with a few illustrations. Or, create a summary in front of the students using the document camera and a piece of paper. Think out loud as you go and, if you can, point to or underline the key points in a copy of the text. Tell how you select what is important.
2. Ask the class to name the steps involved in writing a clear, concise summary.
3. As a bonus activity, you might even try limiting the number of words for the summary. For example, have students write a 25-word summary. This creates a game-like, fun, challenging atmosphere.

Student Participation

1. Have your students work in pairs or groups to create summaries of the text that they have read. They should write the summary on an overhead transparency sheet, or paper to show on the document camera, sign their names, and decorate the summary with illustrations. Try breaking material into sections and assigning each group a portion of the text to summarize.
2. Ask the pairs or groups to share their summaries with the entire class.
3. Ask your students to reflect on what makes a good summary for fiction and for nonfiction. How are they similar or different?

Assessment Tips

- Can your students work in a group to write an effective summary that includes important events in order?
- Ask your students to reflect on how summarizing helps them to comprehend what they read. Provide extra support for students who are struggling by working with a small group to create a clear summary.

Lesson used with permission of Sandy Buscheck, Del Rey School, Orinda, California.

CHAPTER SUMMARY

- Research studies suggest that teachers should introduce all four strategies as quickly as possible to benefit from the power and research behind multiple-strategy instruction (NICHD, 2000; Reutzel et al., 2005).

- There are many effective ways to introduce the Fab Four to your class, including the following:

  - Modeling during fiction or nonfiction and poetry

  - Using characters, props, or icons as metaphors to represent each strategy

  - Supplying mentor texts or texts that support each of the strategies: Select one text per strategy and use high-interest materials for your grade level

  - Gesturing for each of the strategies to provide students with a kinesthetic hook that cues each of the strategies and their uses

- Once you've introduced reciprocal teaching to your class, select a consistent time and setting in which to use it and do so at least twice a week to reap benefits.

- Continually model the strategies all year long, not just in introductory lessons.

- Collect student responses or observe during group work, and adjust your instruction according to your findings. Teach minilessons on one strategy at a time, when necessary.

CHAPTER 3

RECIPROCAL TEACHING
in Whole-Class Sessions

Clarify is when you go back if you don't understand and look at the text again. If it's a sentence you don't really understand, you could reread it. If it's a word, you can look for a part you know, syllables, or sound it out.

—Jacob, grade 3

Engaging Students in Whole-Class Lessons

Once you've worked your way through some introductory lessons (see Chapter 2), you and your students can turn any reading lesson into a lively exchange for learning! When you incorporate the Fab Four with your class, your students won't be in a "sit and get" mode; instead, they'll participate throughout the lessons and will be accountable for learning!

Consider the following examples of engaging whole-class Fab Four lessons at a variety of grade levels:

- First graders gather on the rug as Miss Raines reads aloud from the Big Book *The Night Owl* by Jill Eggleton and pauses every three to four pages to model the Fab Four. She asks the students for help: "I am stuck on a word on this page. Which strategy do I need to use first?" The students quickly signal with the hand motion for clarify, and the teacher follows up by modeling how to clarify the word by rereading and breaking it into familiar parts. The students turn to a partner and choose another word from the page to clarify. Before reading on, Miss Raines uses the same pages and alternates between modeling and inviting partners to try each of the following: how to summarize in a sentence or two, how to ask a question that starts with the word *why*, and how to make a prediction by peeking at the next page. She reads on and pauses every few pages to ask students which strategy she needs using the prompts "I am wondering...," "I think...will happen next," and "Here is what has happened so far...." The students are engaged as they turn to partners to share and use the hand motions for each strategy to cue their thinking and keep them from getting wiggly.

- An enthusiastic discussion begins at each table as Mr. Lopez directs his fourth-grade students to work in groups of five to preview the headings of their social studies text and skim the text for key words about which to make predictions. The students write their predictions on their table group's Fab Four Mat (page 123). Each table leader shares the group's predictions in a whole-class discussion. After reading the first two pages of text, Mr. Lopez models how to ask a quiz question and a thinking question, and he models how to clarify a challenging vocabulary word. Teams scour the text for the best questions and words to clarify as they record their responses on their mats. At the end of the lesson, Mr. Lopez leads the students in a discussion, and the students list the most important points from the text on the board. Next, he challenges the students to pare down the main ideas to write a 25-word summary of the text. The teams hunch over their desks and fervently race to meet the challenge.

- The eighth graders in Mrs. Bridges's classroom turn to their table mates to summarize what happened yesterday in the novel they are reading, *To Kill a Mocking Bird* by Harper Lee. Next, she models questioning using the starter "How do you think...?" She specifically asks, "How do you think Scout felt in this chapter?" Then she models how to clarify challenging paragraphs or sentences by stating, "I didn't get this sentence where it says...so I...." Students do the same using questions that begin with "How do you think...?" and clarifying statements that start with "I didn't get...so I...." Then, Mrs. Bridges models how to skim the text and incorporate that information into a prediction for the next chapter. The students continue working in teams to discuss the chapter using the Fab Four as Mrs. Bridges rotates among the tables to guide student discussions.

One of my favorite ways to reinforce reciprocal teaching strategies is with well-crafted whole-class lessons. Of course, teaching to the whole class all the time is not ideal for differentiating student needs, as a careful mix of excellent instruction in a variety of small-group settings is critical for reaching all students (Allington, 2001). However, when structured properly, the whole-class session can provide students with a sense of community (Kohn, 1996) and support to reinforce reciprocal teaching strategies. Whole-class sessions also offer students a place to establish a common language for the four strategies and afford all students the opportunity to participate in the same piece of literature. When working with all of your students, you can initially scaffold and introduce reciprocal teaching and then move into cooperative groups, pairs, or guided reading groups for a follow-up lesson.

Using whole-class instruction to bring the class together for meaningful activities before and after reading allows your students to benefit from the rich backgrounds and ideas of their classmates. Third-grade teacher Glorianna Chen shares that when she uses reciprocal teaching during whole-class lessons, her struggling readers give thoughtful responses and have a chance to excel in front of their peers. The message to students of all ability levels is that we believe they are capable of reading, understanding what they read, and sharing ideas surrounding the literature or content area text. I have worked with many struggling readers who appreciate being included in class work with grade-level literature, and their comments are insightful and respected by their classmates. When I conduct a class demonstration of reciprocal teaching strategies, I cannot always tell which students struggle and frequently am surprised after the lesson when the classroom teacher tells me who they are, because these students often shine in whole-class sessions.

Meeting Students' Needs by Alternating Whole-Class Sessions With Small-Group Instruction

Although whole-class instruction provides an effective setting in which to introduce and reinforce reciprocal teaching strategies, it has some disadvantages that you should keep in mind. A common drawback is that individual students have diverse needs that cannot all be met in a whole-class session. For example, in a sixth-grade class in one rural school in which I worked, Lincoln Elementary, we introduced and reinforced reciprocal teaching twice a week to the whole class using picture books, the basal reader, a news magazine (*Time for Kids*), and the social studies book. Then, to ensure that we were differentiating for individual needs, we taught twice-weekly guided reading lessons (see Chapter 4) using the instructional level for struggling readers. However, students who were not as attentive during whole-class lessons, like Tommy, Billy, and Evette, learned to focus in a smaller group. Other students who benefited from small-group instruction were shy Bryan and quiet Ishmael, who were reluctant to speak in a large group but opened up in front of fewer students. We learned that these students needed more than the whole-class exposure to reciprocal teaching to make progress in their reading comprehension. An intuitive teacher will use regular running records, observations, and other assessments during a whole-class session to judge when to break into cooperative groups, independent work, literacy centers, or a teacher-led group. By mixing whole-class instruction with other groupings and using engaging whole-class techniques, you can overcome the challenges that whole-class teaching presents.

Following is an example of how to move from whole-group to small-group instruction to meet your students' needs. In this example, I modeled reciprocal teaching strategies using nonfiction reading material in a whole-class lesson, then met with guided reading groups using the same book, and finally pulled the whole class together to end the lesson.

Whole-Group Instruction to Introduce the Book

I introduced one of my favorite nonfiction books, *Sunken Treasure* by Gail Gibbons, to a fourth-grade class. First, I activated the students' prior knowledge by asking them what they knew about lost ships or sunken treasure. Hands waved, and many students offered stories about the *Titanic*. Then, I assigned a student from each table to write the group's responses on sticky notes, bring them up to a K-W-L chart (Ogle, 1986), and place them in the What I Know column. Next, I asked students to preview the text, and I modeled how to make a prediction starting with "I think I will learn...because...." Then, I invited teams to make predictions at their tables. After that, I modeled how to question before reading with "I wonder..." and invited table runners up once again to post the sticky notes from their table discussions on the K-W-L chart in the What I Want to Know column. Kayla and Saul wondered how the divers make the grid. Justin and Clayton wondered how long the *Atocha* remained underwater before someone discovered it. I also read aloud several pages of the book and modeled all four of the reciprocal teaching strategies in a quick think-aloud (see Fast Fab Four lesson, page 174). Then, I asked the students to work in pairs to read the selection, stopping every two pages to work through reciprocal teaching strategies verbally.

Small Guided Reading Groups With the Same Book

During the partner reading time, I met briefly with two guided reading groups that each had a majority of struggling readers (see Chapter 4 for discussion of using reciprocal teaching with guided reading groups), and I used reciprocal teaching in this small, teacher-led group format. The groups of six students each were organized around needs and were flexible as those needs changed. About once a month, I used assessments in which students either wrote or verbalized their use of the four reciprocal teaching strategies.

Whole Group Meets Again

After the students finished with a reading assignment, the whole class convened to contribute to the What I Learned column of the K-W-L chart and to discuss their reactions to the book. I asked each table group to fill out a large sticky note with at least four things they'd learned from the reading and to bring it up to the What I Learned column of the K-W-L chart. In order for students to make the strategies their own (Pearson & Fielding, 1991), I asked students to reflect on how each reciprocal teaching strategy had helped them understand what they had read. Kelsey shared that her favorite strategy was summarizing, because she could remember what she learned and tell her mom in the evening. Leo, a struggling reader, often named the clarify strategy as his favorite, because it helped him figure out challenging words. The book became a class favorite, and students checked out other books on sunken ships.

This chapter outlines essential teaching foundations that facilitate and enhance whole-class instruction, whether you are introducing or reinforcing reciprocal teaching strategies. In fact, every lesson in this book can be converted fairly easily into a whole-class lesson if you choose to do so. I recommend that you reinforce the reciprocal teaching strategies throughout the day during whole-class literature lessons and in content area reading after your class is familiar with them.

Goals of Reciprocal Teaching During Whole-Class Sessions

The goals of using reciprocal teaching during whole-class sessions are the following:

- To establish a common language for using reciprocal teaching strategies
- To increase opportunities to teach and scaffold reciprocal teaching strategies
- To guide students of all reading levels to improve their reading comprehension in grade-level material
- To show students how to use multiple strategies to comprehend what they read
- To engage in reading comprehension discussions using the reciprocal teaching strategies
- To provide a community format for reinforcing the routines and procedures used in guided reading groups and literature circles

Essential Foundations for Effective Whole-Class Instruction

For reciprocal teaching to be effective, regardless of the classroom setting used, certain instructional foundations—scaffolding, think-alouds, metacognition, and cooperative learning—must be in place so students stay engaged and eventually use the strategies independently. (Refer to Chapter 1 for a discussion of these foundations.) When I coach teachers and we observe one another, we look for the four foundations and ways to strengthen them.

In the example I refer to throughout this section, you'll see that all four foundations make for an interactive whole-class lesson as we read a short article from *People* magazine. (In addition to using grade-level materials, I look for short, interesting newspaper, magazine, or Internet pieces to share with students in whole-class lessons. Animal stories seem to consistently grab students' attention.) This article, "From Stray Dog to Movie Star" (Clark, 2008), describes how a trainer spotted and rescued a dog that went on to star in the movie *Beverly Hills Chihuahua*. I have used this article with students of all ages, usually as a read-aloud for elementary and middle school students. (*Note of caution:* I do have to cover up one profanity because the author quotes comedian George Lopez, who says, "This little dog is a badass.")

Scaffolding in Whole-Class Lessons

When we scaffold during whole-class lessons, we put into action the gradual release of responsibility (Pearson & Gallagher, 1983), which includes teacher modeling, student participation or guided practice in pairs or groups, and a wrap-up or reflection on strategy use. I open the session by stating the reason for the lesson, such as, "I am going to show you how I use the four reciprocal teaching strategies to help me understand what I am reading when I read a magazine article." I show the students the icons on the strategy poster as a review (see Appendix E). As I model for students, I point to the text and use a strategy sentence frame as I demonstrate how to predict by skimming the visuals and text: "I think I will learn how the trainer found the dog that starred in the movie, because I saw the word *shelter*. I read in another article recently that animal trainers for movies like to use shelter dogs, because they are more willing to obey than fat, happy dogs who have owners." The students are eager to share predictions. I provide a scaffold for their responses by asking them to turn to a partner and say, "I think I will learn...because..." and to make their predictions, which we discuss in the whole group. I alternate between reading the article and opportunities for thinking aloud with partners, and then return to whole-class debriefing. I also invite pairs to take turns running through all four strategies with their partners using their Fab Four Bookmarks as guides (see page 74) while I circulate and prompt their responses. Reciprocal teaching is unique in having a design that naturally includes scaffolding by either the teacher or student peers every time it is used in the classroom. By using bookmarks, posters, props, and strategy starters, you can provide additional supports to make the learning stick!

Think-Alouds During Whole-Class Lessons

The lesson continues with a series of think-alouds. I read aloud from the article and pause to clarify an idea. "I didn't get the part where it says, 'From the moment he laid eyes on the mutt, Alexander knew he had found a star.' I am not sure how the trainer could that tell this dog was a star without seeing him work," I explained. I continue to read aloud and explain that by reading on, I learned that the dog was a star because "he had attitude" and ripped up newspapers, bounced around, and stuck his chest out. The students giggle at the thought of this. "You are making pictures in your head to see this crazy dog, aren't you?" I tease.

Think-alouds also are inherent in reciprocal teaching, and they are an important foundation for achieving maximum results in reading comprehension. Each reciprocal teaching session includes opportunities for the teacher and the students to make their thinking public. Because reading strategies are not as visible as, say, strategies involved in a science experiment, it is critical to talk through the steps and the thought processes involved in comprehending a text, so good reading strategies become more tangible for students. By witnessing constant think-alouds conducted by the teacher and their peers, students begin to internalize the reciprocal teaching strategies and employ them during independent reading.

Metacognition During Whole-Class Lessons

Another necessary instructional foundation is metacognition, which is easily reinforced during whole-class sessions by reminding students of the strategies and reflecting on their purpose. In my example with the doggie star article, I begin the lesson by asking the students to review the strategies, so they remember the "steps" to using each one. Then, I end the lesson by asking students to reflect on the strategies that they used and that were most helpful during the lesson. Throughout the school day, you can lead additional minilessons involving metacognition by using reciprocal teaching strategies for one or two pages in a content area chapter or when your students are reading a newspaper article. Consider the power of talking about the four strategies—predict, question, clarify, and summarize—throughout the school day to reinforce their usefulness to make sense of text. Students will know the how-tos and employ the Fab Four in their own reading.

Cooperative Learning in Whole-Class Lessons

Throughout my read-aloud of the magazine article, I ask students to turn to partners or table groups—as often as every three to seven minutes—to process the information and promote student engagement. Then, after I've modeled the strategies, I release the students to work in their groups while I circulate and work with pairs of students. Cooperative learning is especially important for keeping students engaged during a whole-class session. All teachers have had the experience when teaching the whole class of having only the same handful of students raising their hands to respond (Routman, 2003). To avoid this pitfall, ask students to turn to a partner to practice or discuss points throughout the lesson. Also, weave in table groups—in which students work with others who sit at their tables—or cooperative groups—in which students are placed in mixed-ability or interest groups—for variety. The cooperative atmosphere of the combination of whole-class and small-group exercises encourages every student to respond to and think about the lesson. Students need time to practice, with and without the guidance of a teacher, in order to eventually become more independent. Working in cooperative groups and pairs with reciprocal teaching provides students with valuable opportunities to practice. When student involvement in the lesson increases, so does their achievement (Routman, 2003).

The Big Picture in Whole-Class Sessions: What Else You Will Need to Do

The best advice in regard to whole-class sessions is to avoid overdoing them. Although there is some security in providing the same instruction to all of your students, educators know that students need other types of groupings—both student- and teacher-led—to meet students' diverse needs. You might want to try reciprocal teaching lessons in guided reading groups and literature circles and vary the groupings depending on the reading material and the grade level. When teaching to the whole class, ensure that students are learning by incorporating opportunities for them to talk. Partners or groups are effective, because when students talk about their thinking with one another, their learning increases, plus you can avoid the common pitfall of only a few students raising their hands to participate in whole-class discussions. Chapters 4 and 5 have many suggestions for using small-group formats, such as guided reading groups and literature circles, for instructing students on reciprocal teaching strategies. By combining the best of what whole-class instruction has to offer with small-group activities, you can ensure that all your students' needs are met.

Assessment Options for Reciprocal Teaching During Whole-Class Sessions

When you use reciprocal teaching strategies with your whole class, there are several simple assessment and observation points that can guide future instruction. Refer to the Rubric for the Reciprocal Teaching Strategies in Appendix A for detailed guidelines on what to look for when observing students engaged in a reciprocal teaching discussion. The following list provides general guidelines for student observation:

- Listen to the students who respond during whole-class sessions. Are they effectively using the four reciprocal teaching strategies?

- During whole-class sessions, provide time for table groups to work cooperatively. Circulate around the room and listen to the students' interactions. Intervene when necessary to model a strategy or coach individual students. Pull aside groups that are having trouble with a particular strategy and teach them the appropriate minilesson from the end of this chapter (see pages 124–128).

- Allow time for student pairs to interact and try the reciprocal teaching strategies. Listen for their effective use of the strategies and assist pairs who are having trouble. For struggling students, model a think-aloud using one or all of the strategies.

- Create a brief written assessment by asking students to fill in the Literature Discussion Sheet for Reciprocal Teaching (see Chapter 5, page 205) either cooperatively, with one student serving as the recorder for the group, or individually. Students should not be asked to write the strategies early in reciprocal teaching instruction, but after a few lessons, have them complete the written record to guide your future instruction. You might use the form every two weeks rather than in every discussion.

- After meeting in groups or pairs, pull the whole class together again and point out specific examples of students who used reciprocal teaching strategies effectively. Share what those students discussed and allow all students to try again.

- Lead a class discussion on each reciprocal teaching strategy. Ask your students to define each strategy and identify what steps are involved. Record their responses on a piece of butcher paper or a dry-erase board.

Lesson 1: Cooperative Table Groups and the Fab Four

BACKGROUND AND DESCRIPTION

In the classes with which I work, I introduce reciprocal teaching over several days or even weeks, using texts that I think will be interesting and engaging for students. After I model think-alouds using the Fab Four characters, teach other guided lessons involving partners, and implement the Fab Four Bookmark (see Chapter 2, page 74), students are ready for cooperative table groups. I have found that having students practice reciprocal teaching strategies in read-alouds (see Chapter 2, page 47) before moving to cooperative table groups leads to success.

There are many quick and practical ways to ask students to work in teams right at their tables so that at a moment's notice you can invite students to work cooperatively without having to move. Allow students to turn to and discuss the reading material and the strategies with their table groups and then signal to all to participate in a whole-group lesson again. I like to alternate throughout a lesson with the following scaffolded steps: (1) I model one of the strategies such as clarifying, (2) students share at tables for just a few minutes to find another example, and (3) the whole class participates in a discussion. Then, we begin the process over again as I model another strategy. We may pause during reading to rotate through the steps several times depending on the text. This type of interactive lesson ensures that students see a number of think-aloud models and that they try out the strategies in a scaffolded, or structured, discussion format. Students can be required to write as a team or with a recorder jotting down the group's responses; however, try not to use written responses every time your students work in teams. Remember, reciprocal teaching is a discussion technique, and any writing should be just a quick note to prompt discussions!

The following are some practical table team options to consider.

- *Four Door Charts for all*—To ensure individual accountability, ask students to each fill out a Four Door Chart during the lesson (see page 110) or a Literature Discussion Sheet for Reciprocal Teaching (see page 205). Collect the forms to assess each student's level of participation and to adjust instruction in each strategy.

- *Table runners*—Assign a "table runner" for each table; this person records the group's responses and shares the information. For example, you can create a poster with four boxes and a space to put sticky notes for each of the strategies, and then as you work through the strategies, the table runners bring the groups' responses up to the chart. Another option is to post four separate charts, one for each of the reciprocal teaching strategies. With either option, the table runners bring a sticky note with the groups' responses to the chart to share and post. Some teachers like to put photos or drawings of the characters on the charts, or the icons work well to make the charts more interesting and to visually represent the strategy use (see Figure 7, page 57).

- *Recorders*—Assign a recorder in each table group to write the group's responses. You might use either the Literature Discussion Sheet for Reciprocal Teaching or the Fab Four Mat (see page 123) to record this information.

MATERIALS

- A copy of the reading material for each student in the classroom
- Fab Four Bookmarks (optional; see Chapter 2, page 74)
- Literature Discussion Sheet for Reciprocal Teaching (see page 205)
- Fab Four Mat (see page 123)

TEACHER MODELING

1. Review and display on a chart the Fab Four strategies predict, question, clarify, and summarize. Ask students what good readers do to understand what they read. Have pairs or table groups review the strategies. Use the Fab Four Bookmark as an optional tool.

2. Another option is to review with students an example from your own reading and explain how the Fab Four has helped you comprehend something (you can simply use an Internet article or a novel you're reading). Ask table groups to quickly discuss how they've used the Fab Four in their recreational or independent reading (Cooper et al., 1999).

3. Introduce the reading material. Tell students that after you model each of the strategies for them, they will work in their table groups to come up with their own examples from the text.

4. Activate students' prior knowledge about the reading material. When reading nonfiction, ask students to tell what they think they already know. First, model how you reflect on your prior knowledge by using the frame "I see...on the cover, and the title is.... I think I already know...." When reading fiction, model how to activate your background knowledge by saying, "This reminds me of...because...." After modeling, give students one minute to discuss their ideas.

5. Read aloud from the text. Pause after one or two pages to conduct a think-aloud with each of the reciprocal teaching strategies, which helps show students how good readers employ all four strategies with the same passage of text. Use the following strategy starters to give students a model for the language they may use in their table discussions (or see Appendix E):

   - *Predict*: "I think I will learn...because...," and "I think...will happen because..."

   - *Question*: "I wonder..." and questions beginning with why, who, what, how, where, and when.

   - *Clarify*: "I didn't get [the word, idea, part] so I [reread, read on, looked for parts I knew]"

   - *Summarize*: "So far...," "This is mostly about...," "First,...," "Next...," and "Then,...."

STUDENT PARTICIPATION

1. After you read aloud and model how to predict, invite table groups to make predictions. Then, signal for groups to stop sharing and conduct a whole-group discussion. If you are using table runners, direct them to record the group's prediction on a sticky note and bring it to the chart to post in the predict section. Allow time for sharing.

2. Alternate these simple steps with each of the four strategies: Model the strategy, allow table groups to discuss, conduct a whole-class debriefing, and then repeat the steps for the next strategy. Table runners may bring group responses to the chart to share.

3. Read another portion of text aloud. (Read just a few pages or headings, whatever fits the text and the age group best. When reading a chapter book, you can pause between chapters to run through the strategies.) Pause every few pages and alternate modeling each of the four strategies with cooperative table discussions and whole-group sharing.

4. Try assigning each table group one of the strategies to focus on during the lesson. Groups share their responses with the entire class. Or, you might rotate the strategies to different tables each time you pause to ask the students to discuss their strategy use.

5. Have each group tell the class how the Fab Four is helping them understand the text. Ask students to reflect and discuss how all four strategies work together as a package for comprehending text better.

ASSESSMENT TIPS

Circulate around the classroom and listen to the table groups during the guided activity after your students have heard a model for a reciprocal teaching strategy. Do the pairs copy the model? Students may offer the same summary as yours. Copying is OK at this early stage if the students understood the model. The following points will help you determine whether your students understood:

- Do your students come up with a sensible but new prediction, question, point, word to clarify (or way to clarify the word that you modeled), or summary?

- Are questions high level or literal? Do students extend and piggyback on one another's ideas?

- Do the students' drawings reflect the character that uses the strategy during reading?

- Can your students verbalize to one another the jobs of each reciprocal teaching team member?

Lesson 2: The Four Door Chart: Discussion Guide and Assessment Tool

BACKGROUND AND DESCRIPTION

The Four Door Chart is a type of folded paper pattern (see page 89). Staff developer Cheryl Caldera introduced me to this practical folding format that students can use to record their responses during reading.

I've used the Four Door pattern in countless demonstration lessons and workshops with teachers to overwhelmingly positive response. Many love the way the Four Door engages students, holds them accountable during the lesson, prompts their ideas, and then ultimately is an assessment tool. Students of all ages from kindergarten to high school enjoy recording their responses on the Four Door. Cathy Bailey, also a literacy coach, agrees and says, "The Four Door increases student engagement and understanding, [and] can be used as a formative assessment or a tool to hold thinking for a discussion."

MATERIALS

- A copy of the reading material for each student in the class

- White paper to fold into a Four Door or the pattern (see page 110)

- A Four Door Chart to use as a model (make a large one or use a document camera)

- A document camera (optional)

- Puppets or props for primary grades (optional; for puppets I created, see www.primaryconcepts.com/rdgcomp/Comprehension-Puppets.asp)

TEACHER MODELING

1. Explain to students that the lesson objective is for them to practice using all four reciprocal teaching strategies: predicting, questioning, clarifying, and summarizing. Model for students how you complete the Four Door Chart and then have them write on their forms and share with their partners. Give students time to decorate their Four Door Charts and write the names of the four strategies, one on each door.

2. Model reciprocal teaching strategies for your students after reading aloud a portion of the chosen text. Alternate modeling each strategy with having students write in their Four Doors and share with their partners. Vary the Four Door Chart with any of the following options. Be sure to model using the same tool that students are using.

- Label the doors with the strategies predict, question, clarify, summarize. Students write page numbers next to their responses. For example, inside the predict door, I might write, "Page 3: I think that..." or "Page 7: I predict that...."

- Label the doors with page numbers or chapter numbers and an illustration. Open each door and write one prediction, question, clarification, and summary for a particular portion of text.

  - Create a chart using elements of the previous two variations (see Figure 11).

- Students turn the Four Door over to write their names and draw an illustration.

3. Model how to predict using the Four Door. Look over headings, pictures, and other visuals. Make an initial prediction. Say, "I think this is about...because I see...," or for nonfiction, "I think I will learn...." Place your Four Door under the document camera or make a large model using construction paper. Model how to open the predict door and write across the entire space. Students then make predictions and write inside their doors.

4. Continue reading aloud, pausing to model each of the Fab Four strategies with your predictions, questions, words or ideas to clarify, and summary. Alternate your modeling and students' participation with each door.

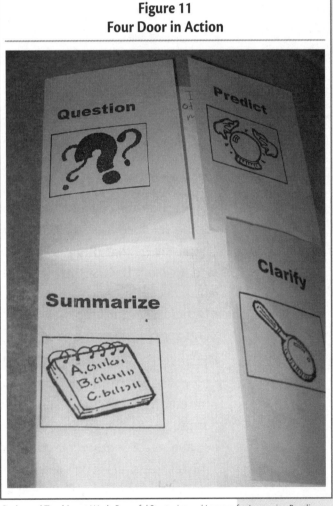

Figure 11
Four Door in Action

Reciprocal Teaching at Work: Powerful Strategies and Lessons for Improving Reading Comprehension (second edition) by Lori D. Oczkus. © 2010. Newark, DE: International Reading Association. May be copied for classroom use.

1. To scaffold the discussion, you may want students to discuss their responses before they write in the Four Door Chart. Discussion choices include the following:

   - First, conduct your think-aloud model, then have students write in their individual Four Door Charts and share with a partner.
   - After your modeling example, students discuss with partners or groups and then write inside their Four Door Charts.
   - If you wish to use the Four Door as an assessment, students should write first and then discuss.

2. Allow younger students to draw predictions, ask a question verbally or write one as a group for everyone to copy, write one or two words to clarify, and finally draw a summary.

   - *Predict*: "I think I will learn...because...," and "I think...will happen because..."
   - *Question*: "I wonder..." and questions beginning with why, who, what, how, where, and when.
   - *Clarify*: "I didn't get [the word, idea, part] so I [reread, read on, looked for parts I knew]"
   - *Summarize*: "So far...," "This is mostly about...," "First,...," "Next...," and "Then,...."

3. Ask students to reflect on the strategies and share with their partners. Lead the students in a discussion about how the reciprocal teaching strategy helped them better understand the text. Younger students may also tell what they liked about the strategy.

- Circulate around the classroom and listen to the responses of the pairs and cooperative groups as they work.

- Collect the Four Doors and analyze student responses. Use your observations from this lesson to help you focus on the next steps in reciprocal teaching. See the Rubric for the Reciprocal Teaching Strategies in Appendix A for assessment guidelines for each of the four strategies. Are any strategies giving students difficulty? Do you need to model them again or use a minilesson (see pages 124–128) on a single strategy to focus your students' attention? Refer to Table 5 (see pages 26–27) for further suggestions when your students have problems using the strategies.

Using the Four Door Chart

Primary   During a read-aloud of the picture book *Charlie Anderson* by Barbara Abercrombie, kindergarten teacher Mrs. Wilson alternates modeling each strategy in her giant Four Door withn allowing the students to sketch and write or draw in theirs. The story, about a cat that chooses one family by day and another by night, engages students with surprises. The students share interesting insights, for example, "I predict the cat will go somewhere else during the day." "I want to ask the cat where it is going." "So far the cat loves visiting the girls at night." "I didn't understand the word *disappeared* because it is so big!"

Intermediate   The eighth graders huddle in table groups as they discuss "Arctic Adventurer" an article from the National Geographic *Extreme Explorer* magazine about African American explorer, Matthew Henson. The teacher, Miss Riser, knows that the many ELLs in the class will benefit from reading the high-interest nonfiction piece. The students filled in their Four Doors as they read independently yesterday, then shared in table groups. Miss Riser modeled an example for each of the strategies. Today, the Four Door serves as a concrete guide for the rich discussions that will take place. The groups buzz with discussion points for each of the strategies as students open their doors and minds to share their thoughts. "At first I didn't get why the ice in the Arctic was more dangerous in the spring, but then I read that when it begins to melt, there are many dangerous cracks," comments Ben. "I was thinking the same thing when I read it, but I thought about the time we went sledding, and my grandpa wouldn't let us go near the ice in the lake, because it wasn't completely frozen," adds Berta. Before dismissing the students, Miss Riser calls on the table leaders and asks them to share what they think are the best of the four strategies from their groups. Each table ranks from 1 to 4 which strategies gave them the most discussion points today. "Our table went crazy for questions on this article. Next, I'd say we spent lots of time summarizing. Then, I'd say we clarified a ton of words like *bleak* and *dwindling*, and last, we predicted easily," reports Juanita.

Instructions for Making a Four Door Chart

The Four Door Chart: A Discussion Guide and Assessment Tool

This chart is an 8.5" × 11" sheet of paper, folded to create four doors that students open and write brief responses behind. Each door is labeled with one of the four reciprocal teaching strategies—predict, question, clarify, summarize. Students can decorate the doors by sketching cartoon characters or drawings that represent each of the Fab Four characters. For example, students may sketch Madam the Powerful Predictor (a fortuneteller) or a crystal ball for predicting, Quincy the Quizzical Questioner (a game show host) or a microphone for questioning, Clara the Clarifier (a sophisticated lady who uses a pointer) or a pair of glasses for clarifying, and Sammy the Super Summarizer (a cowboy) or a lasso for summarizing. Then, students write a one- or two-sentence response inside each door.

Students can use the Four Door Chart during discussions with their teacher and classmates. Their written responses can provide you with a quick assessment tool during reciprocal teaching lessons. If you want to evaluate the quality and depth of students' questioning, for example, collect the completed charts and look for each student's ability to ask higher level questions. If students are asking only literal questions, you will know that they are struggling with questioning and will be able to adjust your instruction accordingly.

Directions for Making a Four Door Chart

1. Place an 8.5" × 11" sheet of white paper horizontally on a flat surface.
2. Fold both sides of the paper toward the middle to form two doors.
3. Using scissors, cut the doors in half horizontally, making four doors.
4. Have students write the words Predict, Question, Clarify, and Summarize on the outside of the doors.
5. Have students write their names on the backs of their Four Door Charts.

Guiding Instruction With a Four Door Chart

Whole-Class Sessions

You can use a Four Door Chart throughout a reciprocal teaching lesson. More specifically, after you discuss each of the strategies, have students write their responses on their charts. If you ask students to write their responses on their charts and then share their responses with partners, the responses can be used as an assessment tool. You can read each student's responses on the four doors and make notes and observations about them. Ask yourself, which students need additional work on predicting, questioning, clarifying, or summarizing? Once you have identified these students, you can group students with similar needs together and teach small-group lessons to target the strategies with which the group members are struggling. Or, you might want to teach struggling students using all four reciprocal teaching strategies but spend more time with the target strategy.

(continued)

Instructions for Making a Four Door Chart
(continued)

Guided Reading Groups

During guided reading groups, you also can ask students to write or draw quick responses on the Four Door Chart, or on sticky notes to add to the chart, and use that information to assess students' progress and growth.

Literature Circles

When using reciprocal teaching in literature circles, students can record individual responses on the Four Door Chart and turn in their charts, so you know how they are participating in the discussions. Students also might prepare Four Door Charts at their desks and bring them to the literature circle discussion as prompts, or a literature circle group may turn in a completed Four Door Chart on which one member of the group recorded everyone's responses.

Reciprocal Teaching at Work: Powerful Strategies and Lessons for Improving Reading Comprehension (second edition) by Lori D. Oczkus. © 2010. Newark, DE: International Reading Association. May be copied for classroom use.

Four Door Chart

Name: _____

Lesson 3: Which One Do We Need?
Name That Strategy!

If you want students to really internalize the Fab Four and use the strategies when they read on their own, then they need this lesson! Students must decide which strategy to call on to solve a particular comprehension problem. Good readers easily and flexibly rotate through the strategies that are needed for the moment during the reading process. It is essential for students to realize that the Fab Four are useful tools that they can call on when reading to unlock meaning in any text.

- A copy of the reading material for each student in the class or Big Book for shared reading with younger students

- Document camera (optional)

- Puppets that you might have handy (optional; for puppets I created, see www.primaryconcepts.com/rdgcomp/Comprehension-Puppets.asp)

1. Explain to students that they are going to play a guessing game using all four reciprocal teaching strategies—predicting, questioning, clarifying, and summarizing—and the lesson objective is for them to know when and how to use each strategy when they are reading along in a text.

2. Read a portion of text and pause to ask students to think about which strategy from the Fab Four you will need to help you continue. Don't tell students which strategy you have chosen; rather, allow them to guess and explain their thinking. Give examples and clues from the four strategies in any order to make the activity like a game and to show that good readers rotate through the strategies as needed during reading. The following are possible examples for how you might word the clues for each strategy. Use these or develop your own to fit your needs. Notice the varying layers of sophistication that are included

for each. You can teach this lesson many times by selecting different examples from texts you are reading.

Predict

- I want to see what will happen next.
- I need to preview the illustrations and text to see what I think will happen in the next part.
- I am thinking about what just happened in the story. Here is what I think the character will do next.
- This author is using chronological order to tell the story, so I think this will come next.
- The text is organized like…, so I can use those clues to help me decide what might happen next.
- Which strategy do I need? (Predict)

Question

- Before reading I am wondering, [who, what, when, where, why, how]…?
- Now I am wondering, [what will the character do next]?
- If I could, I'd ask the character why…or how….
- If we had a test on this section, the teacher might ask us….
- If I could, I'd ask the author….
- I want to see if my partner or group understands this part. I am going to ask….
- Which strategy do I need? (Question)

Clarify

- I don't get this word….
- The confusing part was….
- I don't understand this [paragraph, sentence, chapter].
- This doesn't make sense.
- I am not making a picture in my head.
- I know the prefix of this word but not the rest.
- I have heard of [word, idea] before but am not sure what it means.
- Another word for this is….
- I am sounding out the word and breaking it into parts or syllables.
- I need to look at the suffix or prefix.

- I am thinking of a synonym for the word....
- Which strategy do I need? (Clarify)

Summarize

- So far this is about....
- I can't remember what happened yesterday when we were reading.
- Where did I leave off?
- I want to remember all of the events in order.
- This text is organized by [name the text structure, such as chronological order or problem and solution]
- I need to use the text structure to tell what this is about.
- I need to figure out what the main ideas are in this text.
- Which strategy do I need? (Summarize)

1. Throughout the lesson, students should first turn to partners or table group members to guess which strategy is needed before they participate in a whole-group discussion.

2. Have students make up riddles or "Which strategy do I need?" examples from the text for the class. They might also make up "Which strategy am I?" examples.

3. For younger students, you can conduct the lesson using puppets or by having the students hold a prop or dress up as the characters. Call four students up to wear the puppets or hold props. As you read the riddles, the class makes the hand motion to signal which strategy character is needed. Then, the student with the puppet or prop comes over to the text you are holding and "helps" you use the strategy. Even older students enjoy holding props or dressing as characters when you ask for "Which one do I need?" riddles.

4. As a wrap up to the strategy riddles, ask students to work with you or in teams to create verses to familiar tunes as a review of the strategies. For example, for summarizing, students hum the tune of "Frère Jacques" and create a verse that outlines what they do when they summarize, such as the following:

> Sammy Summarizer, Sammy Summarizer
> Rounds up ideas,
> Makes it short,
> Only tells the important parts.

Gives them in order,
Sammy Summarizer, Sammy Summarizer

From Oczkus, L. (2008). *The Fabulous Four: Reading Comprehension Puppets* (p. 13). Berkeley, CA: Primary Concepts. www.primaryconcepts.com. Reprinted with permission.

I have done this with students of all ages including teachers! Some additional examples include the following:

- Using an instrumental version of rapper Snoop Dogg's "Drop It While It's Hot" in the background for intermediate and middle school students to create raps for each of the strategies (Oczkus, 2009).

- At a workshop, one very bold teacher sang a verse about predicting to the tune of Marvin Gaye's "I Heard It Through the Grapevine."

- First graders created verses for each of the strategies to the tune of "This Old Man."

5. Play a "What's My Strategy?" game like the old TV game show, *What's My Line?* In this popular game show from the 1950s, a blindfolded celebrity panel asked a game show guest what he or she did for a living through a series of yes or no questions and tried to guess his or her occupation. Have intermediate and middle school students role-play as the strategy characters.

6. Post the names of the four strategies in four different spots in the room. As you read your description of a strategy, students walk to that sign.

ASSESSMENT TIPS

- Assess how well your students reflect on the use of the strategies as they make up riddles and respond to yours.

- If you use the hand motions or another means for every student to respond during your think-aloud, such as slates, observe whether students can identify which strategy you are using. (*Option:* As every student responds, keep track of responses using an interactive whiteboard.)

- When students create their own riddles, verses, or examples, watch to see if they are outlining the steps to each of the strategies. Provide guidance when necessary.

116

Predict—Do students include previewing illustrations, pictures, graphs, charts, and headings? Do students include ways to use prior knowledge and what has happened so far in the text?

Question—Do students include the different types of questions that you've taught, including wonders, quiz questions, and thinking questions?

Clarify—Do students include a discussion of the various strategies for clarifying words, including sounding out, syllables, beginnings, and endings? Do the students include rereading, reading on, asking a friend, or thinking of a synonym? Do students discuss visualizing and keeping track of text by rereading?

Summarize—Do students mention selecting main points and ordering them? Do students mention text structures, such as a story map, compare–contrast chart, or topic chart for nonfiction?

Which Strategy Do I Need?

Primary   The first graders in Mrs. Uke's classroom wave their hands wildly to volunteer to be the Fab Four characters during a reading lesson. She selects four students to come up front, sit in chairs, and hold props that represent the strategies and characters. The props include a snow globe for a crystal ball for Madam the Powerful Predictor, a plastic microphone for Quincy Questioner, a pair of oversized glasses for Clara Clarifier, and a cowboy hat for Sammy Summarizer. Once the lucky volunteers settle in, clutching their props, Mrs. Uke begins reading aloud from a Big Book while students follow along in their copies of the text. "Oh no, class. I am stuck on a word here. Which friend do I need?" The students use the hand motion for clarify to show which strategy they think is needed to figure out the word. Some students copy others or use a different hand motion. Mrs. Uke can easily spot the students who do and do not know that the clarify strategy is in demand. She calls on Juan. "You need Clara to help you figure out the word," he explains. Mrs. Uke asks Lauren, the student role-playing as Clara, to come over to the text with her glasses to clarify. Together they point to the word and discuss ways to clarify the problem word, including rereading and breaking it into parts. Students attentively watch their classmate help teach the lesson. The lesson continues as Mrs. Uke pauses every so often and asks, "Who do I need?" to help her predict, question, clarify, and summarize.

Intermediate   The conversation turns thoughtful as a class of sixth graders reflects on characters' feelings in *The Hundred Dresses* by Eleanor Estes, a story about peer exclusion and subtle bullying. Their teacher, Mrs. Jameson, tells students they are going to play a game called "What's My Strategy?" to help them remember the Fab Four. She thinks for a minute, then reveals her first example. "I wish I could ask the author, Eleanor Estes, why she wrote this book. It seems to me that maybe she had something like this happen to her or a child she knew. Which strategy is this? And what are your thoughts?" The students turn to partners. First, they figure out which strategy they think their teacher just used (questioning), then discuss possible answers for the questions their teacher posed about the author. The whole-class discussion begins with comments from several girls who are usually reluctant to share—but not this time. The story has struck a chord. "I think kids, especially girls, have always gone through this sort of drama, and the author just wrote this story to help them think before they do something unkind," comments Vangie. "The mean girl thing isn't new, because this book was written in 1944," adds Lekisha. After discussing the merits of questioning the author, Mrs. Jameson poses another example: "I am trying to get a picture in my head. I need to reread this page. What strategy should I call on?" The students reread the page to discuss their visualizing in pairs and decide the strategy is clarifying, but they are not sure why. Mrs. Jameson explains to the class that clarifying includes a bundle of techniques for staying on track while you read. "If you lose meaning, you need to clarify by either rereading or reading on," she explains. She continues by asking the students to guess which strategy is needed, using examples from predicting and summarizing. When the students close their books, the mood in the room is solemn as students sit for a moment reflecting on the strong feelings evoked from reading this children's book.

Lesson 4: Pass the Mat

Mary Jo Barker, a literacy specialist from Rockwood School District, shared with me this wonderful and engaging lesson idea incorporating the Fab Four with the placemat concept. The placemat is a cooperative learning structure from *Beyond Monet: The Artful Science of Instructional Integration* (Bennett & Rolheiser, 2001). I've added a few of my own "spins" and expect that creative readers everywhere will do the same. Isn't that what good teaching is all about?

- A copy of the reading material for each student in the class
- Copies of the Fab Four Mat (see page 123) or create larger mats on poster-sized or construction paper
- Different colored markers

1. Explain to students that the lesson objective is for them to practice using all four reciprocal teaching strategies: predicting, questioning, clarifying, and summarizing.

2. Model reciprocal teaching strategies for your students after reading aloud a portion of the chosen text. As you talk through one of the strategies and find a specific example, write your response on the mat. Alternate the modeling of each strategy as you think aloud and write, followed by students' writing on their mats and sharing with their table groups.

3. In subsequent lessons, you might select only one of the strategies to model. Choose one with which the students are having trouble.

There are many ways students can write on their mats in teams. The lesson is a great model of cooperative learning, because all students are held accountable as they participate. The following are some suggestions and variations for using this activity in your class:

- Students use different colored markers and sign their names in the center of the mat, then record ideas in their own color (which is helpful as an assessment tool for the teacher).

- Each student is in charge of one of the strategies and fills in the box for that strategy. Every time the reading stops, the students write, share, then rotate the mat.

- Instead of rotating the mat, it stays stationary and the students rotate around it.

- Students rotate the mat at their tables and get a new job every few pages of the text as the class reads.

- Students pass their mat to another table and receive a new one each time they record.

- Table groups might have a mat for just one strategy and then share their thoughts with other groups. Each mat has a place for students in that group to write. For example, at the predict table, each student writes predictions throughout the reading. They might vote on or highlight their best idea to share with the class.

- One student per table is the recorder, and all students chime in for the response.

- Post mats around the room, so students can walk to the charts to record their responses.

ASSESSMENT TIPS

- Circulate around the classroom and listen to the responses of the pairs and cooperative groups as they work.

- Collect the mats and analyze student responses. Use your observations from this lesson to help you focus on the next steps in reciprocal teaching. See the Rubric for the Reciprocal Teaching Strategies in Appendix A for assessment guidelines for each of the four strategies. Are any strategies giving students difficulty? Do you need to model them again or use a minilesson (see pages 124–128) on a single strategy to focus your students' attention? Refer to Table 5 (see pages 26–27) for further suggestions when your students have problems using the strategies.

- Assess your students' use of reciprocal teaching strategies with a variety of reading materials, so you can monitor and adjust your lessons to fit students' needs.

- Are your students' predictions based on clues from the text or its illustrations?

- Are your students' questions literal or inferential, and are they based on the text?

- Are your students able to identify troublesome words and at least two strategies for deciphering them? Are any students identifying difficult ideas and ways to clarify them?

- Are your students' summaries succinct, including only the important points in the proper order? Do your students use language from the text in their summaries? Are their summaries getting at the text's major themes?

Using the Fab Four Mat

Classroom Story

Primary   Mr. Brown sets a Fab Four Mat in the center of each table of four students in his second-grade classroom. The eager students know what to do next, as this is their favorite way to participate in reciprocal teaching lessons. He assigns each student a job for the day. All of the predictors, questioners, clarifiers, and summarizers are raring to go. He holds up the read-aloud for the day, *Fooling the Tooth Fairy* by Martin Nelson Burton. Mr. Brown shows the cover and models a prediction: "I think this is about someone who tried to fool the tooth fairy because of the title and the look on her face. She looks like she knows a secret and like there is no way you could fool her!" The students nod and blurt out (then raise hands after some gentle reminding!) some responses like, "I saw the tooth fairy movie!" "My mom is the tooth fairy!" and "The tooth fairy forgot to come to my house!"

Mr. Brown reads the first four pages of the book and stops after the fourth page. He quickly models each of the familiar strategies: "For summarizing, I can say so far that the boy really wants some money and thinks he can fool the tooth fairy by putting some paper teeth under his pillow. His mom doubts it will work. I predict that the tooth fairy will come and see the paper teeth. I need to clarify something. I didn't get why the boy looked in the dog's mouth, but then I thought about it and realized he wanted to find some loose teeth! Then my question is, I wonder why he needs the money? Now class, each of you should write a one-sentence response to your strategy and draw a quick sketch." Joleen sketches the dog's mouth in the clarify box on her group's Fab Four Mat. Harry predicts that the mom is right and sketches the mom shaking her head. After a few minutes, students share at their tables, and then Mr. Brown continues reading the story. He pauses for students to add new responses after four more pages. He later displays the Fab Four Mats in the hallway.

Intermediate   The fifth graders position themselves around their classroom at the posted charts, one for each of the four strategies. The giant puzzle pieces from the Fab Four Mat will be pieced together but for now are taped separately around the room. Cooperative teams at each station huddle over their basal story, "La Bamba," by Gary Soto. Students read the assigned pages and then as a group dictate to the designated recorder their collective response to write on their piece of the Fab Four Mat. When the teacher, Mrs. Guido, signals, entire teams rotate around the room to the next chart with their books, read the next portion of text, and come up with a response for the chart before them. Camille records her group's prediction, "Manuel will try out for the school talent show, because he thinks it will make him popular." The groups continue rotating, reading, and writing. Between rotations, Mrs. Guido pauses to invite a group or two to share some of their responses. When the lesson ends, the students put all of their charts together on the wall for a gigantic comprehension mat!

Intermediate/Secondary   Miss Ling places large sheets of construction paper on table groups' desks in preparation for the eighth-grade English class. Upon their arrival, she tells students that they will create mats for recording their Fab Four reactions to their reading of the first chapter of *The Call of the Wild* by Jack London, which they completed for homework the previous night. Each student in the groups of four selects a different colored marker and signs his or her name in the center square to show which responses belong to which students. The students choose the strategy closest to them on the mat and write nonstop for two minutes as they prepare to record their predictions, questions, clarifications, and summaries. Then, Miss Ling signals for them to stop to discuss and share their responses. The students rotate the mat to another strategy and again participate in a timed write and share their ideas. Miss Ling encourages students to piggyback on one another's comments. Janielle writes her clarification, "At first I didn't really get the part when the book talks about how the Klondike Gold Rush began in Alaska and would threaten Buck, even though he was thousands of miles from it. That was confusing to me. Then, I read on and realized that maybe someone would take Buck to work in Alaska." "Yeah, I began even before that making predictions that Buck would end up leaving to work up North, because the author mentions the Arctic," adds Sam. Miss Ling selects a strategy to model for the day. "I noticed that many of you are having a hard time finding things to clarify. Readers often need to reread to visualize or make pictures in their heads. I loved the descriptions like the one of the setting in 1897. Turn to that part and watch how I demonstrate by reading aloud and then visualizing. You can always select an example of a passage where you had to visualize to clarify the story line," she explains.

Fab Four Mat

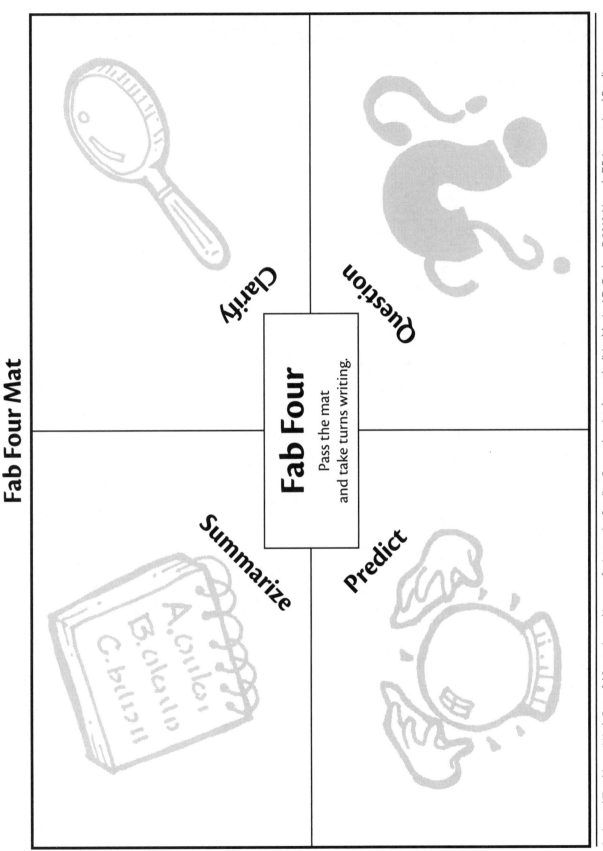

Clarify

Question

Fab Four

Pass the mat
and take turns writing.

Summarize

A. cute!
B. cute!!
C. bruish!!

Predict

Reciprocal Teaching at Work: Powerful Strategies and Lessons for Improving Reading Comprehension (second edition) by Lori D. Oczkus. © 2010. Newark, DE: International Reading Association. This graphic adapted from Bennett, B., & Rolheiser, C. (2001). *Beyond Monet: The Artful Science of Instructional Integration.* Toronto, ON: Barrie Bennett. May be copied for classroom use.

Minilesson: Prediction Stroll Line

Description and Comprehension Strategies

Have students make predictions in groups and share them with others in stroll lines—two lines of students situated across from one another. Comprehension strategies include using textual clues to make logical predictions.

Materials

- Multiple copies of a text with illustrations

Teacher Modeling

1. Ask your students how good readers make predictions. Chart their responses.

2. Model for your students how to use clues from the text and illustrations to make predictions.

Student Participation

1. Assign pages of the text to cooperative groups and have the groups meet to write predictions for their pages. Each group member will need a copy of the predictions to share during the stroll line activity.

2. Have the class form two lines that face one another. Instruct the students who are across from one another to work as pairs and share their predictions and clues with each other. Then, signal all of the students in one of the lines to move one person to the right and the student at the end to move to the front of the line. Have the new partners share their predictions. Continue switching partners and sharing until each student has shared with at least three others.

3. Debrief the prediction-sharing experience as a whole class. List some of the predictions on a piece of butcher paper or a whiteboard. Have students begin reading the text, and use the list to check predictions after reading.

Assessment Tips

- Are your students using text and illustration clues to make logical predictions? Model predicting for small groups of students who are having difficulty providing evidence for their predictions.

Minilesson: Post Your Question

Description and Comprehension Strategies

Students work in pairs then as a whole class to ask questions after reading a text. Comprehension strategies include using a variety of starter words to formulate questions.

Materials

- Multiple copies of the text and paper strips with the question words *who, what, when, where, why, how,* and *what if.*

Teacher Modeling

Model the steps for asking a variety of questions that begin with *who, what, where, when, why, how,* and *what if,* using a meaningful portion of text, such as a chapter.

Student Participation

1. Make cards or paper strips with each of the question words. Mix them up, then turn them over or put them in a container, so students can choose them one at a time.

2. Read the question word and ask student pairs to work together to create a question based on the text that begins with the selected word.

3. Encourage the student pairs to share their questions and answers first with each other and then with the class.

4. Ask your students to reflect on and share ideas for creating good questions.

Assessment Tips

- Can your students use the question words to write their own text questions? Can they ask main idea and inferential questions or only questions about details? Model questioning in small groups for students who need reinforcement, or put students in literature circles (see Chapter 5) to draw question words from a container and use them to discuss a book or article that the class has already read together.

Minilesson: Clarify and Underline a Word or Idea

Description and Comprehension Strategies

Students underline words and ideas they need to clarify and use one color of marker or pencil for difficult words and another for confusing sentences.

Materials

- Document camera, overhead projector, or Big Book
- A copy of one or two pages of the text to project on the screen or copies of one page from the text for each student
- Colored pencils or highlighters
- Two different colors of Wikki Stix

Teacher Modeling

1. Ask students what good readers do when they come to a word that they do not know. Chart student responses, which should include rereading, reading on, looking at beginning or ending sounds, looking for parts you know, thinking about what makes sense in the sentence, breaking the word into syllables, thinking of another word that makes sense, and asking a friend.

2. Ask students what good readers do when they come to a sentence or part they do not understand. Chart student responses, which should include rereading, reading on, thinking about what makes sense, making a picture in their heads, and talking with a friend.

3. Display a copy of the text using the document camera or overhead projector, or show a Big Book page. Underline a word to clarify using a colored marker or pencil. Model for students how to clarify that word. Use the strategy starter "I didn't get the word...so I...."

4. Using the same text find an entire sentence to clarify and underline it in another color. Model how you figured it out. Use the strategy starter, "I didn't get the sentence where...so I....."

5. When teaching this lesson with primary-grade students using a Big Book, you may opt to place two different colored Wikki Stix under the text to mark the words and ideas that need clarifying.

Student Participation

1. Provide one copy per student of a page of text. Immediately following your demonstration, ask students to find a word to clarify in the text. Have them underline it using a highlighter or colored pencil and use a sentence frame to tell a partner how they figured it out, such as "I didn't get the word...so I...." Discuss words in a whole-class debriefing along with ways to figure out tricky words.

(continued)

Minilesson: Clarify and Underline a Word or Idea (continued)

2. Using their copy of the text, ask students to use another color and underline an entire sentence that is tricky. Tell them they may select a sentence that they had to read twice because it was hard to understand, one that was confusing, or one where they didn't make a picture in their heads the first time they read it.

3. If students tell you they get everything and do not need to clarify, tell them to find a word or sentence that a younger student would have difficulty understanding.

Assessment Tips

- Are your students using a variety of clarifying strategies to clarify words and ideas? Collect their papers to see what examples they've selected and discuss them the next day.

Minilesson: Cooperative Group Summaries

Description and Comprehension Strategies

Students work first in cooperative groups and then as a class to construct a summary of a text. Comprehension strategies include summarizing with ideas in the proper order and selecting main ideas.

Materials

- Multiple copies of the text
- Paper strips or sheets
- Overhead transparencies and overhead projector, or a pocket chart, or papers and a document camera

Teacher Modeling

Model the steps for telling a summary with the main events or important facts in the order that they appear within the text. Use a meaningful portion of text, such as a chapter.

Student Participation

1. Break the summary into parts—the beginning, middle, and end. Assign or let cooperative groups choose which portion of the text they will summarize and draw.

2. Have all of the groups share their portion of the summary verbally or in writing. As the tables share their information in order, they can bring their summary piece to a dry-erase board, pocket chart, or overhead transparency at the front of the classroom to construct the group retelling. Drawings are optional.

3. Challenge students in a game-like activity. Try limiting the number of words they can use; for example, see if they can write a 25-word summary!

4. Have the class reread the group summary.

Assessment Tips

- After the group summary, can your students reconstruct their own summaries of the text? Monitor them to see if they tell key events or facts in order. If any of them are having difficulty, model summarizing with a small group or write a class summary together. Eventually, ask groups to write summaries and share them with the class. Then, have the class vote on the summary they think is the best.

- Create a class rubric about what makes a good summary by analyzing summaries that the class and groups have written.

CHAPTER SUMMARY

- Whole-class instruction with reciprocal teaching offers students a sense of community and the opportunity to develop a common language about reciprocal teaching.

- Whole-class instruction needs to be sprinkled with ways to engage and actively involve all students using cooperative learning with partners and small groups.

- Use any materials during reciprocal teaching lessons, such as Big Books, leveled text, magazine articles, textbooks, and chapter books.

- Four foundations must be in place to maximize the effectiveness of reciprocal teaching: scaffolding, think-alouds, metacognition, and cooperative learning.

- Do not overuse whole-class lessons. Students need a mix of small-group exposures as well as they move toward independence.

- Use the written work, such as a Four Door Chart, to plan next lessons to meet student needs.

CHAPTER 4

RECIPROCAL TEACHING
in Guided Reading Groups

Clarify helps me understand words I don't know. So, the next time I see the word, I'll know what it means.

—Francisco, grade 4

Description of Reciprocal Teaching and Guided Reading

Regardless of whether you gather wide-eyed first graders around a kidney-shaped table to read a leveled reader, meet with lanky sixth graders sprawled on a rug to preview a social studies text, or grab a few minutes with high schoolers hunched over a challenging novel to clarify multiple themes, reciprocal teaching offers you a proven guided reading plan. In my travels across the United States, I hear teachers, literacy coaches, and principals from grades K to 12 rave about the easy-to-use lesson design and consistent results that the Fab Four framework yields in small-group instruction.

Some of the feedback I've received from teachers on using reciprocal teaching during small-group instruction includes the following:

> I love using the Fab Four with my second graders in guided reading, because they do more of the work, and I am less tired after the sessions!

> I was looking for a way to reach all readers, especially my struggling fifth graders, and in just three months, they moved from second-grade reading level to fifth-grade reading level on our assessments.

> For years, I've been searching for a method to use in guided reading with my top primary readers in grades 1–2, and reciprocal teaching is it!

> Reciprocal teaching provides a ready-made small-group intervention for our struggling middle school students.

Researchers tell us that struggling readers need frequent quality instruction in small groups (Allington, 2008). Yet, we know all of our students, from strong to struggling readers, benefit from the differentiation that they receive in a more personalized environment (Allington, 2001). Guided reading—small-group instruction that is teacher led and teacher directed—often has been referred to as the heart of a reading program (Fountas & Pinnell, 1996). In this setting, students are organized into flexible groups that change based on regular assessments (Schulman & Payne, 2000). As the term *guided reading* indicates, the teacher guides students through a text, which may be at a slightly more difficult level than the students could read on their own.

Many elementary teachers today employ a strategic type of guided reading that uses meaningful text and good reader strategies, such as making predictions and using various strategies to figure out unknown words. Many of these strategies are borrowed from intervention programs for struggling primary students (Clay, 1985, 1993; Hiebert & Taylor, 1994; Pikulski, 1994) and include the following:

- Rereading a familiar text to build fluency and comprehension
- Previewing illustrations and text prior to reading
- Making predictions
- Reading silently
- Coaching students in strategies for figuring out unknown words
- Participating in word work (e.g., manipulating letters, sounds, word parts, or syllables using manipulatives; writing activities; games)

In addition to the powerful teaching strategies found in early interventions, educators also have learned from the interventions how to (a) assess students by listening to their oral reading, (b) use more natural-sounding leveled texts (i.e., texts that were leveled according to difficulty and certain criteria; Peterson, 1991), and (c) match students' reading abilities to leveled texts (Fountas & Pinnell, 1996). Following is an example of a primary-grade guided reading lesson that incorporates all four of the reciprocal teaching strategies.

Six first graders settle in at the kidney-shaped table, and Mrs. Jimenez is ready for them, armed with her handy Fab Four Dial and Fab Four Chart. The students review the four strategies using the hand motions. Mrs. Jimenez runs through the strategies with Betina as the chosen checker to mark the chart with a check as the group completes each strategy.

Mrs. Jimenez holds up the nonfiction book *Tarantulas Are Spiders* by Norman Platnick and models a prediction as she does a picture walk through the text. "I think I will learn about how tarantulas catch their prey and about their bodies," she offers. Students turn to partners to share predictions. Mrs. Jimenez records some of their predictions, and Betina puts a check mark in the prediction box.

While students read silently, Mrs. Jimenez rotates around the table and asks each student to read to her while she coaches on the strategies that each one needs. The group finishes reading silently, and she asks them to read the book again to a partner.

Throughout the remaining steps of the lesson, Mrs. Jimenez asks the students to imagine turning the dials in their heads to each strategy as she also turns the Fab Four Dial. The students identify tricky words and record them on sticky notes for the chart. Mrs. Jimenez models how to figure out the word *grow* in a think-aloud while students offer words that rhyme with *grow*. Mrs. Jimenez writes down some of their quiz questions, and they each tell something that they learned by sketching a drawing on another note for the group chart.

Betina checks off all four strategies on the chart and smiles for a job well done! Each student tells which strategy they liked working on the most today. "I liked asking questions, because it was fun," shares Abdul.

Interventions With Intermediate, Middle School, and High School Students

The unique literacy needs of intermediate, middle school, and high school students may include struggles with decoding, comprehension, or fluency. Reciprocal teaching originated in middle school, is well suited to meet the needs of adolescents, and consistently yields positive results (Palincsar & Brown, 1986). A group of teacher researchers searching for effective and appropriate strategies to use in a small-group intervention model for intermediate students (Cooper et al., 2000) decided to use reciprocal teaching. They knew that if used consistently, reciprocal teaching could yield dramatic positive results, so they designed an intervention model based on what educators know about effective intervention for intermediate students (Cooper et al., 2001), which includes the successful use of graphic organizers.

Cooper and colleagues (2000) successfully field-tested the following reading strategies in their small-group model, which is designed for intermediate-grade students and adolescents:

- Revisiting familiar texts for fluency and comprehension (Samuels, 1979)
- Reviewing selected content using graphic organizers
- Rehearsing or previewing the text using the illustrations and headings, introducing a graphic organizer, and setting purposes for reading
- Reading the text and then using reciprocal teaching strategies to discuss it
- Responding to and reflecting on one's own thoughts and feelings on the reading selection and self-evaluating one's performance as a reader (Sweet, 1993)

After using what Cooper and colleagues (2000) named the Project Success Model for 76 days of instruction, the researchers found that the students in the research group performed significantly better than the control group on measures of retelling, question answering, and reading comprehension. Also, higher percentages of students in the control group were able to read on grade level after a subsequent period of instruction with the Project Success Model. In subsequent years, the Project Success model became Soar to Success (Cooper et al., 1999), an intervention program that is now used by thousands of schools. Schools that implement the model properly and consistently continue to document positive gains. These promising results make reciprocal teaching a technique worth considering for enhancing your students' reading comprehension skills.

Powerful Small-Group Instruction for All Students

I began using reciprocal teaching in my guided reading groups about 14 years ago and am still constantly amazed and pleased by the consistent results. First, I used it as a small-group intervention, then I began implementing the Fab Four during all of my guided reading lessons with a variety of reading abilities. I've watched students in grades 2–6 grow as much as a staggering two levels in just three to six months, and other educators have experienced similar positive results. Every fall, fifth-grade teacher Kathy Langham finds that the majority of her incoming students, many of them ELLs, read at the third-grade level and leave in the spring at the fifth-grade level and above. Kathy credits the power of the Fab Four.

The settings for guided reading with reciprocal teaching that I've implemented and observed include in-class guided reading groups, after school and in-class interventions, and pull-out programs. Regardless of grade level or setting, promising results are evident when teachers use the Fab Four consistently at least twice per week in a small-group setting.

Many teachers already ask students to predict, clarify, summarize, and sometimes question during guided reading. However, during guided reading, when the four strategies are taught as a package, students have the opportunity to become more metacognitive and flexible in using them. Multiple-strategy instruction works (Reutzel et al., 2005).

This chapter contains many creative options for incorporating guided reading groups and reciprocal teaching strategies. All of the lessons engage students with the text, the teacher, and one another and include strategies to use before, during, and after reading. Guided reading lessons include the following instructional elements:

- Building background or discussing students' prior knowledge
- Picture or text previewing, during which your students form predictions and ask questions
- Silent reading period, in which you move around the table and coach individual students in reciprocal teaching strategies
- Discussing the text, during which you might use a graphic organizer

Throughout guided reading lessons, encourage your students to interact with one another by previewing the text, reading, discussing important text points, asking questions, and reflecting on strategy use together. I have discovered that a well-run guided reading group in which students are led through a reciprocal teaching discussion can serve as a training ground for the eventual use of reciprocal teaching strategies during literature circles (see Chapter 5).

Goals of Reciprocal Teaching During Guided Reading

The goals of reciprocal teaching during guided reading instruction are the following:

- To model the reciprocal teaching strategies and guide students to use them
- To allow all students to benefit from a small-group setting
- To teach comprehension strategies for texts that the students would not be able to read and understand as easily on their own
- To expose students to more teacher modeling of reciprocal teaching strategies
- To group students flexibly, based on regular assessments to better meet their needs
- To guide students through interactive lessons that prepare them for literature circles and other group discussions

Organizing Guided Reading Groups in Your Classroom

The three traditional reading groups of high-, low-, and middle-range achievers are what many teachers and parents think of when they hear the term *reading groups*; however, educators now know that it is not recommended to maintain these traditional groupings all year. I vividly recall being in the "blue bird" group (referring to the name sometimes given to the low-achieving readers' group) all through elementary school. Oh, how I yearned to read at a higher level with the talented "red birds," John and Patty! If only my teachers had known about flexible grouping, maybe I would have developed a better reading self-esteem, which I have to admit I didn't experience until my mid-20s!

Convincing research points to many reasons for flexibly grouping students, and the studies on the negative effects of ability grouping are worth considering when you are deciding how to group your students for literacy instruction. For example, consider that low-range achievers often suffer from low self-esteem and receive lower quality instruction (Slavin, 1987), and that the self-fulfilling prophecy "once a blue bird, always a blue bird" often becomes a reality as a low achiever moves through the grades. Studies on intervention (Cooper et al., 2000, 2001; Pikulski, 1994) indicate that schools should provide their struggling readers with an additional intervention lesson plan for 30–40 minutes three to five times per week. Overall, when you determine the arrangement of small groups, your goal should be to change the groupings based on the students' needs and their proficiency with the text and reciprocal teaching strategies.

You can keep the guided reading groups flexible in many ways so your students are not stuck in the same group all year. The four main ways to group and place students into reciprocal teaching groups are as follows:

1. *Strategy needs groups*—Students are placed in a group because they need work on one specific reciprocal teaching strategy, such as summarizing. You may want to change these groups at least twice a month and sometimes weekly, and use minilessons on the strategy (see the minilessons throughout this book). You can use any of the forms in this book (especially the Literature Discussion Sheet for Reciprocal Teaching, page 205, or the Four Door Chart, page 110) as

formative assessment tools for determining which students need to focus on a given strategy.

2. *Student choice groups*—Students select their reading material based on interest, and you meet in guided reading groups with the students who have selected the same titles. In these groups, a struggling reader who chooses a more difficult book in which he or she is interested often can succeed beyond your expectations. In primary grades, you might display a variety of leveled texts and allow students to sign up for the title that they would prefer to read that week. The response is wonderful, as students jump in and eagerly read their choices. If you work with intermediate-grade students, try putting out a variety of novels, ranging from easy to more challenging, and allow students to select which book they want to read. These interest groups become the guided reading groups for a month. Of course, you can frame the selections by providing titles that all students can access and read.

3. *Intervention for struggling readers groups*—Try to organize a formal after school, in-class, or pull-out intervention that does not replace the regular classroom instruction but is similar to an extra reading super vitamin that is administered for 30–40 minutes three to five times per week. Although you should begin by using literature that is slightly below grade level, once your students are proficient using all four reciprocal teaching strategies, you can change the reading choices to grade-level material (Cooper et al., 1999). In addition to participating in the intervention group, the struggling students should read the core literature with the entire class, participate in mixed-ability guided reading groups, and take literature circle roles (see Chapter 5 for a discussion of literature circles).

   You can use the intervention groups to give struggling readers the advantage. In several classrooms, I have introduced reciprocal teaching strategies to intervention students over many months during guided reading. Then, when they are proficient in the strategies, I introduce the rest of the class to reciprocal teaching strategies with the intervention students serving as the resident reciprocal teaching experts. The intervention students love their roles as the authorities on reciprocal teaching.

4. *Ability groups*—In first- and second-grade classrooms, I meet a few times a week with groups whose members read at the same level. Students are given an overall reading assessment that tells at what

grade level they are reading for both instruction and independent reading, then they are grouped with students at similar levels. Teach reciprocal teaching strategies to the groups, using materials that fit each group's reading level. I try to minimize the use of this type of ability grouping after second grade because of the negative effects that ability grouping can have on students' self-esteem and achievement. These ability-based guided reading groups are part of a broader grouping plan in which all students participate in whole-class instruction and mixed-ability literature circles.

Table 10 outlines the four flexible groupings and suggests ways to assess your students' placement in the appropriate groups.

Materials for Guided Reading: Thinking Beyond "Little Books"

Many teachers and schools use leveled texts or "little books" with guided reading groups. The books often are organized in bins according to reading level or Reading Recovery level (Peterson, 1991) and are matched to students' abilities according to where they place on an assessment (usually a record of a student's reading level as measured by his or her score on oral reading passages). Although these materials are incredibly valuable to guided reading, especially in grades K–3 when students are first learning to read, you may consider using many other rich materials during guided reading.

Some great reading material sources, especially for grades 3–6, are

- Your school district's adopted reading series (ideal for reciprocal teaching practice because of the wide variety of genres and shorter reading selections).

- Newspaper articles (great for minilessons on high-interest topics).

- Poems (ideal for brief, practical lessons for both summarizing and analyzing word patterns when clarifying).

- Magazines (short articles on high-interest nonfiction topics can be used in small groups).

- Picture books for nonfiction topics (work well with primary or second-language students because of opportunities for the use of all four strategies on every page).

Table 10
Guidelines for Placing Students Into Reciprocal Teaching Groups

Type of Group	Assessment for Placement	Suggestions
Strategy needs	• Assess students' proficiency in each reciprocal teaching strategy using a variety of tools, including observation during discussion, many of the forms in this book (e.g., the Literature Discussion Sheet for Reciprocal Teaching, page 205, and the Rubric for the Reciprocal Teaching Strategies in Appendix A).	• Change strategy groups often, perhaps every time the class reads a new text selection. • Have students who have difficulty using reciprocal teaching strategies in a given genre (e.g., summarizing nonfiction texts) work on the classroom text or an easier text to practice the strategy.
Student choice	• Have students choose the title that they want to read, which will become the criteria for group placement. • Have students give first and second choices of texts to read.	• Place books where students may peruse them before choosing a title. • Meet with each group regularly to lead the reciprocal teaching discussion.
Intervention for struggling readers	• Place students in this group based on reading level. Intervention students should be at least 1–2 years below their grade level in reading skills. • Use an overall reading assessment to measure a student's grade level of reading. The assessment should include reading passages at a variety of grade levels, in addition to comprehension items or a retelling. • Continue performing ongoing oral-reading and comprehension checks with the students.	• If possible, give this group their extra 30-minute dose of reading instruction using reciprocal teaching strategies in an intervention after or before school. Otherwise, incorporate intervention group time into regular class time at least three times per week. • Introduce this group's members to reciprocal teaching first, making them the experts for literature circles.
Ability level	• Listen to and score students' oral reading. • Also, score students' overall comprehension to find their reading and grade levels.	• In grades 3–6, rely more on flexible and interest groupings and less on ability grouping. • Use leveled texts with this group.

- Novels (ideal for chapter-by-chapter use of reciprocal teaching strategies).
- Real-world texts, such as maps, menus, travel brochures, and directions for machines like how to program the DVD player (fun to read and offer short selections for use in guided reading groups).
- Social studies, science, and health textbooks (can be used in small-group settings to teach students how to read nonfiction texts).

Content Area Textbooks and Guided Reading

Although many text types can be used with reciprocal teaching in guided reading groups, in this section I elaborate on textbooks, because many teachers struggle with how to use them to teach reading comprehension. Social studies and science textbooks are practical and available resources for guided reading groups and reciprocal teaching strategies. One day when I visited Glorianna Chen's third-grade class, the students in her guided reading group were working their way through a chapter in a science text (see Figure 12). They were busy previewing the headings and pictures, making predictions about what they thought they would learn, and reading silently. Glorianna explained to me that she was going to meet with one group per day to preview and begin reading the science chapter. Her rationale for using the science text during guided reading was twofold and simple: (1) She has found it efficient to use the content area material that she needs to cover within guided reading sessions, and (2) she has found that many students pay better attention to the text in a small-group setting.

Textbooks are a ready source of material to use to practice reciprocal teaching strategies. I especially enjoy predicting with textbooks, because they are loaded with illustrations, maps, charts, and other nonfiction text features that make great minilessons for educators to focus on during guided reading lessons. I call mixed-ability groups up to the reading table to preview, predict, and read silently. After reading, my students make quick summaries and ask one another questions. We choose one idea and one word that we need to clarify. Although I cannot get very far in the text with a group using this method, I can send the students back to their desks and ask them to work through the next text chunk with reciprocal teaching strategies, or I can conduct interactive whole-class lessons with the remaining portions of the text selection.

Figure 12
Glorianna Chen Works With Students in a Guided Reading Group

Reciprocal Teaching at Work: Powerful Strategies and Lessons for Improving Reading Comprehension (second edition) by Lori D. Oczkus. © 2010. Newark, DE: International Reading Association. May be copied for classroom use.

Students can record their Fab Four ideas for the content area reading on a Four Door Chart (see Chapter 3, page 110).

Assessment Options for Reciprocal Teaching During Guided Reading

Many excellent opportunities exist for assessing individual students' use of reciprocal teaching strategies during guided reading groups. The small-group format allows for more student participation and increased opportunities for observing them in action with the strategies and various types of texts. Refer to the Rubric for the Reciprocal Teaching Strategies in Appendix A for detailed guidelines on what to look for when observing students who are engaging in a reciprocal teaching discussion. Also, refer to Table 5 (see pages 26–27) for ways to overcome the difficulties that students experience with reciprocal teaching strategies.

The following guidelines will help you assess reciprocal teaching during guided reading lessons:

- Observe your students during reciprocal teaching discussions. Listen closely to them as they predict, question, clarify, and summarize. Use the Rubric for the Reciprocal Teaching Strategies in Appendix A as a checklist at the guided reading table. Either focus on one student per day and note how he or she uses all of the strategies, or focus on one strategy and observe all students' use of that strategy.

- Coach and assess individual students during silent reading. When your students are busy reading on their own during guided reading, take turns sitting next to students for quick, individual coaching sessions. Take a few notes regarding student progress during these quick assessments, so you can keep track of strategies with which each student struggles (see the Rubric for the Reciprocal Teaching Strategies in Appendix A). Coaching students during guided reading lessons gives them individual attention and gives you time to assess them. (See Table 11 for prompts to use during guided reading.)

Table 11
Guided Reading Coaching Strategy, Protocol, and Prompts

Selecting a strategy to coach
Move around the group and choose strategies to coach based on any of the following criteria:
- Coach every student on the focus strategy you just modeled in a minilesson.
- Coach each student on a different strategy—the one he or she needs to practice based on your observations. Use a note-taking chart.
- Ask each student which strategy he or she wants to practice!
- Coach the strategy that naturally fits the portion of text the student is reading (e.g., a logical place to make a prediction).

Coaching protocol
1. Student reads a small portion of text aloud to you (e.g., sentence, paragraph, page).
2. Select a strategy to coach (see above choices).
3. Model for the student if necessary (e.g., "Watch me...").
4. Guide using language prompts for the strategy (e.g., "I didn't get...so I...").
5. Ask the student to tell you what he or she just learned (e.g., "I learned to summarize using the headings.").

(continued)

Table 11
Guided Reading Coaching Strategy, Protocol, and Prompts (*continued*)

Reciprocal Teaching Strategy		Coaching Prompt(s)
Predict	I think...will happen next, because.... I think I will learn.... I bet.... I predict.... Maybe....	Tell me what you think will happen next in the text. Why do you think that is so? How is this text organized? Based on that, what do you think will happen next? Look at the headings to make a prediction. Study the pictures to make your prediction. Skim the words in the text. What do you think this is about?
Question	I wonder... Who, what, when, where, why, or how. What if.... Why do you think...?	What is a question that you could ask about this page? What is the answer? How did you get that answer? Ask a wonder question starting with "I wonder...?" Ask a quiz question: who, what, when, where, why, or how. Ask a thinking question that starts with "Why do you think...?"
Clarify	I didn't get the [word, sentence, part, chapter] so I....[reread, read on, looked for parts I know, broke into syllables, substituted a synonym]	Identify a difficult word, sentence, or part. How did you figure it out? Give at least two ways. What is a word or idea that would be difficult for a younger child to read? Show me a place where you had to read twice to get a picture in your head. Is there a metaphor or figure of speech that you need to clarify?
Summarize	This is mostly about.... So far.... First..., Next..., Then..., Finally.... In the [beginning, middle, end],.... The theme is....	Summarize this [paragraph, page, chapter]. Or, summarize what we have read so far. What is this mainly about? Is there a problem to be solved? If so, what? Tell me the main idea. Use the topic sentence or heading to help you.

- Use brief, written responses from students during guided reading lessons as informal assessments of their progress with reciprocal teaching. Assignments may include having your students write predictions, questions, summaries, or ways to clarify words or ideas on sticky notes for the group's graphic organizer. Have your students put their names or initials on the notes, so you can identify and assess each student's work. Also, have students fill out any forms in this book that apply to the strategy or strategies that you are modeling and guiding (e.g., use the Literature Discussion Sheet for Reciprocal Teaching, page 205, or the Four Door Chart, page 110).

During guided reading, teachers coach individual students and prompt them to use the strategies during reading. To give you a better idea of what coaching reciprocal teaching strategies looks like during guided reading, I've included these brief examples at a variety of grade levels. For more detailed examples of coaching prompts, see the lesson on coaching (page 164) and the coaching prompts presented in Table 11 (pages 142–143).

- The "silent" reading in Mrs. Jimenez's first-grade classroom is not so silent, but nobody seems to mind! She rotates around the table and coaches each student as he or she reads aloud one page to her from *Fly Facts* by Janice Marriott and Andy Keylock (2008). Billy needs help formulating questions, so Mrs. Jimenez reads one sentence and models. Then, they read the next page "The mother fly lays about 120 eggs" (p. 12), and she gives him a question starter, "Can you ask a 'How many?' question about this?" Billy beams as he asks and then answers the question, "How many eggs does the mother lay?" Sondro needs help clarifying words. Mrs. Jimenez asks him to sound out the word *maggot* by looking for parts that he knows. Elizabeth struggles when asked to create a quick summary of what she learned on the page, so Mrs. Jimenez guides her to reread. Together, they make up a "This is mostly about…" sentence using the heading and main ideas. Mrs. Jimenez marks her notes to indicate which strategy each student worked on and a plus, check, or minus for how well they did, so she can continue to monitor and support their progress during guided reading.
- The group of sixth graders hunch over their book, *Mummies & Their Mysteries* by Charlotte Wilcox, devouring the topic. Mr. Jones rotates to several students to coach the use of their reading strategies. He asks Roberto to predict by reading headings and skimming for key words. He has made progress on this important strategy but needs practice. Next, Gina asks a literal question about page 17 but needs guidance in asking higher level questions.

Mr. Jones rereads a paragraph and asks, "Why do you think...?" They read the next paragraph together, and Gina asks, "Why do you think people care about what food they find in mummies' stomachs?" She smiles, feeling smart! Erik pauses on the word *hieroglyphs* as he reads aloud to Mr. Jones. Together they brainstorm ways to figure it out, including using syllables and rereading. "What is the main idea on this page?" asks Mr. Jones, and Jennifer rereads, looking for a topic sentence to rephrase. He praises her for her ability to find the main idea.

What to Do With the Rest of the Class During Guided Reading

A burning issue that concerns many teachers regarding guided reading is what to do with the rest of the class while you are working with a small group. Staff developer Susan Page uses familiar routines and what she calls smart work to keep her students engaged in meaningful ways. Familiar routines are activities that students are trained in fully and participate in regularly. *Smart work* is a clever term that I borrowed and have used in dozens of schools, and students enjoy using the term and all that it implies. The students' routines that become smart work might include reading alone or with partners, filling in graphic organizers, preparing a read-aloud for a cross-age buddy, and participating in word work with spelling words. I prefer asking students to spend much of their smart work time reading in real texts rather than filling out worksheets that isolate reading skills.

A creative solution for keeping students busy during guided reading groups is to train the rest of the class to participate in literature circles (see Chapter 5) while you meet with one group. It also is very helpful not to feel that you have to meet with every group every day. Doing so is nearly impossible and will probably cause you undue stress. However, you should try to meet with students in grades 2 and 3 several times a week in a guided reading setting and with students in grades 4–6 at least once a week. The exception is, of course, the struggling readers group that needs to meet three to five times a week either during class or before or after school in a special teacher-led intervention group.

Master teacher and staff developer Regie Routman wisely warns against just having kids "do a lot of stuff." Rather, she encourages teachers to ask themselves if what we are asking children to do will help them become readers and writers (Routman, 2003). There are many new, wonderful resources that address this complex issue of managing students and providing meaningful activities for them, so you can meet with guided reading groups. One current favorite is the practical work of "the sisters," Gail Boushey and Joan Moser, and their popular title *The Daily 5* (2006). They suggest a model that promotes student independence and includes training students to do the following while the teacher meets with other groups: read to yourself, read to someone, work on writing, listen to reading, and participate in spelling and word work.

In addition, once you've modeled and taught comprehension lessons, students can practice the strategies as independent work. These might include writing "I wonder…" questions before, during, and after reading; sketching a series of "So far…" and Next,…" drawings as students read; or marking the text for discussions (Oczkus, 2004, 2009). Another option is using the Four Door Chart for different purposes. Students might fill every door with just one of the strategies, such as questions, summaries, or tricky words. Sometimes I ask students to put page numbers on their doors and write about the focus strategy inside, such as questioning or summarizing.

If you prefer workstations or centers, Diller (2005) provides many practical ways to organize your room for student independence. In his landmark title, *Deeper Reading: Comprehending Challenging Texts, 4–12*, Gallagher (2004) shares many creative and easy-to-implement ideas that translate well to smart work options. I love his "Snow Globe" lesson, in which students draw snow globes and sketch the setting of a particular chapter inside the globe. I've compiled these and additional resources for easy access in Table 12, which you can

---

Table 12
Professional Resources for Keeping Students "Busy" During Guided Reading

Boushey, G., & Moser, J. (2006). *The daily 5: Fostering literacy independence in the elementary grades*. Portland, ME: Stenhouse.

Diller, D. (2003). *Literacy work stations: Making centers work*. Portland, ME: Stenhouse.

Diller, D. (2005). *Practice with purpose: Literacy work stations for grades 3–6*. Portland, ME: Stenhouse.

Gallagher, K. (2004). *Deeper reading: Comprehending challenging texts, 4–12*. Portland, ME: Stenhouse.

Hoyt, L. (2009). *Revisit, reflect, retell: Time-tested strategies for teaching reading comprehension*. Portsmouth, NH: Heinemann.

Oczkus, L.D. (2004). *Super six comprehension strategies: 35 lessons and more for reading success*. Norwood, MA: Christopher-Gordon.

Oczkus, L.D. (2009). *Interactive think-aloud lessons: 25 surefire ways to engage students and improve comprehension*. New York: Scholastic; Newark, DE: International Reading Association.

Opitz, M.F., & Ford, M.P. (2001). *Reaching readers: Flexible and innovative strategies for guided reading*. Portsmouth, NH: Heinemann.

Routman, R. (2003). *Reading essentials: The specifics you need to teach reading well*. Portsmouth, NH: Heinemann.

use to find ideas to keep your students meaningfully engaged while you meet with small groups.

The Big Picture in Guided Reading: What Else You Will Need to Do

Although reciprocal teaching during guided reading sessions strengthens students' reading comprehension, there are other types of lesson plans that students may need to further their reading comprehension skills. Guided reading requires your understanding of all the comprehension strategies that students need as well as the classroom management techniques associated with small-group instruction.

Students in grades K–2 may need guided reading lessons that focus more on decoding and word-level strategies. Those guided reading lessons also may focus on word work in which students build words from the selection's vocabulary using magnetic letters or letter cards (Cunningham & Cunningham, 1992). Sometimes you may opt to lead primary-grade students in an interactive writing lesson in which they take turns helping the group write a message on a chart.

Students in grades 3–12 who are reading sophisticated novels may need time to have an open discussion in which they can discuss their feelings, the author's craft, character motives, themes, opinions about the text's content, or connections that they have to the text. These lively exchanges may not fit neatly into the boundaries of reciprocal teaching strategies, yet it is valuable to take the time during guided reading lessons to discuss the emotional issues related to the reading experience.

For more information on using guided reading groups in your classroom, see the book suggestions in Table 13.

Table 13
Books on Guided Reading

Allington, R.L. (Ed.). (1998). *Teaching struggling readers: Articles from* The Reading Teacher. Newark, DE: International Reading Association.

Fountas, I.C., & Pinnell, G.S. (1996). *Guided reading: Good first teaching for all children.* Portsmouth, NH: Heinemann.

Fountas, I.C., & Pinnell, G.S. (2001). *Guiding readers and writers (grades 3–6): Teaching comprehension, genre, and content literacy.* Portsmouth, NH: Heinemann.

Opitz, M.F., & Ford, M.P. (2001). *Reaching readers: Flexible and innovative strategies for guided reading.* Portsmouth, NH: Heinemann.

Routman, R. (1999). *Conversations: Strategies for teaching, learning, and evaluating.* Portsmouth, NH: Heinemann.

Schulman, M.B., & Payne, C.D. (2000). *Guided reading: Making it work (grades K–3).* New York: Scholastic.

Lesson 1: A Guided Reading "Generic" Plan for Fiction or Nonfiction

Although you should vary your lessons on reciprocal teaching in guided reading depending on your students' grade level and reading selections, some consistent and effective reciprocal teaching routines are worth considering for fiction or nonfiction. These routines include the following:

- All four reciprocal teaching strategies
- Before-, during-, and after-reading applications of reciprocal teaching
- Reflections on strategy use

There are some important differences to keep in mind when teaching a guided reading lesson using nonfiction instead of fiction. Predicting is slightly different with nonfiction, because you can ask students what they think they will learn instead of what they think will happen next. Summarizing with fiction may center on story elements, including a problem and the main events, but summarizing with nonfiction varies depending on how the text is organized, and it requires students to select the main ideas and supporting details. Also, when teaching with nonfiction texts, it is helpful to discuss text features such as captions, diagrams, maps, and indexes during guided reading lessons.

During your lessons with small groups, you may want to visually cue the students in their strategy use with any combination of the following: the icons (see Appendix E); the Reciprocal Teaching Spinner (see page 230); a comprehension chart on chart paper, a dry-erase board, or a file folder; or the Fab Four Bookmark (see Chapter 2, page 74). You may wish to incorporate two charts, one with all four strategies on it and one for students to write on sticky notes to display their thoughts for each strategy. You may also want to hang a comprehension graphic organizer for the content. I like to combine my charts.

Also, because cooperative learning is an essential foundation, ensure that students turn to partners and talk about points throughout the text, even in the small-group setting. You can also use the role sheets from Chapter 5 (see pages 211–216) and give each student a job during the guided reading group.

MATERIALS

- Multiple copies of the text to read with the guided reading group
- Chart paper to create a comprehension chart, or the Basic Comprehension Chart for Guided Reading Groups (for fiction or nonfiction; see page 153)
- Reciprocal Teaching Guided Reading Lesson Plan Guide (see page 154)
- Copies of the Fab Four Chart (see page 160)
- Copies of the Clarifying Bookmarks (see page 183)
- Coaching suggestions from Table 11 (see pages 142–143)
- Sticky notes, and pencils or pens

TEACHER MODELING AND STUDENT PARTICIPATION

You may wish to use the Reciprocal Teaching Guided Reading Lesson Plan Guide along with the following more detailed suggestions. Once you've taught the lesson described, the shortened version on the Reciprocal Teaching Guided Reading Lesson Plan Guide provides a handy reference to use while you teach subsequent lessons.

Before Reading: Predict and Summarize

1. Discuss the book's title, cover illustrations, and information on the back cover. Model predictions for your students and have them make some initial predictions.

2. As an option, record your students' predictions on a comprehension chart—a concrete place for chronicling discussions, responses, and reflections. Create your own chart or use the Basic Comprehension Chart for Guided Reading Groups (for fiction or nonfiction; see page 153). Use the appropriate chart throughout the lesson as necessary to monitor your students' reading comprehension and discussions.

3. If you are using fiction, discuss students' past experiences that relate to the book to activate their prior knowledge. If you are using a nonfiction text, ask your students what they know about the topic. Fill in the section of the chosen chart to record predictions.

4. If you are in the middle of a text with a group, summarize the last reading selection before previewing the current one. Refer to the comprehension chart that you have selected to use.

5. Have students work in pairs or as a group with you to preview illustrations in fiction texts, or headings, illustrations, captions, and maps in nonfiction texts. When there are no illustrations in either text, have your students skim and scan the chapter or pages for a minute or two. Model for them how to skim, scan, and hunt for key words. Allow students to offer predictions verbally or on sticky notes, and remind them to monitor their predictions as they read. Ask them, "What do you think you will learn?" "What do you think is going to happen?" "What clues did you use?"

6. Encourage students to think about questions that they would like to have answered. Begin with "I wonder...."Add their predictions and questions to the comprehension chart that you have selected for this lesson.

During Reading: Question and Clarify

1. Encourage students to hunt for portions of text that would be good sources of questions to ask others after reading. Provide sticky notes for recording the questions and give an example that your students can follow.

2. Remind students to use their copies of the Clarifying Bookmarks to help them with words or ideas that are tricky. Ask them to be prepared to share with the class one difficult spot in the text and how they clarified it. You may wish to model this activity before asking students to do it. Provide sticky notes.

3. Have students read the text selection silently while you rotate to individuals and coach them in the reciprocal teaching strategies. Do not use round-robin reading because it does not promote reading comprehension (Opitz & Rasinski, 1998).

4. Encourage students to reread the text to ask questions or identify clarifications. Sticky notes are an optional place for students to write their questions or clarifications. They should initial their notes and can place them directly on the group's guided reading chart. You can save the notes after the lesson to document students' progress in strategy use.

After Reading: Question, Clarify, Summarize, and Check Predictions

Remember that the four reciprocal teaching strategies can be discussed in any order. However, I often use the following sequence, because students are so enthusiastic about asking their questions after reading. Then, I alternate between modeling each strategy and allowing students to practice each one.

1. Model questioning for your students and invite them to share their questions with partners or the group. As an option, write the questions on the guided reading chart that you have selected, or have your students write questions on sticky notes to attach to the chart. Invite students to ask one another their questions. Encourage students to use good social skills by prompting answers politely and making eye contact.

2. Refer to the predictions made prior to reading that are recorded on the chart, and model how to check a prediction to see if it came about or was changed during the reading. Have students take turns checking other predictions against what they have read.

3. Model one word or idea and how to clarify it. Have your students share their points to clarify and the strategies that they used for clarifying (refer to the Clarifying Bookmarks).

4. Either model a summary, guide the group in creating a summary, or invite individual students to summarize the text. Discuss any interesting text points and decide which ones belong in the summary. Fill in a Fab Four Chart.

5. For a fictional text, discuss any other points that you or the students wish to talk about, including personal connections, character motives, favorite parts, surprises, and emotions.

    For nonfiction selections, reflect on the nonfiction text features—such as headings, maps, and visuals—and ask your students how they used the text features to help them understand the reading.

6. Ask your students to reflect on the four reciprocal teaching strategies and invite them to tell the class which strategy helped them the most and why. Give examples and model reflection, if necessary.

ASSESSMENT TIPS

- Keep your individual coaching notes and records of your observations of students during guided reading lessons by using the Reciprocal Teaching Observation Chart for Guided Reading (see page 168). Use any or all of the informal assessments in Appendix A as an assessment guide.

- As you work your way through the lesson plan, have your students write some of their predictions, questions, points or words to clarify, and an occasional summary on either sticky notes or forms from this book (such as the Literature Discussion Sheet for Reciprocal Teaching, page 205).

- Keep a guided reading observation notebook with one page designated for each student. After a lesson, remove any sticky notes initialed and dated by your students and place each one on the respective student's page in the notebook. Over time, your records will show how individual students have grown in their use of the four reciprocal teaching strategies. Then, you can form temporary groups of students who are having trouble with the same strategy or strategies and meet with the groups to teach more guided reading lessons or the minilessons on pages 178–184.

Basic Comprehension Chart for Guided Reading Groups

What We Know
(our experiences, background knowledge, and/or connections with the text)

Our Predictions
(make predictions before reading and check their accuracy after reading)

Our Questions
(who, when, what, where, why, how, and what if)

Our Words or Ideas to Clarify	How We Clarified

Our Summary

Reciprocal Teaching Guided Reading Lesson Plan Guide

Fiction Lesson Plan	Nonfiction Lesson Plan

Before Reading
Activate prior knowledge
• "Have you ever...?"
• "What do you know about...?"
Predict
• Preview illustrations/chapter books
• Skim and scan
• "I think...will happen because..." (start graphic organizer)
  • Setting
  • Characters
  • Problem
  • Events
  • Ending
  • Character feelings
	Before Reading
	Activate prior knowledge
	• "What do you think know or think about...?"
	Predict
	• Preview illustrations/chapter books
	• Skim and scan
	• Predict the following:
	• What are you wondering about
	• Use table of contents
	• Start a graphic organizer, such as a K-W-L chart or Venn diagram.
	• Write predictions
	• "I think I will learn...because..."

During Reading Read [silently, chorally, with partners] to find out predictions **Question/Clarify** • Reread to find a point/word to clarify • Or, reread to ask a question • Teacher circulates and models and asks individuals to predict, summarize, question, or clarify	**During Reading** Read [silently, chorally, with partners] to find out predictions **Question/Clarify** • Reread to find a point/word to clarify • Or, reread to ask a question • Teacher circulates and models and asks individuals to predict, summarize, question, or clarify
After Reading Predict • Return to predictions to confirm or change Question • Take turns modeling, then partners ask questions about the characters, events, theme Clarify • Discuss/model words or points to clarify and say "I didn't get the part where..., so I..." • Discuss ways to clarify Summarize • Summarize as a group or page by page • Fill in a graphic organizer with setting, characters, problem, events, ending, feelings • Which strategy helped you the most today and why? • Give examples	**After Reading** Predict • Return to predictions to confirm or change Question • Model for students as you question using headings/main ideas • Partners ask questions Clarify • Discuss/model words or points to clarify and say "I didn't get the part where..., so I..." • Discuss ways to clarify Summarize • Summarize as a group,or page by page with partners • Return to fill in graphic organizer with what was learned • Which strategy helped you the most today and why? • Give examples

Lesson 2: Using Graphic Organizers During Guided Reading

Many students are visual learners who benefit from the use of graphic organizers during instruction. Although you can use graphic organizers, specifically comprehension charts during whole-class instruction, comprehension charts are especially effective for guiding small-group instruction, because they assist students who need visual aids to guide their reading and boost their comprehension. Also keep in mind that you may not wish to use a graphic organizer every time you meet with your groups, because writing on a chart slows down the discussion considerably. Teach a mix of lessons with charts and what I call "grab and go" lessons where you simply grab appropriate books, go sit down with students, and run through each of the Fab Four verbally (see the Fast Fab Four lesson, page 174). Eventually, you may occasionally ask older students to fill in their own graphic organizers during their literature circles or cooperative groups.

There are two types of charts I like to use during small-group guided reading. One is the Fab Four Chart, a place to record student responses for each of the four strategies (see page 160). This handy chart helps guide your discussion and ensures that all four strategies are covered in a class period. You can easily sketch this chart at your guided reading table on chart paper, a dry-erase board, a colored file folder, or piece of construction paper. Write the name of the group on the chart and save each one for informal assessments when you wish to look back at student comments that are recorded on it. Sometimes I call this file folder a "game board" and use it even when I informally gather a group at a table or on the floor. I often assign a student to be the checker, and that student puts a check mark in each of the boxes as we fill in the chart with sticky notes.

The other type of chart you might choose to use is a combination of the Fab Four Chart and one of various graphic organizers, such as a description web, sequence, problem/solution, main idea/details, or

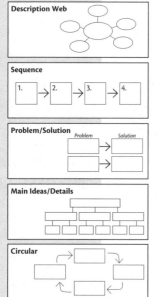

Description Web

Sequence

1. → 2. → 3. → 4.

Problem/Solution

Problem   Solution

Main Ideas/Details

Circular

circular. You can create a "combo organizer" simply by placing one of the graphic organizers in the appropriate box on the Fab Four Chart. When working with fiction, I often combine the Fab Four Chart with the Story Map Prediction Chart (see page 161) to create a Fab Four Combo Chart specifically for fiction (see page 162). I sketch the graphic organizer in the Predict box and the Summarize box on the Fab Four Chart. I tell students that we will fill in the summarize box after we read. At the beginning of the lesson, we predict by skimming the text and predicting how it is organized. At the end of the lesson, students summarize by writing what actually happened on sticky notes. Students place their sticky notes on the chart.

Because reciprocal teaching is a discussion technique, you should not require your students to write long pieces for the comprehension chart but only brief reminders on the sticky notes. The notes give your students ownership of the chart and keep the focus on the discussion, not the written responses. You can ask them to put their names on their responses. That way, you have a formative assessment to use in planning other lessons or moving students into different groupings.

MATERIALS

- Chart paper, a dry-erase board, or large sheets of butcher or construction paper

- A supply of pencils, markers, sticky notes, and tape

- Any of the following charts:

    - Basic Comprehension Chart for Guided Reading Groups (see page 155)

    - Story Map Prediction Chart (see page 161)

    - Fab Four Combo Chart: Story Map/Fiction (see page 162)

    - Fab Four Combo Chart: Nonfiction/Compare–Contrast (see page 163)

    Or your own combo chart using the Fab Four Chart and graphic organizers, as needed

- Copies of Clarifying Bookmarks (see page 183)

TEACHER MODELING

1. Select a text to use with your reciprocal teaching guided reading group. You may group particular students together, because they need work on the same strategy, are at the same reading level, or have

selected the same text to read. (See page 136 for more information on forming groups.)

2. Sketch a Fab Four Chart in front of your students. Be sure to allow a place for jotting down notes about what your students already know and/or connections that they make to the text (see the top portion of the chart), and also include places for noting predictions, questions, clarifications, and summaries (see the bottom portion of the chart).

   Tell your students that they will use the chart to guide them through that day's reading.

3. Model how your students can make connections to and predictions about the text and use their background knowledge by previewing the text and noting a connection and a prediction on sticky notes. Post the sticky notes directly on the Fab Four Chart.

4. Optional: Model and show students how to use and select a graphic organizer, or sketch the organizer directly inside the summary box of the Fab Four Chart. Explain before reading why you've selected a particular graphic organizer (it's fiction with characters and a problem, or it's nonfiction with four headings and details) and how it will help students keep track of the reading. Model how to predict using the organizer and throughout the reading fill it in when you summarize.

5. Alternate modeling each of the Fab Four strategies and then invite students to discuss with a partner and write their responses on sticky notes, or you can record students' responses on the chart.

6. Model a summary and guide students as you summarize together and fill in the summary box of the Fab Four Chart. If you are incorporating one of the graphic organizers in the Fab Four Chart, then alternate modeling and inviting students to fill in the organizer as you summarize together.

STUDENT PARTICIPATION

1. Ask your students to read the text silently after they have added their predictions, connections, and experiences to the chart or you have written them there. You can ask the students who finish early to reread the text and write questions for the group to answer. Another option for early finishers is to have other reading material available at the guided reading table.

2. Model the reciprocal teaching strategies one at a time and then ask your students to follow your example. For instance, when all students have finished reading, discuss their predictions. Discuss whether they

changed their predictions while reading. Then, model a question and ask your students to ask questions of their own. (Students usually love asking questions, so let them do it.) Have them record one question each on a sticky note for the chart. Then, model a clarification and ask your students to come up with clarifications of their own. They may also write their clarification points on sticky notes for the chart. Finally, model a summary and then ask the group to help you summarize. Record the group's summary on the comprehension chart. See Figures 13 and 14 for examples of comprehension charts completed by students.

3. Continue to use modeling throughout many reciprocal teaching sessions, but gradually release the responsibility to your students. For example, invite student volunteers to model the first prediction, question, clarification, or summary.

4. Ask your students to discuss how reciprocal teaching strategies helped them comprehend the text during the lesson.

Figure 13
A Guided Reading Chart About Spiders, Completed by a Second-Grade Guided Reading Group

Reciprocal Teaching at Work: Powerful Strategies and Lessons for Improving Reading Comprehension (second edition) by Lori D. Oczkus. © 2010. Newark, DE: International Reading Association. May be copied for classroom use.

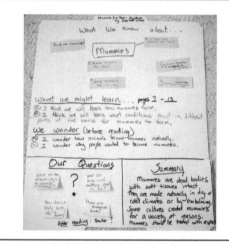

Figure 14
A Guided Reading Chart About Mummies, Completed by a Sixth-Grade Guided Reading Group

Reciprocal Teaching at Work: Powerful Strategies and Lessons for Improving Reading Comprehension (second edition) by Lori D. Oczkus. © 2010. Newark, DE: International Reading Association. May be copied for classroom use.

- When your students contribute to a comprehension chart, have them put their names or initials on their responses. If you are taking dictation of their discussions, simply write the students' initials next to their responses. This way, you can make notes to yourself and keep track of individual students' progress during reciprocal teaching discussions. You might choose to transfer the sticky notes used on the chart to a page for each student in a guided reading observation notebook.

- Do not judge your students' writing skills based on their comprehension chart responses. Remember that the chart is a discussion guide and a visual reminder for students, not a writing assessment. Instead, look for the quality of their responses as they use each reciprocal teaching strategy.

- When coaching individual students, use the coaching prompts in Table 11 (see pages 142–143) to help you to guide your students to use the four reciprocal teaching strategies more effectively.

- If your students are having difficulty clarifying ideas, be sure to continue modeling at least one point to clarify per session or text. Discuss how to clarify ideas by using the Clarifying Bookmarks. Emphasize rereading as an effective clarifying strategy.

- If your students are having trouble summarizing on their own, summarize as a group. Then, student pairs can work together to reiterate the summary. Watch for word-for-word text retellings and encourage your students to use their own words when they summarize.

- Form temporary, flexible strategy groups of students who may need to work on one particular strategy or all four. Teach the minilessons at the end of this chapter (see pages 178–184) to students who need extra support. Also, refer to Table 5 (see pages 26–27) when your students struggle.

Fab Four Chart

Our Connections
What do we know about...?
Have we ever...?

Predict	**Question**
I think I will learn.... *I think this is about....*	*Who, what, when, where, why, how, what if?* *Why do you think...?* *I wonder....*
Clarify	**Summarize**
I didn't get..., so I.... Words/ideas to clarify How we clarified	*This is about....* *First..., Next..., Then..., Finally....* *In the [beginning, middle, end]....*

Story Map Prediction Chart

Before Reading (Use text and illustrations to predict.)	**After Reading** (Fill in what actually happened.)
Setting:	**Setting:**
Characters:	**Characters:**
Problem:	**Problem:**
Main Events:	**Main Events:**
Resolution/ending:	**Resolution/ending:**
Theme or lesson:	**Theme or lesson:**

Fab Four Combo Chart
Story Map/Fiction

Our Connections
What do we know about...?
Have we ever...?

Predict	Question
Predict before reading the book or chapter.	*Who, what, when, where, why, how, what if?* *Why do you think...* *I wonder...*

Predict (left column):

Setting:

Characters:

Problem:

Events:

Ending/theme:

Clarify	Summarize

Clarify (left column):

I didn't get the [word, idea, part],

so I (check the ones you used):
__**Reread**
__**Read on**
__**Broke the word into parts**
__**Visualized**
__**Used a synonym**
__**Asked a friend**
__**Other:**_____

Summarize (right column):

Summarize after reading the book or chapter.

Setting:

Characters:

Problem:

Events:

Ending/theme:

Fab Four Combo Chart
Nonfiction/Compare–Contrast

Our Connections
What do we know about...?
Have we ever...?

Predict	**Question**
I think I will learn... because...	
Clarify	**Summarize**

Lesson 3: Coaching and Meeting Individual Needs During Guided Reading

BACKGROUND AND DESCRIPTION

During guided reading sessions, I tell the students to think of me as they would a sports coach who compliments them and gives helpful hints as they, the athletes, play the game of reading. Sometimes during guided reading lessons, I wear a hat or visor that says *Coach* on it to illustrate the point that the students are doing the work with my guidance. Students love this real-life comparison.

So, how can you effectively coach individual students in reciprocal teaching strategies during a guided reading group? Picture the coaching sessions in this lesson taking place in a spot that makes sense for your classroom. Perhaps you meet with small groups at a kidney-shaped table, with you seated on the inside. Maybe you are into less formal settings for reading groups, so you can meet with students on a rug or in beanbag chairs. Either way, the physical arrangement of the setting is important to conducting this lesson. It is helpful to read with and coach each student privately without interrupting the other students as they read silently.

If you work at a kidney-shaped table with your students, move from the table's center to the outside. Sit or crouch next to each student for just a few moments to check his or her use of one reciprocal teaching strategy and provide necessary guidance before moving on to coach the next student. You may not make it to every student in the group during one lesson, but you can make a note of which students need to be coached during the next lesson. By moving around the outside of the table to work with your students, you can keep the coaching sessions quiet. If you use a reading workshop model, then the coaching techniques in this lesson and the guided reading coaching prompts (see Table 11, pages 142–143) will help you as you confer with individual students. (See the Conclusion for reading workshop suggestions.)

This lesson offers prompts to use for each of the reciprocal teaching strategies during guided reading sessions. Use the prompts with individual students and keep track of your coaching sessions using the Reciprocal Teaching Observation Chart for Guided Reading (see page 168). During this lesson, your students will do the following:

- Be held individually accountable for one of the four reciprocal teaching strategies
- Be asked to verbalize a think-aloud for the reciprocal teaching strategies
- Be guided by you in the reciprocal teaching strategies

MATERIALS

- Multiple copies of reading material for a small group of students
- Fab Four Chart (optional; see page 160)
- Multiple copies of the Fab Four Bookmark (see page 74) with reciprocal teaching strategies for student and teacher reference
- List of coaching prompts (see Table 11, pages 142–143)
- Reciprocal Teaching Observation Chart for Guided Reading (see page 168)

TEACHER MODELING

1. Begin the guided reading group by introducing a new book or, if your class is already engaged in a text, by reviewing what the group has read so far. If you wish, pass out copies of the Fab Four Bookmark for students to use to guide their strategy use and discussions throughout the lesson. Preview the portion of text that the group will read during this lesson by looking at headings and illustrations and making predictions. If the text has no illustrations, then read aloud the first few paragraphs and skim over each page for vocabulary that stands out. Have your students write predictions about the text on sticky notes and post the notes on the group's Fab Four Chart.

2. Review all of the reciprocal teaching strategies or focus on one strategy. Quickly model each strategy, using examples from the text that the group is reading. When you focus on one particular strategy, ask your students to closely observe your think-aloud. Tell them that they will have a chance to practice the strategy or strategies with you as you coach individual students.

3. As you move around the group, choose strategies to coach based on any of the following scenarios:

   - Coach all students on the focus strategy that you taught in the minilesson prior to reading

- Coach each student on a strategy that you think he or she needs to practice based on your previous observations
- Ask your students which strategy they want to practice or demonstrate for you

4. If a student needs to be coached on a particular reciprocal teaching strategy, provide a model of that strategy and ask him or her to try again with the next paragraph or page of the text. Give the student specific examples, such as, "I noticed that you were having trouble with summarizing this page. I can model that for you, so you can see how to summarize. Watch how I tell the events in order. Also, I reread the paragraph to remember all of the main points. You can try summarizing again with the next page." Coach a few students that day and the rest the following day. If your students are done reading silently, and you have not coached everyone, then you can coach the students that you missed the next time they meet in a guided reading group.

STUDENT PARTICIPATION

1. Ask your students to begin to read silently and tell them that you will coach them in their use of reciprocal teaching strategies. Select a student with whom to work and sit next to him or her. Ask the student to read a sentence or two aloud. Then, either you or the student can select a reciprocal teaching strategy for the student to model.

2. Ask a student to work on one reciprocal teaching strategy in the portion of text that he or she is currently reading. Then, use one of the prompts in Table 11 (see pages 142–143) to help the student get started with the chosen strategy.

3. When the student finishes modeling the reciprocal teaching strategy, give him or her very specific compliments, such as, "I like the way that you used clues from the heading to make a logical prediction" or "That question is one that I had to use several clues from the text to answer. Good job!"

ASSESSMENT TIPS

- Use the Rubric for the Reciprocal Teaching Strategies in Appendix A for guidelines on each reciprocal teaching strategy.
- Take notes on individual students during guided silent reading and group discussions, marking which strategies the students demonstrate and a few notes about what they do. The following list provides some examples:

Oct. 8—Juan summarized the paragraph on page 1. Left out two of the five main ideas.

Sam clarified the word *follow* by making an analogy to the word *swallow*.

Rachael asked a literal question about page 13.

Use your notes to guide the next few lessons. Which strategies do your students need to work on the most?

- Use the information that you gather on the Reciprocal Teaching Observation Chart for Guided Reading (see page 168) to help you flexibly group students according to their strategy use. Form student groups and teach focus lessons or minilessons on the strategies with which the students are having trouble.

- Provide extra support for students when they need reinforcement by teaching the optional minilessons for Reciprocal Teaching in Guided Reading Groups found at the end of this chapter (see pages 178–184).

- Check each student's ability to use the strategies in concert. Have each student read a passage and verbally give you a response for each strategy. Use Table 5 (see pages 26–27) for additional suggestions when your students struggle with a specific strategy.

- Ask students to self-assess by asking themselves, which strategies are helping me the most? Which strategies do I find myself using in other reading situations? Ask your students to give examples of how they use the strategies at home and when they are reading at their desks independently or with a partner.

Reciprocal Teaching Observation Chart
for Guided Reading

Key for Reciprocal Teaching Strategies Coached: P = predict Q = question C = clarify S = summarize					
Student Name	**Strategies Taught/Date**				
1.					
2.					
3.					
4.					
5.					
6.					
7.					

Lesson 4: Watch Your Qs and Cs During Reading!

This is one of my favorite lessons, because it engages students during guided reading with a meaningful task that promotes the independent and flexible use of several strategies. (Besides, the students get to write on sticky notes, one of their favorite "grown-up" things to do!) Many students have been taught to watch for their predictions during reading, but good readers do much more than just anticipate what is next. They also naturally ask questions and clarify. By requiring that students be on alert for these thoughts, you are promoting metacognition that boosts reading comprehension. While reading silently, the students choose to either question or clarify points by placing a sticky note labeled with a Q for question or a C for clarify directly on the page next to the text. During the debriefing time, the students discuss their thoughts and the places they marked. Watch Your Qs and Cs makes an excellent literature circle, center, or workstation activity as well.

- Multiple copies of reading material for a small group of students
- Two different colors of sticky notes
- Fab Four Chart (see page 160)
- List of coaching prompts from Table 11 (see pages 142–143)
- Reciprocal Teaching Observation Chart for Guided Reading (see page 168)
- Watch Your Qs and Cs Record Sheet (see page 173)

1. Begin the lesson with a review of all four strategies and explain that students will focus on Qs (questions) and Cs (words or ideas to clarify) during reading today. Ask what students know about asking questions. Ask what students know about clarifying words or ideas.

2. Read aloud a portion of text as students follow along. Model how to ask a question. Focus on a wonder ("I wonder..."), quiz questions (who, what, when, where, why, how, what if), or a thinking question

("Why do you think...?"). Write the letter Q on a sticky note and put it next to the paragraph you asked your question about. You do not have to write the question on the note.

3. Read aloud another portion of text or use the same part and model how to clarify a word, sentence, idea, or concept. Begin your clarification with "I didn't get..., so I...." Mark your point or word to clarify in the text by placing the sticky note in the book. You do not have to write the word or part, just the letter *C*. Tell students you expect them to be able to explain why they marked that particular spot. Explain how you figured out the tricky part and include strategies such as reading on, rereading, thinking of synonyms, chopping the word into parts, and sounding it out. You may wish to find a confusing sentence or paragraph that warrants rereading, or find a part you had to read twice to get a picture in your head.

STUDENT
PARTICIPATION

1. As students read silently, provide them with access to two different colors of sticky notes to write their Qs and Cs on. You can require that they find a certain number or leave it open.

2. Rotate around to individual students and coach them as they try finding their Qs and Cs. Prompt and model. When a student tells you that he or she doesn't have anything to clarify, ask if the student can find something a younger child would have trouble with.

3. As you move around the group, choose strategies to coach based on any of the following criteria:

   • Coach all students on the focus strategy, either a Q or C, that you taught in the minilesson prior to reading.

   • Coach each student on a strategy that you think he or she needs to practice based on your previous observations.

   • Ask your students which strategy they want to practice or demonstrate for you.

4. If a student needs to be coached on a particular reciprocal teaching strategy, provide a model of that strategy and ask him or her to try again with the next paragraph or page of the text. Give specific compliments such as, "You found the tricky part! I like the way you reread to figure out that word."

5. End the lesson by having students do a group summary in the form of a drawing, or they can dictate to you and you write one for them.

You may also ask each student to tell one thing they learned. Or, ask partners to summarize first, then discuss as a group.

6. Ask the group of students to reflect on which strategy helped them the most today, either clarifying or questioning and tell why.

7. Occasionally, use the Watch Your Qs and Cs Record Sheet as part of the lesson. Discuss specific points students found in the text to clarify and question.

- Use the informal assessments in Appendix A for guidelines on each reciprocal teaching strategy.

- Take notes on individual students during guided silent reading and group discussions, marking which strategies the students demonstrate and a few notes about what they do.

- Are the students clarifying words only or ideas as well? Do they use a variety of fix-up strategies?

- Are the students asking wonders, quiz questions, and thinking questions?

- Are their questions a mix of in the book and higher level, critical thinking or inferential questions?

- Use your notes to guide the next few lessons. Which strategies do your students need to work on the most?

Minding Your Qs and Cs !

Primary The second graders eagerly approach the guided reading table anxious to meet and continue reading a nonfiction title, *Cloud Forest* by Nic Bishop. Mrs. Rosenberg tells the students they will find Qs and Cs today as they read. Even though the students are familiar with the procedure and know the routine, Mrs. Rosenberg takes a few minutes to conduct a think-aloud for the group. She models how to figure out several words and tells the students she is not going to choose them as her word today, as she is waiting to find the trickiest one of all. "Oh, I see this super tricky word *overlapping* on page 12, so I write it on my yellow sticky note," she explains as she models sounding it out and checking the picture to see how the leaves overlap. The students read independently as Mrs. Rosenberg rotates around the circle to coach each student as they quietly whisper read to her. Each one gives her either a word to clarify or a question to ask. Pencils are in motion as the students write their tricky words, which they share and place in the Clarify box of the Fab Four Chart. Mrs. Rosenberg passes out pink sticky notes to mark questions that start with "How do the...?" She models, "How do the plants survive in the cloud forest?" The second graders nod, feeling grown up and scholarly as they begin rereading the text to write their "How do the...?" questions on their sticky notes. They pass around the popular plastic microphone, and each one asks a question and places it on the Fab Four Chart. Questions include "How do the birds eat and survive in the cloud forest?" "How does the hummingbird feed in the cloud forest?" and "How does the gecko catch insects?" The recess bell rings, and their ticket out is to each tell one thing they learned about the cloud forest as they quietly toss a stuffed frog around the table. The Qs and Cs adorn the chart with sticky notes full of good thinking!

Intermediate   The fourth graders gather on the class rug to read *Because of Winn-Dixie* by Kate DiCamillo with their teacher, Mr. Ling. After summarizing yesterday's chapter and discussing Opal's choice to give Winn-Dixie a bath, the students predict that Opal will talk her father into keeping the dog and telling her more about her mom. Stacks of sticky notes are available in the center of the group, so students can grab them to mark their texts with a Q for question or a C for clarify. Mr. Ling quickly models a question, "Why does Opal want to keep the dog?" The responses flow, "She needs someone, because she doesn't have many friends." "Opal loves dogs and maybe has always wanted one." Mr. Ling circulates around the group. As each student whisper reads a paragraph or two aloud, he asks, "Would you like to question or clarify?" Arem wants to clarify, "I didn't get what Opal meant by saying that she and the dog were both orphans." Mr. Ling coaches him by suggesting that he read on. Arem lights up, "Oh, I get it now. The dog and the girl do not have moms."

Arem places a C next to the paragraph and reads on. The other students are lost in the story, but occasionally someone reaches for a sticky note, labels it with a Q or C, and reads on. Mr. Ling calls time, and the students grab one more sticky note to mark a spot and then eagerly share their Qs and Cs with the group. The group agrees they want to watch the movie to compare and contrast the story line with the book. Tomas adds, "I liked the picture in my head better than the one in the movie, though!"

Intermediate/Secondary   The seventh graders gather in their table groups to read and mark their Qs and Cs as they read *The Invisible Man* by H.G. Wells. Miss O'Leary introduces the book by having students discuss science fiction titles they've read or movies they've seen, and after just a few minutes, asks the students to predict by reading the chapter title and very first paragraph, and then by skimming and scanning the chapter. Students open the predict door on their Four Door Charts and write a few thoughts starting with "Maybe...," "I'll bet...," and "I think..." statements. "Please find at least two Qs and two Cs as you read the chapter to yourselves and mark them with your sticky notes." After a few minutes, Miss O'Leary joins a table and asks the students to pause as she guides a discussion. "Please mark a Q that you have so far. Mine is a wonder. I wonder who this stranger is." The students quickly mark their notes with Qs, then proceed with a lively discussion. "I wonder why the lady let him in the inn." "How much of the invisible man can you see?" "Does the author use flashbacks to tell us how he became invisible?" Miss O'Leary rotates to each table to spend five to seven minutes leading a discussion, modeling examples of Qs or Cs, and prompting students to elaborate on their responses. Before the bell rings, she asks students to first discuss a summary with their table groups, then write a quick three-sentence summary to turn in as they leave.

Watch Your Qs and Cs Record Sheet

Directions: After marking your book with sticky notes to show your questions and words and ideas to clarify, fill in this sheet with more detail. Share with a partner or your group.

Before Reading **Predict** Turn to a partner and, after previewing the text, make a prediction for pages ____ to ____. Sketch or write your prediction below.	

During Reading
Wonder Questions
1. On page _____ I am wondering:
 	
2. On page _____ I am wondering:
	During Reading
	Clarify Words
	List of at least 2 words to clarify.
	1. Word _____ page _____
	   How I figured it out:
	
	2. Word _____ page _____
	   How I figured it out:

Quiz Questions Write two questions. Start with *who, what, when, where, why, how,* or *what if.* 1. 2.	**Clarify Sentences** Find one or two confusing sentences. Page _____ How did you figure them (or it) out?
Thinking Questions Write two questions for your group to discuss. 1. Why do you think... 2. Why do you think...	**Clarify Scene** Draw a picture, or find a part you read twice to get a picture in your head. Look for descriptions and metaphors. Page _____
After Reading **Summarize** Draw or write a brief summary for pages _____ to _____.	

Reciprocal Teaching at Work: Powerful Strategies and Lessons for Improving Reading Comprehension (second edition) by Lori D. Oczkus. © 2010. Newark, DE: International Reading Association. May be copied for classroom use.

Lesson 5: Fast Fab Four

BACKGROUND AND DESCRIPTION

A Fast Fab Four lesson is exactly that, fast! This simple lesson has two quick versions of reciprocal teaching that will allow you to rotate around the room to as many groups of students as you can or simply meet at your table with one group to quickly run through all the strategies in record time!

There are two ways you might use the Fast Fab Four:

1. *Teacher rotates to tables*—Predict as a class, and the students begin reading silently or aloud in table teams. Rotate to each group and run through all four strategies once, using them in any order. Move to the next group and do the same. Try to reach as many groups as you can. Provide prompts to each group and model one or two of the strategies at each table. There is no writing or recording, to keep the fast feel of this lesson.

2. *Guided reading groups at the table*—Conduct the lesson at your reading table with a guided reading group. The students read a few pages and then pause. Using the Fab Four Dial, ask students which strategy they want to use first. Allow them to quickly turn and talk or share with the small group for each of the strategies, moving quickly through each one. Again, there is no writing, and the discussion should be brief to keep the pace fast. Model one of the strategies in a think-aloud, but not all of them, in this fast version of the Fab Four!

MATERIALS

- Multiple copies of reading material for a small group of students or for students to read at their desks
- Fab Four Dial (see page 177) or Fab Four Bookmark (see page 74)

TEACHER MODELING

1. Tell students you are going to whip through the strategies for each chunk of text.

2. Use the Fab Four Dial or Fab Four Bookmark to guide the discussion. Move the dial or refer to the bookmark as you prompt students to

share responses for each. Select one of the strategies to model for them as you read from the text and give an example.

3. Move around the classroom to each table. The class may read independently and silently. When you arrive at a table or if students are at desks, address 4–6 of them at a time and engage them in a Fast Fab Four run through for the text they are on. If some students are ahead, then select a portion of text most of them have read already.

4. You may call students up to you and base your groupings on students who need a particular strategy. So, for example, if one group needs to work on asking better questions, then call them up and model one question. Then, ask them to think of a question. Before they leave the table, quickly run through the other three strategies.

5. During a readers' workshop you might also try a Fast Fab Four. As you circulate to groups of students who are reading different texts, ask them to discuss how the strategies are helping them and coach them as they give examples of predicting, summarizing, clarifying, and questioning.

1. Students read silently, and as they read, they watch for examples of words to clarify, questions to ask, or predictions. You may even provide them with sticky notes to mark their texts as they go. Then, when you get to their group, they can go back and refer to the marked sections of text as examples of the Fab Four.

2. After you meet with students, they resume reading independently as you rotate to other groups.

• Use the informal assessments in Appendix A for guidelines on each reciprocal teaching strategy.

• Take notes on individual students during guided silent reading and group discussions, marking which strategies the students demonstrate and a few notes about what they do.

• Use your notes to guide the next few lessons. Which strategies do your students need to work on the most?

Fast Fab Four

Primary   "Ready to fly through the Fast Fab Four?" Mrs. Pummer asks the small group of second graders as they gather on the rug to read and discuss a leveled text, *Tiger's Tales* by Michaela Morgan. "Turn the dial in your heads to predict," she suggests, and the six students immediately thumb through the book to picture walk and share a prediction with a partner.

Manny blurts out, "I think the cat lives in the bookstore and reads the books." "Yeah," adds Adam, "and he tells the other cats the stories at night!" "I think he gets locked in," chimes in Marisa. Mrs. Pummer encourages the students to read the first 10 pages silently. Then, they continue the Fast Fab Four by pausing to give a quick summary using the prompt, "So far…." The tricky words to clarify are *related*, *panic*, and *frightened*. Mrs. Pummer models a "what" question, and partners formulate quick questions, including, "What kinds of stories does the cat tell at night to the street cats?" and "What do people do when they see the cat in the library?" The group discusses what will happen next when the cat is locked in the library. Kelly notices the sign that reads, "Closed for the holidays." The students gasp in horror as they worry and predict the fate of the trapped kitty! They read on, totally hooked until the end of the book when they will run through another Fast Fab Four.

Intermediate   Fourth graders quietly read their basal story about the *Titanic* by Robert Ballard. Mrs. Gomez previewed and predicted with the entire class, and students discussed their predictions at their table groups. Now the entire class is quietly reading. Mrs. Gomez circulates to each table of six students and brings her reciprocal teaching Fab Four Dial with her. At the first table, the students stop reading as Mrs. Gomez leads them in a quick discussion of each of the strategies for the pages they are reading at that moment. That group resumes their reading as she moves to the next group and invites the next table of students to suggest which strategy they want to discuss first. Each group takes about five minutes to run through a Fast Fab Four. If Mrs. Gomez can't cover all the tables today, she plans to finish tomorrow.

FAB FOUR DIAL

Directions: This dial can be used during whole-class sessions, guided reading groups, or literature circles. An enlarged version of the Fab Four Dial can serve as a wall chart. In either case, students turn the dial to the next strategy until all four strategies have been covered in a given lesson (a brad and a pointer can be placed in the center of the dial and turned as the strategies are discussed). The purpose of this activity is to let your students know that the reciprocal teaching strategies work together as a package and that all four strategies must be used during reading.

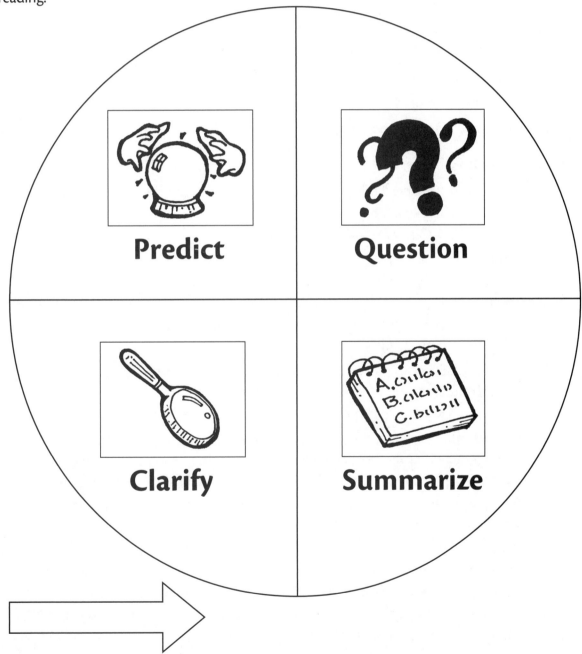

Minilesson: Word Pop Prediction

Description and Comprehension Strategies

When you read a magazine article, you most likely preview the headings and captions, and then skim and scan the text and words a bit to get the gist. Students also benefit from skimming and scanning (Oczkus, 2004) as part of the prediction process, as it helps them anticipate the overall text content and some of the important vocabulary. When you couple a picture walk (Clay, 1993) with looking over the words, students learn a lifelong useful tool for predicting in any text.

Materials

- Multiple copies of a text
- Fab Four Chart (see page 160)
- Document camera or overhead projector

Teacher Modeling

1. Ask students to review predicting. What are some ways they predict (e.g., look at the pictures, illustrations, headings)?

2. Tell students you are going to show them how to skim and scan through the text, because that is what good readers do to help themselves as they peek at the content and vocabulary to decide what the selection is about. You can use the analogy that skimming and scanning is much like scrolling down a computer screen and selectively reading or scanning with your eyes. Scanning helps us get the idea as readers, but we are not reading from left to right.

3. Use a text the students can see or have copies of. If possible, model using the document camera, overhead projector, or interactive whiteboard.

4. Read aloud some of the text and show students how to make a prediction based on pictures and headings. Then, take your two index fingers and place them on the sides of a page of text at the top. While running your fingers simultaneously down the sides of the page, call out words and phrases you read as you quickly scan the text. Then, pause and say, "Now I think…, because I saw some clues that make me think this is about…." Model skimming and scanning again while students follow along.

5. If you teach primary-grade students and wish to try this lesson, then an alternate is to do what I call "Grab a Word." Instead of scanning down the text with your fingers, ask students to look up at the ceiling, count to three, and then tell students to look down at the page and "grab" the first word they see. They look ahead and

(continued)

say their word aloud. Then, ask students to share their words and use those words to help them make predictions. Use the starter "I see the words..., and I think...will happen..., because..." to guide the discussion (or for nonfiction, "I see the words..., so I think I will learn..."). Kids of all ages love doing this!

Student Participation

1. Alternate modeling and guiding students as they skim and scan.

2. Students practice with partners.

Assessment Tips

- Are student predictions becoming more sophisticated when they skim and scan?

- Do you need to coach students, so they will select key vocabulary and words that will help them predict?

- Ask students how skimming and scanning can help them when they read.

Minilesson: Question Starters

Description and Comprehension Strategies

Many ELLs and primary-grade students experience difficulty formulating questions. One way to scaffold questioning for students is to provide question starters. Some students only need the first word or two of a question as they learn to ask good questions, while others may need more extensive three- and even four-word prompts.

Materials

- Multiple copies of a fiction or nonfiction text
- Sticky notes

Teacher Modeling

1. Select a portion of text to read aloud to students. Pause and think aloud, "I am going to ask a question on this part, so I need to reread. I think I will ask a 'what' question because that goes with this sentence best. What...?"

2. Model for students using a variety of question starters including the following:

   - I wonder....
   - [Who, what, where, when, why, how, or what if]...?
   - What do you think...?

Student Participation

1. You may need to provide varying levels of questioning scaffolds for students in a particular group or for individuals. Model using the starter first and then ask the students to try it. Assign a question word that goes with a particular portion of text, for instance, "On page..., ask a 'where' question." Then, take it one step further and provide a two-word starter, such as, "Can you turn this sentence into a question that starts with 'How many...?'" Some students will need a three-word or longer starter in order to successfully ask a question, for instance, "Let's ask a question about this part that starts with 'Why did the...?'"

2. Students read further and pause several times to ask one another questions using the question starters.

Assessment Tips

- Have students write their questions on sticky notes. Collect and assess them.
- Are students asking only literal questions? Are they asking critical thinking questions?
- Can students use the starters and ask logical questions that go with the text?

Minilesson: Clarify Bookmark

Description and Comprehension Strategies

In this lesson, students use the Clarify Bookmarks to guide their discussions as they look for words and ideas they need to clarify in the text.

Materials

- Multiple copies of the chosen text
- Chart paper (or a file folder to display the chart at the table)
- Clarifying Words Bookmark and Clarifying Ideas Bookmark (see page 183)

Teacher Modeling

1. Make a two-column chart with the headings "Clarifying Words" and "Clarifying Ideas."

2. Ask your students what good readers do when they need to clarify a word. Ask students to refer to the strategies listed on the Clarifying Words Bookmark. Pass out the bookmarks and go over the content with students.

3. Read aloud a portion of the text and model how to clarify a word. Have the students put their fingers under the word you are clarifying on their copy of the text. Tell which strategies you used to help you figure it out. Use the strategy starter "I didn't get the word..., so I...."

4. Review how to clarify ideas using the Clarifying Ideas Bookmark.

5. Read a portion of text and model how to clarify a sentence or idea, which may include a description, metaphor, idiom, illustration, map, or entire chapter. Model how a reader might need to clarify the confusing parts of a text, even though he or she may know all the words. Make sure that your students have copies of the text and are looking at the correct portion of text as you model clarifying. Use the strategy starter "I didn't get the [sentence, part, chapter, illustration, map, metaphor, idiom], so I [reread, read on, thought of a synonym, talked to a friend]."

Student Participation

1. After reading a selection, invite your students to put words that need to be clarified on sticky notes. Place the sticky notes on the two-column chart. Discuss what strategies may be used to figure out each word. Use the bookmark to guide the discussion.

(continued)

Minilesson: Clarify Bookmark (continued)

2. After reading, invite your students to write on sticky notes for the chart any ideas or parts of text that were confusing or the page numbers where the ideas can be found in the text. Discuss strategies for clarifying ideas, and place the suggestions on the chart.

Assessment Tips

• Are your students using the clarification strategies in their own reading? As the group reads, watch to see if students refer to their bookmarks to clarify. Every time the guided reading group meets, choose one word and one idea from the reading to model clarifying strategies to quickly clarify.

Clarifying Words Bookmark

1. Identify the difficult word.

The word _____
is tricky, because

a. I had trouble pronouncing it.

b. I didn't know what it meant.

c. I didn't know what it meant, and I couldn't pronounce it.

2. Try to clarify the difficult word.

I tried the following strategies to understand the difficult word:

____ I checked the parts of the word that I know (prefixes, suffixes, base words, and digraphs).

____ I tried blending the sounds of the word together.

____ I thought about where I have seen the word before.

____ I thought of another word that looks like this word.

____ I read on to find clues.

____ I tried another word that makes sense in the sentence.

____ I reread the sentence to see if the word I figured out made sense.

Clarifying Ideas Bookmark

1. Identify the confusing part, which might be a sentence, paragraph, page, or chapter.

A confusing part is
_____
_____ ,
because

a. I didn't understand _____ .

b. I can't figure out _____ .

c. It doesn't make sense.

d. I don't get _____ .

e. This part isn't clear, because _____ .

2. Try to clarify the confusing part.

I tried the following strategies to understand the confusing part:

____ I reread the parts that I didn't understand and some text before that part.

____ I read on to look for clues.

____ I thought about what I know about the topic.

____ I talked to a friend about the reading.

____ I visualized.

Minilesson: Draw or Dramatize Summaries

Description and Comprehension Strategies

Summarizing is fun when you incorporate drawing or dramatizing in your lessons. After reading, give students the option to draw a part from the text or to dramatize a scene. Either way, this game-like lesson will keep your students guessing.

Materials

- Multiple copies of the chosen text
- Slates or paper to draw on
- Markers

Teacher Modeling

1. Ask students what they know about summarizing.

2. After reading, model the drawing part of this lesson by telling students you will sketch a scene from the selection on your dry-erase board and the students will guess what scene it is. Students should turn to the part in the text that they think you drew. Students reread the part together.

3. Select one page or scene from the text to pantomime. After you quickly act it out, call on students to guess which scene you are dramatizing and have them locate it in the text. Tell students if they guessed correctly or not. Reread the part of text you acted out.

Student Participation

1. When it is time to summarize, give each student a choice of either using a small dry-erase board to sketch a scene from the reading or to pantomime something from the text. Give students one minute to flip through the text and find a part to draw or act out. Each student in the group shares their drawing or dramatization while the group guesses the scene.

2. Or, you may wish to have all the students work as a team to pantomime or draw the same scene as they summarize the text together.

3. Help the group construct a verbal summary using the scenes they acted out and drew.

4. Ask pairs of students to repeat the summary to each other.

Assessment Tips

- Listen to the students as they summarize. Can they select main ideas and vocabulary from the text and incorporate these elements into brief summaries? Do students only select details or interesting parts rather than main ideas to use in their drawings and dramatizations?

CHAPTER SUMMARY

- Reciprocal teaching strategies enhance comprehension when they are taught during small-group, guided reading instruction. The small-group format allows for further scaffolding of the four reciprocal teaching strategies.

- Students have the opportunity to use reciprocal teaching strategies in a variety of texts, including grade-level and leveled texts.

- Primary and intermediate intervention programs have influenced guided reading practices.

- The four main ways to group for guided reading include organizing strategy needs groups, student choice, intervention, and student ability level.

- A powerful intervention for struggling readers introduces them to reciprocal teaching strategies during guided reading instruction. After several months of using guided reading and reciprocal teaching with struggling students, have them introduce the strategies to the rest of the class. The intervention students become the resident experts during whole-class and literature circle lessons.

- Comprehension charts provide effective visual tools for monitoring and guiding students in using the four reciprocal teaching strategies.

- Students need to engage in meaningful activities during seatwork time (see page 145 for suggestions).

- Assessment procedures during guided reading include observing, coaching individual students, reflecting on strategy use, and collecting brief written responses from students for a chart or discussion purposes.

CHAPTER 5

RECIPROCAL TEACHING

in Literature Circles

After every chapter, I summarize to let people know what's going on so far. It helps you know what you're reading.

—Belinda, grade 4

Description of Reciprocal Teaching and Literature Circles

"Does anyone have another question we can discuss?" asks Owen, the discussion director of his fourth-grade literature circle. Hands shoot up, and Owen calls on his classmates as they take on the roles of predictor, questioner, clarifier, and summarizer to discuss the novel *Tales of a Fourth Grade Nothing* by Judy Blume. The lively discussion continues. The students enjoy their "book club" time so much that their teacher, Mrs. Hada, also incorporates the reciprocal teaching literature circle format when they read material from the social studies curriculum.

The Fab Four reciprocal teaching strategies provide an easy and natural literature circle structure as students each take on one of the strategies as a role during discussions—predictor, questioner, summarizer, and clarifier. Fab Four literature circles make a powerful impact on student comprehension scores at any grade level, from third graders reading leveled readers to sixth graders reading *Bridge to Terabithia* by Katherine Paterson to 10th graders discussing a controversial current event article on inappropriate forms of text messaging. The discussions are lively and engage the students as their comprehension soars with reciprocal teaching.

According to Vygotsky (1978), learning is social, and students use language and discussions to construct negotiated understandings. The cooperative nature and scaffolded support of reciprocal teaching make it a natural match for student-led discussion circles. A literature circle provides a unique environment for boosting comprehension with reciprocal teaching strategies, because it is a natural setting in which students can take turns using each reciprocal teaching strategy—predicting, questioning, clarifying, and summarizing. In addition, reciprocal teaching can be incorporated easily into a literature circle format at a variety of grade levels. Just ask the sixth graders at Stedman School in Denver, Colorado, and the fourth graders at Bowles Elementary in Fenton, Missouri: They will tell you that the combination of reciprocal teaching and literature circles improves reading comprehension and, most of all, is fun.

Book clubs are popular among adult readers, so I often begin my literature circle training with students by asking them if they've heard about book clubs or if any of their parents are in one. I tell the students that we are going to learn a grown-up way to interact and discuss books, just like they're in a book club. The hands go up, and students share comments such as the following:

My mom is in a book club, and they read Oprah books.
My sister was in one with her friends, and they read Twilight books!
My aunt is in one, and they eat lots of snacks at her book club.
They pick the books they want to read in book clubs.

When I draw the comparison from literature circles to book clubs students perk up, pay attention, and know they are in for something special that follows a real-world model. This analogy helps me build on the book club format as I train students in the social skills involved in discussing books. I share ways adults talk about books quite naturally with comments like, "I really liked the part where…, because…," "I didn't get the chapter…, because…," or "I wonder about the author's idea for…." We also discuss the option of choosing a reading selection and forming book clubs based on book titles and choice.

It was out of necessity that I finally developed a model for reciprocal teaching in literature circles. I had been meeting with a group of six struggling fourth graders twice a week for reciprocal teaching sessions. The group worked hard and, after three months of guided reading lessons with reciprocal teaching, most of them had improved one year in their reading levels. Then, their classroom teacher decided that the students could not miss any more regular class time for the intervention sessions. Although I understood her frustration, I desperately wanted to find a way to continue helping the students hone their use of reciprocal teaching strategies. It was then that I asked the struggling students to be my experts and help me introduce reciprocal teaching strategies to their entire class. Beaming with pride at their accomplishments, they gladly assisted me in modeling for the class and leading the literature circles. By the end of the school year, all of the struggling students had raised their reading levels, comprehension abilities, self-esteem, and motivation to read.

For those teachers who like the structure of official roles (Daniels, 1994) in literature circles, the reciprocal teaching roles of predictor, questioner, clarifier, and summarizer work well. I add a fifth role—a discussion director—to assist with additional, essential reading comprehension strategies such as making connections and visualizing to improve comprehension, and with tasks such as filling in graphic organizers (see Figure 15).

Figure 15
Students Participate in a Literature Circle

Reciprocal Teaching at Work: Powerful Strategies and Lessons for Improving Reading Comprehension (second edition) by Lori D. Oczkus. © 2010. Newark, DE: International Reading Association. May be copied for classroom use.

If you do not want to assign reciprocal teaching roles, another option is to allow your students to discuss the strategies freely. Then, one student can record the group's collective predictions, questions, points or words to clarify, and summary (Routman, 1999). Roles or no roles, I hold every student responsible for knowing how to use all the reciprocal teaching strategies when reading a given text. I often do this by calling on students from each of the literature circles at random to give examples of the strategies.

Goals of Reciprocal Teaching During Literature Circles

The goals of reciprocal teaching during literature circles are the following:

- To deepen comprehension using a highly cooperative peer setting and reciprocal teaching strategies
- To provide opportunities for students to practice the four reciprocal teaching strategies in a variety of texts—fiction, nonfiction, required books, choice books
- To release more responsibility for strategy use to the students

- To guide students in becoming metacognitive and independent in their use of reciprocal teaching strategies

Reciprocal teaching adds a "read and learn to comprehend" dimension to literature circles because it gives students the basics for comprehending texts well. I decided to try using reciprocal teaching strategies in literature circles because many students with whom I worked were reading and not comprehending what they were reading. I knew research indicated that gains could be made with reciprocal teaching strategies even when peers interact (Palincsar, Brown, & Martin, 1987), and literature circles provide more opportunities for scaffolding reading strategies. More teachers are starting to incorporate reciprocal teaching into their literature circles, which may already include other wonderful models and variations that promote discussion (Daniels, 1994; Hill, Johnson, & Noe, 1995; Samway & Whang, 1995).

An added benefit of using reciprocal teaching in literature circles is that the reciprocal teaching model teaches and reinforces basic reading comprehension strategies. Some primary-grade teachers with whom I work prefer reciprocal teaching during literature circles because their students are still learning to read and reciprocal teaching is easy to implement with primary students. Teachers are attracted to students' growth in the four basic reciprocal teaching strategies that become tasks during the literature circle model. Some teachers gradually introduce reciprocal teaching during guided reading groups and whole-class sessions over the school year as part of their plan to teach students to read. By the spring, their students are capable of participating fully in reciprocal teaching during literature circles.

Practical Steps for Introducing Literature Circles to Your Students

When it is literature circle time in Mrs. Garcia's fifth-grade classroom, her students sit in circles of five on the classroom floor, huddled over their books. While one group's members ask questions after reading a text and another group acts out a chapter summary, Mrs. Garcia might meet with a third group to listen in and guide the students as they discuss ideas and words to clarify. Her literature circles run smoothly, because she has provided her students with ample support in reciprocal teaching in a variety of ways before introducing them to reciprocal teaching in literature circles. For example, she taught whole-class and guided reading lessons to model the reciprocal teaching strategies with both fiction and nonfiction texts. When she introduced reciprocal teaching literature circles to her class, she asked for volunteers to model the strategies, and she continued to do so every day since then. Mrs. Garcia's literature circles did not come together in just a few lessons; she carefully introduced them with a lot of support. You will need to do the same for your students.

The question teachers often have about literature circles is, What is the best way to get started? It can seem overwhelming thinking about the training in both the reciprocal teaching strategies and the positive social skills that your students will need to begin. This chapter contains many practical lessons to get you started and to help your class stay on track as you implement literature circles. Most important, your students need to be well grounded in the four strategies before you begin any sort of cooperative groups. I suggest teaching lessons from Chapter 3 on whole-class sessions for at least a month or two before letting students loose to work on their own. Students also need training in the social skills that are required for literature circles to flow smoothly. I recommend heterogeneously grouping students, so all types of learners benefit from working together. Then, you can decide which books to use and how often to meet. If you want your students to experience growth in reading from employing the reciprocal teaching model, twice a week is ideal. I've found that it is much easier to train students in the literature circle procedures if the text we use initially is easy to read and short.

In the schools in which I have worked we have used two very effective ways to begin using literature circles in the lessons. Following is a brief description of each so you can determine which you might like to try with your class. You can find the full lessons for these options later in this chapter.

Fishbowl: It's Your Role!

- Pass out role sheets (see pages 211–216) in four different colors and make sure that at every table, all four of the strategies are represented—predict, question, clarify, and summarize—and that a discussion director is also chosen.
- Select one group to be your model group that the class will observe. (This doesn't need to be your strongest readers, as you are closely leading this group!) It is helpful to display a copy of the

role you are demonstrating on the overhead or document camera and model each step on the card.

- After each member completes his or her role or job, before going on to model the next role, invite all of the members around the room who hold the same role card to repeat the steps with their groups. For example, talk the predictor through his or her job in front of the class. Prompt the student who is modeling, "Let's see what your first task is on the card. Here it says you are supposed to...." Each of the predictors takes a turn at their tables to go through the same steps with their groups while you circulate and assist.
- Then the class focuses their attention on your model group again, and you prompt the questioner for her or his job followed by all the questioners trying it out at their tables.
- The lesson continues, alternating modeling with trying out the roles until all five roles complete a turn.

This first lesson takes about 45 minutes to an hour but is well worth it. You may from time to time choose to return to this lesson to improve the quality of the roles or even just to model one of the jobs. By alternating strong, step-by-step modeling with practice and feedback, students actively participate in a scaffolded first experience in a literature circle.

Jigsaw Expert Huddles

This unique lesson is a different spin on a jigsaw (Aronson, Blaney, Stephin, Sikes, & Snapp, 1978). In a jigsaw, each student in a group of four or five is in charge of a portion of the material, in this case one of the reciprocal teaching roles or discussion director. Students with the same roles meet in a huddle with the teacher to practice their "job" before performing in front of peers.

- Each group member holds a colored jigsaw puzzle piece for one of the following roles: predictor, questioner, clarifier, summarizer, and discussion director.
- During the training session, all students keep two books on their desks, their independent reading novel and the text the group will read during literature circles.
- Each jigsaw expert comes to the front of the room to join you as you stand in a circle or huddle with the small group to model, practice, and discuss their jigsaw role and the text they will use with their group (see Figure 16). For example, the predictors come

Figure 16
Students in a Jigsaw Huddle

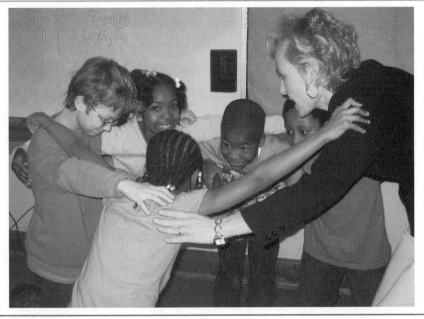

to the front of the room for a huddle while classmates read silently from their independent books. When the predictors return, groups predict under their leadership using the book or reading material.

- When the teacher signals, students go back to reading their other book while the next role, questioners, come up front for a quick huddle. The questioners return to their groups, and the groups discuss questions in the literature circle book.

- The rotation continues, and the class continues to move in and out of the two books during training sessions. Each of the other roles, clarifier and summarizer, alternate between meeting to learn the job and practice in a huddle and then returning to their groups to lead a discussion of their assigned strategy.

- Once all of the roles have met to huddle and have returned to work with their groups, you can invite the groups to run through their discussions with another chunk of text without meeting with the like-role huddles.

This is a very effective way to train students and you can choose to return to this method any time to refine and teach a new level of sophistication to each of the roles.

In order for any literature circle model to flow smoothly, you should train your students in reciprocal teaching strategies, social skills, and other necessary procedures. Table 14 outlines the training that students need and some basic ways to conduct it. Many of these fundamentals are incorporated into the lessons in this chapter. In addition, Table 15 provides a quick reference for getting started with reciprocal teaching and literature circles.

Table 14 **Training for Reciprocal Teaching in Literature Circles**		
Training That Students Need Prior to Literature Circles	**Why?**	**How to Model and Teach**
Reciprocal teaching strategies—predict, question, clarify, and summarize	• Students need a deep understanding of all four strategies, so they can participate fully in discussions. • Each student needs to be ready to give a response for each strategy.	• Model and guide through reciprocal teaching strategies during whole-class lessons with partners, during guided reading lessons with small groups, and when using role sheets during guided reading as a training ground for literature circles.
Social skills—taking turns, being polite, practicing active listening skills, and building on others' comments	• Literature circles will not run smoothly without the necessary social skills. • Students can learn a lot from their peers, but social skills must first be modeled, taught, and reinforced.	• Ask one group to model social skills for the class. Choose model groups often. • Have the class respond to the model group by discussing the Reciprocal Teaching Observation Chart for Guided Reading (see page 168).
Necessary procedures—minilessons on how to use materials and act out roles, filling out graphic organizers, and completing other response activities	• Students need to know basic procedures in order to function effectively within literature circles. • Students should know the routines associated with literature circles to allow them to focus on what they are reading.	• Discuss and model minilessons on procedures for materials, roles, and responses. • Model these activities with one group in front of the class. • Practice or guide students in these procedures during guided reading sessions with one group at a time.

Table 15
Getting Started With Reciprocal Teaching and Literature Circles

1. Decide how you will organize the groups.

- *Heterogeneous groups:* In order to provide a rich reciprocal teaching experience for all students, opt for creating literature circles that are heterogeneous.

- *Interest groups:* In addition to organizing heterogeneous literature circles, give students opportunities to form groups based on their shared interest in a particular text. Offer several different books for students to choose from, and they form groups based on their book choices. To ensure that the books are not too challenging or easy for some students, offer a variety of texts but try to keep the material at the students' grade level.

- *Struggling readers as "experts":* If you've met regularly with struggling students to use reciprocal teaching strategies with them, invite the struggling students to be the experts when you introduce the Fab Four to the whole class. Try to include one struggling reader Fab Four "expert" in each literature circle. This way, the struggling readers have the opportunity to shine as they train the heterogeneous groups to use reciprocal teaching strategies.

2. Select books to use.

What books work best for introducing reciprocal teaching literature circles?

- *Easy-to-read, high-interest, short materials:* When first introducing a class to reciprocal teaching in literature circles, use short, easy-to-read, high-interest books and articles. During the introductory phase, you do not want the students to become bogged down with material that is too difficult to read and understand.

- *Novels, content area reading, required reading, leveled texts:* Once the students know the reciprocal teaching routine and strategies, you can switch to textbook and novel chapters and the school district's grade-level anthology. Struggling students can read with a group member as a partner, or you can assist students who need extra support in the actual reading of the material.

3. Decide how often circles will meet.

A minimum of twice a week is necessary to keep the discussion and interest in the reading material going.

4. Introduce and teach the Fab Four strategies.

Use lessons from Chapters 3 or 4 first, for at least 4–8 weeks, to familiarize students with the strategies in a supportive and structured setting. Make sure your students know how to use all four strategies well and in cooperative table groups before teaching them the literature circle roles. You may also bring the role cards (see pages 211–216) into your guided reading group and guide the students as they learn to use them.

5. Select an introductory lesson from this chapter.

- Fishbowl: It's Your Role! (see page 206)
- Jigsaw Expert Huddles (see page 217)

(continued)

6. Turn any other lesson in this chapter into an introductory lesson.

If you use a fishbowl or group to help you model, then you may also turn either of these lessons into an introductory lesson. So, for example, if you use the Rotating Roles lesson (see page220) with a sample group and the class observes that group as you guide them, then other groups may try the procedure.

7. Teach and reinforce social skills.

- Share Table 14 (see page 194) and directly model and teach the desired behaviors.
- Each time groups meet, select a "focus social skill of the day," such as making eye contact. Mention and model it and ask students to briefly discuss the importance of the skill.
- When literature circle time ends, hold a debriefing session in which each discussion director shares how the group did socially. Provide specific feedback on the social skill of the day.

The Big Picture in Literature Circles: What Else You Will Need to Do

Although I highly recommend reciprocal teaching strategies for use in literature circles, I have reservations about exclusively using reciprocal teaching strategies in this setting. I try to consider and incorporate other important strategies that promote reading comprehension, such as making connections and inferences and discussing a text's theme (McLaughlin & Allen, 2002; Oczkus, 2009). You also may want to continue using other literature circle models (Daniels, 2002; Hill et al., 1995; Samway & Whang, 1995) to ensure that your students have the opportunity to work collaboratively with a variety of essential reading strategies. See Table 16 for other books that discuss literature circles.

In some classrooms, I use reciprocal teaching exclusively with certain texts and reserve other literature circle models for use with other designated texts. For example, a sixth-grade teacher with whom I work was concerned because she had already taught her students to use Daniels's (1994) literature circle roles of discussion director, passage picker, summarizer, artful artist, word finder, and connector. She felt that it would be confusing to introduce her students to another set of jobs in order to use reciprocal teaching in literature circles. I suggested that she might want to use Daniels's model with fiction and the reciprocal teaching model with nonfiction, including textbooks. This idea may be

Daniels, H. (1994). *Literature circles: Voice and choice in the student-centered classroom.* York, ME: Stenhouse.

Daniels, H. (2002). *Literature circles: Voice and choice in book clubs and reading groups* (2nd ed.). Portland, ME: Stenhouse.

Hill, B.C., Johnson, N.J., & Noe, K.L.S. (1995). *Literature circles and response.* Norwood, MA: Christopher-Gordon.

Hill, B.C., Noe, K.L.S., & Johnson, N.J. (2000). *Literature circles resource guide: Teaching suggestions, forms, sample book lists, and database.* Norwood, MA: Christopher-Gordon.

Marriott, D. (2002). *Comprehension right from the start: How to organize and manage book clubs for young readers.* Portsmouth, NH: Heinemann.

Morris, B., & Perlenfein, D. (2003). *Literature circles: The way to go and how to get there.* Westminster, CA: Teacher Created Resources.

Samway, K.D., & Whang, G. (1995). *Literature study circles in a multicultural classroom.* York, ME: Stenhouse.

Vasquez, V. (with Muise, M.R., Adamson, S.C., Heffernan, L., Chiola-Nakai, D., & Shear, J.). (2003). *Getting beyond "I like the book": Creating space for critical literacy in K–6 classrooms.* Newark, DE: International Reading Association.

limiting, because reciprocal teaching works well with either fiction or nonfiction. However, if you prefer to continue implementing a literature circle model that you already find successful, then try reserving certain texts for the reciprocal teaching model.

Adding a Means for Including Other Strategies: The Discussion Director

Another practical way to include strategies that fall outside reciprocal teaching in literature circles is to incorporate the special role of discussion director. When I first designed the reciprocal teaching literature circle model complete with role sheets (see pages 211–214), I had only four basic roles—a predictor, questioner, clarifier, and summarizer. As the students began working their way through the strategies, I found that something was missing. My literature circle model limited students by omitting some important reading strategies. I felt the need to have students discuss what they already knew about a topic and what they wondered about it before reading a nonfiction text. When they were engaged in fiction, I wanted students to make connections between the text and their own lives and to discuss open-ended responses. The reciprocal teaching roles were simply not enough to encompass all of the discussion points that I wanted students to share.

I decided to include a literature discussion director who would play a sort of catchall role for reading strategies and social skills. The discussion director involves the students in other important reading comprehension strategies that good readers should use. Because fiction and nonfiction require slightly different responses and strategies, I designed two role sheets for the discussion director that include reading strategies and social skills necessary for working with these text types (see pages 215–216). The discussion director also may lead the group in creating a graphic organizer or an artistic response to the reading. After the first time that I used the discussion director role, the reciprocal teaching literature circles worked much more smoothly, and I felt reassured that I was including other important reading comprehension strategies in my lessons.

Training Students in Essential Social Skills for Literature Circles

Social skills, or the lack thereof, can make or break your literature circles. Students need to learn proper discussion etiquette to avoid common problems that emerge during literature circles, which include the following: everyone talking at once or not talking enough, not making eye contact, rarely piggybacking on one another's comments, exhibiting poor listening skills, being rude, straying from the topic, and interrupting. One fifth grade where I met twice weekly to teach literature circles needed quite a bit of training in the social skills. The teacher felt it was her most challenging class ever, and the group even had a reputation around the school for being difficult. So, we provided scaffolds for their literature circles that ensured they'd exercise their best behavior. After just six weeks, the students participated fully in literature circles using appropriate social skills.

Following are the steps we used to explicitly teach social skills for literature circles:

1. We introduced literature circles by talking about book clubs, and we asked students what behaviors should constitute the ground rules in our literature circles.

2. We allowed students to pose first and second preferences for book titles, then moved students around to form suitable groups that would work well together.

3. We filled out a T-chart I sketched on the board with the headings "Looks Like" and "Sounds Like" (see, for example, the Reciprocal Teaching Observation Sheet, page 203). We brought out our icon and strategy starter posters (see Appendix E) during book clubs and modeled one or two behaviors each lesson.

4. Each day prior to breaking into groups, we conducted a five-minute minilesson to introduce the "focus social skill of the day." We also taught a "focus strategy of the day" (discussed in more detail in the next section). For example, for the focus social skill of how to piggyback on one another's comments, I'd select a group to demonstrate briefly with me walking and talking students through an example. The class discussed and commented on the topic.

5. As I moved around to each circle, I reinforced the social skill in focus and in the lesson debrief with the whole class.

6. We revisited the focus social skill again at the end of the lesson, calling on each discussion director to report on progress.

7. Once in a while, the class gathered around a model group to observe them in their literature circle for a longer period of time and to run through all the roles in 10 minutes. Students used the Reciprocal Teaching Observation Sheet (see page 203) to check off behaviors.

By constantly teaching and reinforcing social skills, you and your students will get more out of the literature circle experience. A fishbowl observation setup, the focus skill of the day, and lots of modeling give students the scaffolding they need to interact well in groups.

Including a Whole-Class Minilesson on the Focus Strategy of the Day

How can you reinforce and continue to model reciprocal teaching strategies? One way to effectively demonstrate them and keep building on student needs is to also teach a focus strategy of the day. Observe your students and how they use each of the four reciprocal teaching strategies. Select one of the strategies—predict, summarize, clarify, or question—that your students need to work on and model it in a minilesson with the whole class. Then, during group work, students should make an effort to use the same strategy. For example, you might model how to use syllables to figure out a word in a minilesson, and the clarifier in each group leads the students in using syllables as a word-attack strategy. During the debriefing, students share how they used the focus strategy. Or, during a minilesson, model how to predict based on events that have happened so far in the text. During the literature circle, the predictor follows your example and leads his or her group in making predictions based on prior events. (Use any of the minilessons from the end of each chapter in this book as focus strategy of the day lessons or create your own!)

When I worked in Mrs. Valentine's fifth-grade class, I spent just a few minutes each day conducting a quick think-aloud and modeling in either one of the student texts or my own novel, newspaper, or magazine article. Using examples from your reading is a wonderful way to show your students that the strategies aren't just for school but are for the rest of our lives (Oczkus, 2009). Besides, as I mentioned previously, students enjoy listening to stories about your life outside of school. Have you ever noticed how your students perk up when you start talking about your personal life (the kids, dog, broken down car, anything)? They like hearing about our reading, too!

The students really enjoyed it when I brought in examples from my novel, *Hotel on the Corner of Bitter and Sweet* by Jamie Ford. The story is about two children, a Chinese boy and Japanese girl, growing up in Seattle during World War II. They become friends at a private school where they are both taunted and teased. The girl's family ends up in an internment camp, and the boy sneaks away to visit her. I brought this book in every week for about a month and modeled a quick prediction, summary, question, or point to clarify each day. The students loved it and begged me for more. One day I used an example to clarify. In the scene, Henry, the main character, is wandering around the abandoned Japanese town searching for his friend. "Class, I need to clarify here. As I read the description of the Japanese town, I need to make a picture in my head of 'the barren streets to the cold sky, plumes of black smoke snaking skyward from places unseen.... Avoiding the strange looks on the faces of the few men and women who passed him' (p. 72)."

During reading that day, the groups discussed descriptive passages and visualizing from their novels during the clarify step of the lesson.

When I brought the class together to debrief at the end of the literature circle time, each clarifier from around the room shared how their group used visualizing to help them understand their text better. One day, we were short on time, and I signaled for the groups to just begin. "Aren't we going to have a focus strategy of the day?" asked Lana. I was thrilled that the class was hooked on the routine. Using a focus strategy of the day is a great way to model a think-aloud and strengthen strategy use.

Assessment Options for Reciprocal Teaching in Literature Circles

Assessment of students' achievements during literature circles can be approached from a variety of angles. Sometimes I require students to produce a group product such as a written response for all four reciprocal teaching strategies, and on other occasions I ask individual students to turn in a written piece. Students need to know that they should be ready at all times, because at any time you might call on them to share their knowledge with the group.

The following assessment opportunities can be used alone or in combination to provide important data to inform your instruction in reciprocal teaching strategies and literature circle procedures:

- Circulate around the classroom and observe your students during reciprocal teaching literature circles. Take notes on how your students are performing each strategy in the groups (use the Rubric for the Reciprocal Teaching Strategies in Appendix A as a guide). Also, make notes regarding your students' social skills. Observe whether they take turns, ask for clarification, signal agreement, or use other group-process skills. As needed, teach the minilessons from any of the chapters in this book.

- During your observations, choose a group that is doing well with all four strategies. After the literature circle session is over, invite the whole class to surround the group that you have selected. Have the chosen group model reading a page of text and working through reciprocal teaching strategies. Invite the class to respond to and evaluate the group's modeling in addition to making note of the social skills that the group models. If time constraints do not allow for the group members to model the strategies at the end of the literature circle session, then ask them to model the strategies at the beginning of the next session.

- Hold all groups accountable for the work that they do during reciprocal teaching in literature circles. Tell the groups that they each must choose one member to record their reciprocal teaching responses on the Literature Discussion Sheet for Reciprocal Teaching (see page 205).

- Hold individual students accountable for their work during reciprocal teaching literature circles. Rather than asking a group to turn in one Literature Discussion Sheet for Reciprocal Teaching, you can require that every student turn in a copy of the form. Or, you can simply have each student write a response to the four strategies on a sheet of paper or a Four Door Chart. Hold students verbally accountable for their learning, too. Let them know that you may call on them anytime, and they must have responses ready when you do.

- Observe all the groups and join one group for a few minutes while group members discuss reciprocal teaching strategies. Coach, model, and praise the students in the group as needed. Also, be prepared to coach a group in any reciprocal teaching strategy with which it is having difficulty. Use Table 5 (see pages 26–27) when students are struggling.

- Invite students to use the Self-Assessment Form for Reciprocal Teaching Literature Circles (see page 204) to evaluate their own progress with the use of reciprocal teaching strategies. Have the discussion leaders share with the class how the group did. Model the strategies based on difficulties that show up in the evaluations and coach each group as needed.

- Provide the whole class with additional modeling of and practice with reciprocal teaching strategies by using the minilessons (see pages 235–238) before breaking into reciprocal teaching literature circles. Reteach the minilessons to individuals and groups of students who are struggling with particular strategies.

Reciprocal Teaching Observation Sheet

Observer's Name: _____

Group Members' Names: _____

Looks Like	Sounds Like
What does the model group look like? (Check all that apply.)	**What does the model group sound like?** (Check all that apply.)
___ They sat still (no fidgeting). ___ They looked at each other when talking (nodded heads, smiled). ___ They looked back at the book.	___ They were polite to one another. ___ They were nice when they disagreed ("I see what you mean, but I think…"). ___ They stayed on topic. ___ They piggybacked on one another's comments ("I agree. I want to add…"). ___ They didn't interrupt one another. ___ They helped one another. ___ They praised one another ("Good job," "Nice prediction," and so on). ___ Everyone participated in the discussion.
Compliment What is one compliment that you could give the model group?	**Compliment** What is one compliment that you could give the model group?
Improvement How could the group improve the way that they look when they work together?	**Improvement** How could the group improve the way that they sound?

Self-Assessment Form
for Reciprocal Teaching Literature Circles

1. I participated in the discussion

   _____ a lot _____ some _____ a little _____ not at all

2. I listened to others in the group

   _____ a lot _____ some _____ a little _____ not at all

3. I looked at others when they were talking

   _____ a lot _____ some _____ a little _____ not at all

4. I gave answers for all four reciprocal teaching strategies.

   Predict _____ yes _____ no

   Question _____ yes _____ no

   Clarify _____ yes _____ no

   Summarize _____ yes _____ no

5. Here is a drawing of what I did best today.

6. Here is a drawing and writing to describe what I could do next time to improve.

Literature Discussion Sheet for Reciprocal Teaching

Group Members: _____

<table>
<tr><td>

Predict

Fiction

I predict that _____

_____

_____

_____ ,

because _____

_____

_____ .

Nonfiction

I think I will learn _____

_____

_____ ,

because _____

_____

_____ .

</td><td>

Question

Here are questions I can ask my group (who, what, when, where, why, how, what if):

1. _____

_____

_____

_____

2. _____

_____

_____

_____

3. _____

_____

_____

_____

</td></tr>
<tr><td>

Clarify

1. _____ is a difficult word, because

_____ ,

  so I (check the strategies that you used)

  __ checked parts of the word that I know.

  __ sounded out the word.

  __ thought of a word that looks like this.

  __ read on to find clues.

  __ reread to find clues.

  __ tried another word.

2. _____ is a confusing idea, because

_____ ,

  so I (check the strategies that you used)

  __ reread.

  __ read on.

  __ thought about what I know.

  __ talked to a friend.

</td><td>

Summarize

Here is a one- or two-sentence summary:

_____

_____

_____

_____

_____

_____

_____

_____

_____

_____

_____

_____

_____

_____

_____

_____

_____

</td></tr>
</table>

Lesson 1: Fishbowl: It's Your Role!

BACKGROUND AND DESCRIPTION

How do you know whether your students are ready for literature circles with reciprocal teaching strategies? First, students need to be very familiar with each reciprocal teaching strategy and they also need training in the social skills that are necessary for polite and meaningful exchanges with their peers (see page 198).

In this lesson, students actively engage in the Fab Four by alternating back and forth several times as observers of a fishbowl group (Kagan, 1989), then as participants in their own groups. I find this method far more effective than forcing students to watch an entire demonstration of all four strategies at once. When I taught my fishbowl lessons that way and the groups tried to work independently, students did not remember what to do, and the long demonstration became boring for them to observe. Step-by-step modeling may take longer, but it is worth it during this training phase!

Throughout the fishbowl lesson, a demonstration group guided by the teacher walks through each role in front of the class. Immediately following each role (predictor, clarifier, and so forth), the groups around the room mirror the demonstration and try it on their own. After just a few minutes of working in their groups, the teacher calls the class to observe the fishbowl group again as they model the next role. This structure of alternating a thorough demonstration for each role with the fishbowl then allowing group members to immediately try out the same role is a very explicit and engaging way to introduce reciprocal teaching literature circles.

Role sheets are extremely helpful when you first start literature circles in your class. When I first started, I didn't have them, and without role sheets, I found that many groups raced through the four roles and, after only a few minutes of discussion, proudly raised their hands, announcing, "We're done, Mrs. Oczkus!" The role sheets that I designed for each reciprocal teaching strategy guide students in their jobs. I have been pleased with the results: The students use the role sheets to stay focused and on task. As an option, you can have students rotate roles within the group, so each student gets a chance to play each role and use each role sheet (see the Rotating Roles lesson, page 220). Rotating roles is usually the student favorite, so I suggest trying it at some point. Later, when the students are more proficient in the roles, you can abandon them entirely if you wish. In situations in which the students become especially proficient in reciprocal teaching strategies, you eventually can set aside the role sheets and continue the reciprocal teaching discussions in a less structured fashion. It is up to you to decide just how much you want your students to rely on the role sheets during reciprocal teaching literature circles.

MATERIALS

- Role sheets duplicated on tag board and folded to display for each reciprocal teaching role (see pages 211–216)
- A copy of the Reciprocal Teaching Observation Sheet (see page 203) for each student
- The role sheets to display on the overhead projector, document camera, or interactive whiteboard
- A copy of the reading material for each student
- Optional: clipboards
- Four Door Chart (see page 110) or the Literature Discussion Sheet for Reciprocal Teaching (see page 205)

TEACHER MODELING

Prior to this lesson, your students all should be proficient in the four reciprocal teaching strategies. They should have learned the strategies in either guided reading groups or whole-class lessons. Notice the teacher modeling in this lesson is actually done by a student under the direction of the teacher. You may at any time give an example of the strategy when the model student or group is struggling.

1. Introduce reciprocal teaching in literature circles by telling your students that they are going to see what a literature circle using reciprocal teaching strategies looks like by observing a fishbowl group. They will need to pay careful attention, as they will be held responsible for either one of the strategies or the discussion director role.

2. Review reciprocal teaching strategies via a class discussion or by modeling each strategy for your students. Give each student in the class a role sheet, making sure that at every table all four strategies and the discussion director are represented.

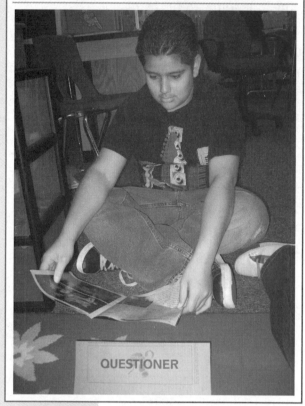

Figure 17
Student Acting as Questioner

QUESTIONER

Reciprocal Teaching at Work: Powerful Strategies and Lessons for Improving Reading Comprehension (second edition) by Lori D. Oczkus. © 2010. Newark, DE: International Reading Association. May be copied for classroom use.

3. Select a group of students to be your model fishbowl group. Have the students in the group display signs indicating which role they are playing—predictor, questioner, clarifier, summarizer, or discussion director (see Figure 17).

4. Ask each student in the model group to perform his or her role one at a time and walk the group members through a reciprocal teaching discussion in front of the class. Immediately following the walk-through of each job, invite all of the other students in the class who hold the same role card to try out their role in their teams. After a few minutes, signal for the class to pay attention and conduct another walk-through with the next role and invite students to try that strategy at their tables. For example, the fishbowl predictor takes a turn with you directing, then all the predictors at the tables take turns. Then, the class observes the fishbowl questioner asking a question with your guidance before all the questioners try it in their groups. To effectively model each role, you should do the following:

• Display the role sheet on the overhead or document camera and walk through the steps throughout the demonstration. Begin with the discussion director.

• Invite the student demonstrating a role to go through each step with your guidance. For example, help the predictor read each step on the predictor role card and then execute it with his or her group. Provide a language frame, such as "I think...will happen, because...." Provide one example of a prediction for the predictor to build on, or you can require that he or she develop another one.

5. Notice that there is a discussion director role card for fiction and another for nonfiction. You may wish to run this fishbowl lesson twice, once for each genre. Strategy use is slightly different in

each genre as well. (For example, summarizing might be based on sequence of events in a fiction text and on main ideas in nonfiction.)

1. Give each student a copy of the Reciprocal Teaching Observation Sheet, so students can keep track of what the model group does well and what they need to improve. I like to use clipboards when they are available, so students can stand or sit around the model group and write easily. Also, clipboards make students feel grown up and like true observers! The observers stay at their desks, or you can call them to stand in a circle around the table where the model group is working.

2. Ask the class for feedback along the way, such as, "What did the predictor just do in this step? How did the group members respond? What did they do well? What should they do next?"

3. Continue alternating modeling with the fishbowl group and then inviting the class to participate in their groups. Have groups write their responses to the strategies on either a Four Door Chart or the Literature Discussion Sheet for Reciprocal Teaching. You may wish to follow this order for the roles:

   - The discussion directors go first and follow directions on the role card. Then, discussion directors ask the predictors to take a turn.

   - The predictors follow directions on the role card and ask the groups to preview the text and think of a prediction. The predictors give a prediction first and then invite their group members to share theirs.

   - Next, the discussion director either selects a mode of reading or polls the group for how they want to read the selected pages—silently, aloud in pairs, or aloud by pages or paragraphs. The group begins in its chosen manner.

   - After reading, the discussion director asks the model group members who would like to go next—the questioner, clarifier, or summarizer. Each student takes a turn and performs his or her role before asking the rest of the group to follow suit (that is, the questioner asks a question first, then asks others to do so, and so on through the roles).

   - The discussion director should compliment group members' participation and good strategy use. The group discussion should end with the predictor predicting what will happen in the next segment of the text.

4. Lead the class in a discussion of the Reciprocal Teaching Observation Sheet. Ask the class to give the fishbowl group compliments and suggestions regarding both strategy use and proper literature circle etiquette.

ASSESSMENT TIPS

- Observe your students in their literature circles and take notes, so you can group students who are having trouble with a particular strategy for a quick minilesson on that strategy.

- Some forms in this book (for example, the Literature Discussion Sheet for Reciprocal Teaching) can be used for written assessments. Students may fill out the chosen form either as a group or individually. After you review the forms, group students according to the strategy with which they need the most help. Teach the minilessons on pages 235–238 or any of the minilessons in this book to the groups who need support.

- Continue modeling from time to time with one student group in front of the class, so students can discuss the strategies and social skills necessary for an effective reciprocal teaching literature circle. If you don't have time to model all four, conduct a fishbowl for one of the strategies, such as summarizing.

- If groups experience difficulty, try meeting with one literature circle at a time. Have the rest of the class stay at their desks reading quietly. After working with one group, send members back to their seats and call another group to work with you in a literature circle.

Classroom Story

Role Sheet Training for Students

Primary   All eyes are on the fishbowl group as they try out the reciprocal teaching roles in Mrs. Baumgartner's third-grade classroom. Mrs. Baumgartner prompts the predictor. "Read your role sheet, Tim. What does it say you need to do first?" she asks as she projects the predictor role sheet on the overhead projector for all to see. Tim takes a moment to read the first step and then hesitantly faces his group and tells them to look over the cover, headings, and illustrations and describe what they see in the article. "Good job!" Mrs. Baumgartner encourages him as he smiles and the group members raise their hands to share their ideas. "Class, did you see what Tim did? And I like the way Jocelyn piggybacked her comment on Mike's prediction," she comments. The class buzzes with quiet discussions as all of the predictors work their way through the directions on their predictor role sheets and the first chunk of text. Mrs. Baumgartner circulates to the tables to guide the discussions. After a few minutes, Mrs. Baumgartner signals the class to observe the fishbowl group again as they read the next chunk of text and the questioner takes a turn.

PREDICTOR

FOLD HERE

PREDICTOR

(predicts what the story or text will be about)

1. Ask your group to look at the cover, next heading, or next illustration.
2. Encourage group members to discuss what they see.
3. Ask all group members to write their predictions on their Literature Discussion Sheet for Reciprocal Teaching.
4. Share your predictions first. Then, encourage all group members to share their predictions with reasons for them.

QUESTIONER

FOLD HERE

QUESTIONER

(asks questions about the text—who? where? when? what? why? how? and what if?)

1. Ask your group members to write one or two questions that could be answered by reading this text.
2. Ask your questions first. Call on a volunteer to answer your question.
3. Ask for other volunteers to ask their questions. Don't allow *yes* or *no* questions!

CLARIFIER

*(finds areas where a word or idea needs to be explained—reread, read ahead,
use what you know, break a word into chunks, and think about what makes sense)*

1. Ask the group to reread this portion of text and look for confusing ideas or words. (What if you had to explain the book to a kindergartner?)

2. Ask the group to write one confusing or difficult word or idea.

3. Share your word or idea first. Tell how you figured it out using the Clarifying Bookmarks.

4. Ask for volunteers to give their words and ideas. Ask how they figured them out. If someone has a difficult word or idea that he or she didn't figure out, ask group members for ways to clarify the unclear word or idea.

FOLD HERE

Reciprocal Teaching at Work: Powerful Strategies and Lessons for Improving Reading Comprehension (second edition) by Lori D. Oczkus. © 2010. Newark, DE: International Reading Association. May be copied for classroom use.

SUMMARIZER

FOLD HERE

SUMMARIZER
(tells in own words a brief summary of the important point or points)

1. Ask the group to summarize this part of the text in writing on the Literature Discussion Sheet for Reciprocal Teaching.

2. Share your summary first.

3. Ask if anyone would like to add to your summary or give his or her own.

DISCUSSION DIRECTOR FOR FICTION

FOLD HERE

DISCUSSION DIRECTOR FOR FICTION

(keeps the discussion going, fills in the comprehension chart, and helps the group evaluate its performance)

Before Reading

1. Ask the predictor to go first.
2. After the predictor's turn, decide how the group will read the text—aloud, silently, or in pairs.

After Reading

1. Ask who would like to go next—the questioner, clarifier, or summarizer. Keep the discussion going. If the group did not finish reading the book, the predictor can take another turn to ask, What will happen next?

2. Ask each group member to share his or her connection on paper strips for text-to-self, text-to-text, and text-to-world connections. Glue the connections to a chart, or just talk about them.

3. Compliment the group for their behavior and use of reciprocal teaching strategies. Invite the group members to compliment one another: "Good eye contact," "Great idea," or "Good turn-taking."

DISCUSSION DIRECTOR FOR NONFICTION

FOLD HERE

DISCUSSION DIRECTOR FOR NONFICTION

(keeps the discussion going, fills in the What I Know and What I Wonder Chart, and helps the group evaluate its performance)

Before Reading
1. Ask everyone to share his or her I Know strips and tell what each knows about the topic.
2. Ask everyone to share his or her I Wonder strips. Glue the strips to the What I Know and What I Wonder Chart.
3. Ask the predictor to take a turn making predictions.
4. After the predictor's turn, decide how the group will read the text—aloud, silently, or in pairs.

After Reading
1. Ask who would like to go first—the questioner, clarifier, or summarizer. Keep the discussion going.
2. Return to the I Wonder strips. Ask if anyone had his or her question answered in the reading. Ask if there are any new questions.
3. Compliment the group members for their behavior and use of reciprocal teaching strategies. Invite the group members to compliment one another: "Good eye contact," "Great idea," or "Good turn-taking."

Lesson 2: Jigsaw Expert Huddles

This lesson is an alternate literature circle lesson that you might prefer to teach when you train your class in reciprocal teaching roles. I first developed this lesson to use with third graders who needed lots of structure as I introduced and strengthened the literature circle roles in their classroom. Since, then I have shared this lesson with thousands of teachers who've found it to be not only a helpful way to train students in each of the reciprocal teaching roles but also a lesson that can be used on occasion to strengthen the use of the strategies.

- Jigsaw expert cards (role sheets) copied in different colors, (see pages 211–216)

- Multiple copies of reading material for the class

- Independent reading material, one self-selected book per child

- Optional: Four Door Chart (see page 110) or Literature Discussion Sheet for Reciprocal Teaching (see page 205)

- Optional: Fab Four Bookmark (see page 74)

1. In this lesson, you will call up each role (predictors, questioners, clarifiers, summarizers, and discussion directors) to work with you as you model their "job" for them and then ask them to practice in the small-group setting before going back to their tables to lead their groups. Demonstrate how to use the jigsaw prompts and directions on their puzzle pieces.

2. Call the discussion directors to work with you first. If you like the huddle concept, then ask the team to stand in a circle during the lesson as you model and they practice using the text they will read with their group.

3. Next, call up the predictors. Read a portion of the text and model the strategy. Ask students to share their predictions.

4. Invite each of the other strategy jigsaw roles up—the clarifiers, questioners, and summarizers. Immediately after each group comes to train with you, the students return to their groups and run through their jigsaw pieces with the group. Circulate and assist.

5. Use the strategy starters for each strategy as you model to guide the students in the language of the strategies.

   - *Predict*: "I think I will learn….," "I think…will happen, because…."
   - *Question*: Who, what, when, where, why, how, or what if; "I wonder…;" "What do you think?"
   - *Clarify*: "I didn't get…, so I…."
   - *Summarize*: "This is about….," "First…," "Next…," "Finally…."

STUDENT PARTICIPATION

1. During the training sessions when other students are waiting at their tables for group members to return from the huddle, the students read their independent reading books.

2. Students participate as group members by taking part in the discussions led by the jigsaw roles.

3. Optional: Ask individual students to write their responses on a Four Door Chart, Literature Discussion Sheet for Reciprocal Teaching, or use either tool as a group record sheet.

4. An alternate use of the jigsaw pieces is to divide the class into five expert strategy groups—the predictors, questioners, clarifiers, summarizers, and discussion directors. Each role meets in their expert groups in corners of the room to discuss their role and the reading material. You might meet briefly with each expert group to assist students in their strategy use as they prepare to meet in reciprocal teaching literature circles. Then, have students form literature circles that include one person for each of the four roles.

ASSESSMENT TIPS

- Group members should reflect on their strategy use and social skills and offer one another compliments and suggestions for improvement.

- Classmates can offer suggestions for groups who are having trouble with reciprocal teaching strategies or social skills, such as taking turns, listening to one another, and commenting politely.

- Vary the written responses of groups. Collect a group's Literature Discussion Sheet for Reciprocal Teaching that one member has recorded for the other students. On other occasions, ask each group member to fill out one of the sheets. Use these written records as a way to find out which students need help with certain strategies.

- If your students are having trouble with summaries, ask each group to submit a group summary and share it with the class. Have the class vote on the best summary (Hacker & Tenent, 2002).

- Encourage students to assess themselves on the strategies and their participation in the literature circle using the Self-Assessment Form for Reciprocal Teaching Literature Circles.

Jigsaw Expert Huddles

Intermediate   A hush falls over the classroom as the fourth graders quietly read their different independent reading books. Besides their independent reading books, every student also has on his or her desk a jigsaw puzzle piece with the role of predictor, questioner, clarifier, or summarizer. The class continues to devour their books of choice while their teacher, Mrs. Weaver, calls the jigsaw predictors up to the front of the room where they join her to stand in a huddle. Armed with their jigsaw puzzle pieces and the book for literature circles, the students form a circle ready to work their way through a chapter in the nonfiction book, *Great Hearts: Heroes of Special Olympics* by Rebecca Weber. "OK, team, predict," Mrs. Weaver begins, "let's figure out how you are going to predict today. First, let's think about what's happened in the book so far to help us predict. We learned that the Special Olympics started as a small day camp in the Shrivers' backyard and today has thousands of events in 150 countries and has helped millions of intellectually disabled people. The rest of the book is about the stories of some of the athletes. We are reading only chapter one today. Let's skim the photos, captions, and some of the words to predict." She continues by modeling how to picture walk. "I see a boy named Ryan doing so many active things in these photos including horseback riding, playing baseball, swimming, skiing, and playing hockey. I saw the words *Down Syndrome* and information about that. I predict that I will learn that he has Down Syndrome and we will learn what that is." Mrs. Weaver asks the group to each use a picture walk with a partner and practice asking each other what they predict and why. The predictors are primed and ready to head back to their tables to lead their groups in predictions for the chapter. When they return, the group members put their independent reading aside and pick up their copies of *Great Hearts: Heroes of Special Olympics* as the predictors lead their group in their practiced predictions. "I think this is about a very special, hard-working, adventurous athlete named Ryan," shares Olivia, "because I see him doing so many different sports in the pictures!" When they are done predicting, the class resumes reading their independent books, and Mrs. Weaver invites the questioners to run through a model question or two and helps them practice before they lead their group.

Lesson 3: Rotating Roles

BACKGROUND AND DESCRIPTION

Of all the lessons in this book, I think this one might be students' all-time favorite! When we rotate roles, the students read a designated chunk of text, run through one of the roles, and then pass their role card one person to the right and receive a new role. By the end of a class period, the students have had a chance to be all the reciprocal teaching roles: predictor, questioner, clarifier, summarizer, and discussion director.

MATERIALS

• Role sheets (see pages 211–216)

TEACHER MODELING

Introduce this lesson to your class in one of these three ways:

1. Use the fishbowl method or demonstrate with one group.

2. Train students in small groups during guided reading.

3. Circulate to the groups and model for each. Guide students as they take turns and use the strategies. Prompt students to give better responses.

STUDENT PARTICIPATION

1. Each student takes a role card.

2. The discussion director calls on the predictor to begin by giving a prediction about the text.

3. Next, the discussion director selects the mode of reading for the page or designated portion of text from the following list:

   • Silent reading
   • Reading chorally
   • Reading aloud
   • Reading by paragraph or page
   • Reading with a partner

4. After reading, the discussion director calls on students or volunteers to take turns with the other roles—summarizer, questioner, and clarifier, in any order. Or, you may require students to take turns in a prescribed order.

5. After a set number of pages, the discussion director calls "pass," and the group members pass their role sheets to the right.

6. The process begins again.

- At the end of the lesson, ask teams to reflect on which strategy was the most helpful in this text and which was the most challenging to use.

- Observe as students work in their literature circles. How are they using each of the strategies? Are students giving substantial responses, or do you need to model and prompt them?

Rotating Roles

Intermediate　The fifth graders in Mrs. Preble's class sit cross-legged on the floor in circles of five students each with chapter books perched on their laps. The Chet Gecko mystery series by Bruce Hale is a class favorite, and each circle is reading a different title. In the center of each tight circle is a little container of marbles the groups have collected for their good comments and behavior. "I just gave this circle a marble, because when Paige predicted, two other group members commented on and extended her ideas. Good job!" Mrs. Preble praises them with this specific compliment and the group beams. In another circle, the discussion director, Roberto, tells the group to pass their cards to the right. As soon as the members hold their new cards, Roberto calls on the predictor to do his job. For Chapter 1 of *The Big Nap*, Justin predicts that the main character is bored and needs a mystery based on the chapter title, "Chairman of the Bored," and what he saw when he skimmed the chapter, including the terms *nothing, bored,* and *no mysteries there.* Juanita comments that she doesn't think the author is going to introduce the problem yet, because he never does in the first chapter in this series.

Roberto decides the mode of reading for the first two pages is reading aloud, and he volunteers to do it. When he is done, he calls on the questioner, Samantha, who asks, "How much is Chet getting paid to work on a mystery?" Justin answers, "I think 75 cents a day." The group quickly rereads and confirms his correct answer. Juanita takes her turn and selects a phrase to clarify and says she didn't get when it says "it is safer to...dance the hootchy-koo in front of a raging bull" (Hale, 2005, p. 1). Laura chimes in, "I know. It is safer to wiggle and dance in front of a bull than it is to go on the big kids' playground. Bulls might hurt you, and sixth graders, too!" Laura then summarizes for the group and starts with, "So far Chet has chatted with some sixth graders on their playground and has lunch with his friends while looking for a mystery."

Roberto asks the group to pass their cards to the right and the entire process begins again. By the end of the class period each student has taken on each role. (Figure 18 shows students in their literature circle group.)

**Figure 18
Students Rotating Roles in a Literature Circle**

Reciprocal Teaching at Work: Powerful Strategies and Lessons for Improving Reading Comprehension (second edition) by Lori D. Oczkus. © 2010. Newark, DE: International Reading Association. May be copied for classroom use.

Lesson 4: Using What I Know and What I Wonder Strips

BACKGROUND AND DESCRIPTION

In addition to predicting prior to reading, students also need opportunities in reciprocal teaching literature circles to activate their background knowledge and record what they want to know about a topic. This lesson connects reciprocal teaching literature circles with the additional strategies that good readers use before reading (Hoyt, 1999; Ogle, 1986).

Teachers at all grade levels can easily implement What I Know and What I Wonder strips with any nonfiction reading material, including articles, leveled books, and textbook chapters. For example, Mr. Herman's sixth-grade students worked independently at their desks prior to meeting with their literature circles to discuss a social studies chapter about ancient Greece. Each student wrote on two strips of paper. The first strip was for recording one fact that he or she knew about ancient Greece. After previewing the chapter's headings, illustrations, and maps, the students each wrote on the second strip something that they wondered about the topic. Later, during the literature circle session, the students shared their strips and posted them on a chart.

The What I Know and What I Wonder strips give you the opportunity to teach the whole class the additional background information and vocabulary necessary for understanding the reading material before a literature circle session. I use this lesson as a transitional, teacher-led step that prepares students for working with nonfiction materials in their reciprocal teaching literature circles. This lesson does the following:

- Requires the activation of students' prior knowledge about a topic
- Encourages students to wonder about what the text will contain prior to reading it

Tell your students how their prior knowledge helps them understand what they read. Then, introduce your students to the background knowledge necessary for understanding the chosen text's topic. Teach your students how to wonder about a topic prior to reading, and show them how wondering helps develop their reading comprehension.

- Two colored construction paper strips per student
- A piece of chart or construction paper for each literature circle
- A copy of the reading material for each student
- Tape or glue

1. Tell your students that good readers think about what they know before they read, and then model that strategy. Preview the text's cover and title (or the first page if you have chosen a chapter). On a What I Know strip, write one fact that you know about the text's topic.

2. Next, tell your students that good readers wonder about the topic of a text that they are going to read. Show your students how to preview the illustrations and other graphics in the text that you have chosen. As you view the various items, say aloud what you are wondering. Write a What I Wonder statement on the second paper strip, using the opening phrase "I wonder...."

1. Invite your students to work in cooperative table groups or pairs to come up with one What I Know strip and one What I Wonder strip about the chosen text. Have the groups share their strips and give a rationale for their statements.

2. Have your students individually preview the chapter or book again and come up with two more What I Know and What I Wonder strips with their names on them.

3. Have literature circles meet, and instruct their discussion directors to lead a sharing of the group members' What I Know and What I Wonder strips. Have each group tape or glue its strips onto the piece of chart or construction paper that you have provided (see Figure 19 for an example).

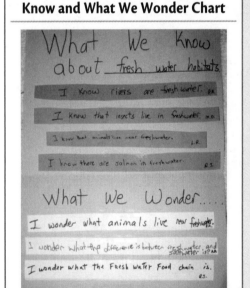

**Figure 19
A Student Sample of the What We Know and What We Wonder Chart**

Reciprocal Teaching at Work: Powerful Strategies and Lessons for Improving Reading Comprehension (second edition) by Lori D. Oczkus. © 2010. Newark, DE: International Reading Association. May be copied for classroom use.

- Have each literature circle discuss how thinking about prior knowledge and questions before reading helps them learn to understand what they read.

- Collect your students' What I Know and What I Wonder strips. Ask yourself, are my students activating appropriate background knowledge on the topic? Are they wondering about the text by using clues from the illustrations or the text prior to reading?

- Identify students who are having difficulty with the What I Know or What I Wonder strips. Some students may need background information for a particular topic or have difficulty studying illustrations and other text clues. Support these students in a small-group setting in which you model with both fiction and nonfiction texts how to wonder about a topic before reading.

Lesson 5: The Do All Four Challenge!

When Palincsar and Brown (1984) created reciprocal teaching, they intended for the teacher and students to take turns modeling all four strategies (thus the name "reciprocal" teaching). I like to reserve this way of carrying out lessons for small groups of three or four students or for partners, because being in charge of all four strategies, rather than just one at a time, is a challenge. However, when you assist and guide students in this exercise, their reading strategy use is strengthened dramatically. Using all four at the same time makes sense, because good readers employ all the strategies to some degree every time they read. I like to conduct a real-world think-aloud to show students how in a given reading situation a reader puts all the strategies to use almost simultaneously.

Reading maps and following recipes are fun, engaging, and concrete ways to demonstrate using all four strategies. For example, when reading a recipe, you predict by skimming over the recipe; clarify by rereading certain directions or vocabulary; ask questions and wonder how ingredients may mix together, how much time you need, or how this recipe fits into certain menus; and summarize each step throughout the preparation. You may even want to try passing out recipes for kid-friendly foods, such as pizza, pretzels, or sweets, and ask students to discuss their Fab Four use. Map reading is another one of my favorite examples that is great fun and fast for modeling all four strategies with students.

This lesson provides another way for you to vary your lesson delivery and differentiate instruction for all the learning styles in your room. In some classrooms, we simply pair cross-age tutors, younger and older students, for this variation (also see cross-age tutor suggestions in Appendix B). The Fab Four Bookmark provides a guide as students work their way through the strategies. You may also wish to use the Reciprocal Teaching Spinner (see page 230) or other visual to help prompt the students.

MATERIALS

- Fab Four Bookmark (see page 74)
- Reading material
- Optional: Reciprocal Teaching Spinner (see page 230)

TEACHER MODELING

1. Tell students that in their literature circles today they will take turns running through all four strategies, which is what good readers do as they read on their own.

2. Read aloud a portion of text. Pause and, for each of the four strategies, give your thoughts and a quick example from the text. For example, "When I read this sentence, I wondered and asked the question...." "This word made me stop and clarify." "I thought of a question on this part." "To summarize so far, this is about...."

3. Read another portion of text and pause to run through the four strategies again. Do so swiftly.

4. Ask students to discuss what you just did for each strategy. What are the steps to using each one?

STUDENT PARTICIPATION

1. Ask students to practice running through all four strategies with partners when it is their turn. Use the Fab Four Bookmark as a guide.

2. Encourage students who are listening to partners to use active listening. Then, encourage the other students to comment on the students' strategy use (e.g., compliments, questions).

3. Have students try the challenge of using all four strategies with fiction and then nonfiction. Discuss the differences.

4. Students may also work in teams of four and run through all four strategies when it is their turn.

ASSESSMENT TIPS

- Can your students quickly run through all four strategies? Which strategies are most challenging for your students?
- Continue modeling all four and providing time to practice in partners and groups.

Lesson 6: Practicing Reciprocal Teaching Strategies With the Reciprocal Teaching Spinner

BACKGROUND AND DESCRIPTION

The third graders in Mrs. Nichols's class huddled around their Reciprocal Teaching Spinners in their literature circles. When the spinner in one group landed on *Question*, Jason enthusiastically blurted out, "Yeah! I finally got a question!" His question, based on the text that the group had read, was, "How many insects does a bat eat in one night?" Then, the rest of the group members watched intently as Nora took her turn with the spinner. "I hope I get *Clarify*, because I have a great word to clarify this time," she explained. Nora landed on *Question*, too, and sighed, but she grinned as she asked, "What are some of the insects that bats eat?" The other students raised their hands to answer, and the spinning and discussing continued until all the group members had taken a turn.

The Reciprocal Teaching Spinner is a useful, game-like tool to use with your students during reciprocal teaching in literature circles. The spinner strengthens reading comprehension skills by giving students the opportunity to use each reciprocal teaching strategy on multiple levels. However, similar to most of the activities and lessons in this chapter, the activity's success relies heavily on your students' proficiency and experience with reciprocal teaching strategies, because they must be ready at any moment to model any of the four strategies.

You can make your own spinner and add other reading comprehension strategies, such as making connections, or include reaction prompts, such as "My favorite part is...," or "I like the way that the author...."

MATERIALS

- A Reciprocal Teaching Spinner (see page 230) made with tag board for each literature circle
- A spinner (for each literature circle) made from a pencil and paper clip in the following manner:

1. Unbend the outer loop of a paper clip until it is straight.

2. Place the paper clip on the Reciprocal Teaching Spinner with the paper clip's remaining curved end directly over the spinner's center.

3. Hold the paper clip in place by putting the point of a pencil into the clip's curved end.

4. Spin the paper clip by quickly pushing the straightened section of it clockwise or counterclockwise.

- A copy of the reading material for each student in each group
- Fab Four Bookmark (see page 74)

TEACHER MODELING

1. Ask your students to review all four reciprocal teaching strategies in table groups or in pairs. Using the Fab Four Bookmark, students take turns defining the strategies.

2. Read aloud a page of text to your students while they follow along. Then, spin the Reciprocal Teaching Spinner several times and model each reciprocal teaching strategy in regard to the text. When modeling predicting, demonstrate how to predict what may come next in the reading.

STUDENT PARTICIPATION

1. Select a group of students to model how to use the Reciprocal Teaching Spinner with a text that they have read. Discuss possible solutions when two students spin and land on the same strategy: Have the class members decide if that student should create a new prediction, question, clarification, or summary, or perhaps add to the one that the other student previously generated.

2. Ask the class to discuss the model group's Reciprocal Teaching Spinner discussion. Elicit their compliments and suggestions, and discuss how the students can create another response when someone already has landed on the same strategy. The following list offers some examples:

- *Predict*: Come up with another possible prediction or add a detail to the prediction that another student has made.

- *Question*: Ask another question using a different question word.

- *Clarify*: Choose another word or idea to clarify.

- *Summarize*: Repeat or improve the summary that another student has given.

- Ask your students to reflect on the reciprocal teaching strategy use in their literature circles. Which strategy did they hope they would land on with the spinner? Why? Observe the groups to see what students do when two of them in a row land on the same strategy. Does the second student copy the previous student's response or generate a new response?

- Teach the minilessons throughout this book to either the entire class or to small groups to reinforce the reciprocal teaching strategies. Evaluate your students' strategy use with the Rubric for the Reciprocal Teaching Strategies in Appendix A.

Reciprocal Teaching Spinner

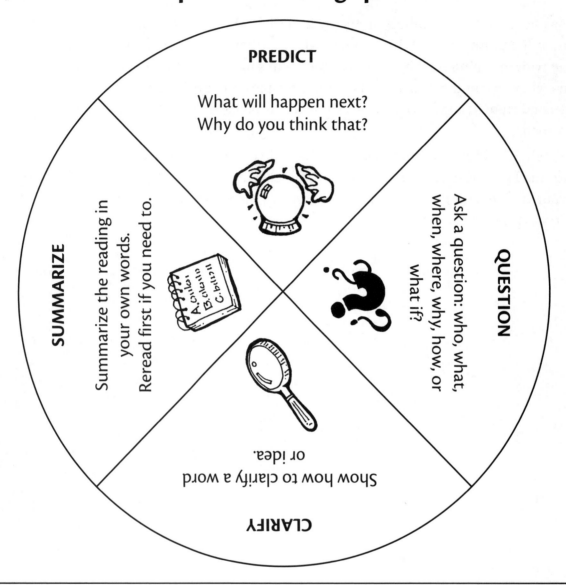

PREDICT

What will happen next?
Why do you think that?

QUESTION

Ask a question: who, what, when, where, why, how, or what if?

CLARIFY

Show how to clarify a word or idea.

SUMMARIZE

Summarize the reading in your own words. Reread first if you need to.

When you land on a strategy that someone else already landed on, you can...

PREDICT	**CLARIFY**
• Give a new prediction.	• Choose another word or idea to clarify.
• Or, add a detail to the last one.	• Or, give more ways to clarify the same word or idea.

QUESTION	**SUMMARIZE**
• Ask another question that begins with a different question word.	• Give a new summary.
	• Or, add to the previous summary.

Lesson 7: Fab Four Free-for-All!

Once you've thoroughly trained your students in the four strategies, taught the social skills, and practiced them many times, your students will be ready to try a free-for-all. You may want to run the training sessions during guided reading, so you can scaffold and support students as they learn to run this style of discussion.

Although the term *free-for-all* may suggest chaos, this lesson is far from unorganized. The students enjoy the free-for-all, because they use the Fab Four as a tool kit in a very independent and flexible way. The students simply have free reign over the strategies they now have in their toolbox and can call on any strategy that is needed for the task. In a Fab Four free-for-all, students read the text together, and when someone feels the need to use one of the strategies, he or she simply signals, and the discussion director calls on that person to begin a discussion point. Students will surprise you at their ease in moving from one of the strategies to the next and back again quite naturally. Following are some highlights of a free-for-all:

- The students freely discuss, politely taking turns and piggybacking on one another's comments.
- The discussion is metacognitive, because students are very aware of which strategy they are using at the moment. Students use hand signals to indicate which reading comprehension strategy they are using. If you teach at the high school level, you probably will not use the hand motions (except maybe with newcomers who do not speak as much English).
- The comprehension and content of the text are center stage.
- The students discuss the strategies in any order throughout the lesson.
- The students naturally include other strategies, like making connections and evaluating.

- Fab Four Bookmark (see page 74)
- Reading material
- Optional: Four Door Chart (see page 110)

TEACHER MODELING

1. Tell students that in their literature circles today, they will exercise the freedom that real readers do and use the strategies predict, question, clarify, and summarize in any order and only as the students feel the need for them. Have students turn to partners to review the strategies and use their Fab Four Bookmarks to do so.

2. Option: Allow students to use the hand motions (see page 52) for the strategies when they wish to speak or to indicate and label which strategy they wish to share. This is beneficial for ELLs, elementary students, and struggling readers.

3. Read a portion of text aloud. Pause and, for one of the strategies, give your thoughts and invite and encourage the students to piggyback on your comment. Say something like, "What would you like to say about my idea?"

STUDENT PARTICIPATION

1. The discussion director asks the class to do any of the following to begin the literature circle:

   • Discuss and summarize what they read yesterday.

   • After the discussion director summarizes he or she asks if students agree.

   • Lead a discussion on what may happen today by skimming the pages then making predictions.

   • Decide as a group how to read the selection (designated amount of pages)—alone, silently, paragraph by paragraph, page by page, or any other way they can come up with.

2. Students alternate reading the selection with pausing after every few pages to discuss the strategies in any order.

3. The discussion director ensures the following:

   • Every student in the group contributes freely, or the director calls on a student, "So, what do you think about...?"

   • Students do not talk over one another.

   • The conversation keeps going.

4. If there is a lull in the discussion, the director can ask the group to try one of the strategies, such as summarize, and encourage several students to verbalize their thoughts.

- Call on the discussion directors and ask them to report on their group's strategy use.

- Individual students may fill out a Four Door Chart after the lesson to demonstrate what they learned.

- Record your observations of each group of students as they discuss the strategies. Is there a strategy they are overrelying on or one they rarely call upon? Model and teach minilessons to help students with problem strategies.

- Continue modeling all four strategies and providing time to practice with partners and in groups.

Free Choice of Strategies

Intermediate   I popped in to visit the literature circles in Mrs. Buscheck's fourth- and fifth-grade combination classroom and witnessed a wonderful example of reciprocal teaching in action. (I even ran to my car to retrieve my video camera to tape the lively discussion!)

The fourth graders place their chairs in an oval shape to face one another and discuss *Hatchet* by Gary Paulsen. The choice I give the groups is to either take on roles for the Fab Four or work with a discussion director (or as we like to refer to it, the "DD") and then run a free-for-all. This group selects a free-for-all. The students open their books and skim over yesterday's chapter. Several students begin using the hand motions simultaneously to signal their strategy use. Clayton makes the crystal ball hand motion, Ben the signal for connections, and Rebecca and Yuri the pause motion. The DD, Yuri, begins to call on the students whose hands are motioning. Following is a transcript of a portion of that rich interaction:

Clayton:	[signaling a connection] So far this reminds me of the book, *Patty Reed's Doll,* because she is going places and finding water like Brian.
Yuri:	How could he make all that [pauses to label his thinking first]. This is a question. How could he make all that weaving? What did he make it out of?
Several students:	[in unison] Branches!
Clayton:	[signals prediction] I predict that since Brian realizes he has glass on the watch he can take some sticks, a rock, and some brush and when the sun is shining and try to make a fire.
Rebecca:	[signals for a clarification during Clayton's prediction; it doesn't distract from his discussion points, but rather signals how her thinking is connected to his ideas.] I don't get it. Is the rock in his hut he made?
Yuri:	I think it is in his hut. [signaling a connection] I am adding on to Clayton, this reminds me of the episode on *Survivor* last season when they use glass in the sun and waited and waited to start a fire with a spark.
Several students:	Oh yeah, I remember that.

Ben: [frantically makes the signal for connection until Yuri calls on him at last] This is like what Clayton and Yuri said. This part reminds me of another *Survivor* episode where they took apart a camera to use some of the glass to make a fire.

Several students: [heads nodding]

Yuri: Would anyone like to summarize this chapter?

Ben: He found the berries, and he ate a lot of them. He went and wove branches and made a door on a cave and, and… [hesitates]

Yuri: [prompting] He fought off the mosquitoes.

Ben: Yeah, he fought off the mosquitoes.

Elise: [trying her own version of the summary] He finds berries and eats a lot and gets swollen.

Clayton: [signals to clarify] What does *whine* mean in this sentence? It said that he heard the close vicious mosquitoes whine.

Several students: [making buzzing sound.]

Rebecca: You know how mosquitoes make that buzzing noise in the summer and when they bat against something? Yeah, that's it.

Clayton: I noticed a really big A-plus writing when the author described his face as cut and bleeding, swollen and lumpy, bloody and scabbed over. I can really picture that.

Several students: Ohh.

Minilesson: I Predict That I Will Learn....

Description and Comprehension Strategies

Prior to meeting with the literature circle, students will preview a nonfiction text, and, based on text and illustration clues, they will predict what they think they will learn from the reading. Comprehension strategies include using text clues to predict.

Materials

- One copy per student of a nonfiction book or article (each group may use a different text)
- Sticky notes
- Fab Four Chart (see page 160)

Teacher Modeling

1. Select a nonfiction book or article, and model how to preview the cover and illustrations to predict what you think you will learn from the reading. You may also model predicting using the table of contents and the starter "I think I will learn..., because...."

2. Write at least one sentence on a sticky note that starts with "I predict that I will learn..., because..." and model the clues that led you to believe that you would learn about your prediction.

Student Participation

1. Invite your students to work alone or in pairs before joining their literature circles to write at least one "I predict I will learn..., because..." statement. Ask some students to share their responses with the class. Assist students who are having trouble.

2. When the literature circles meet, have them share their ideas and post them on a group chart. Encourage your students to check their predictions after reading to see which ones were correct or which were changed during reading.

Assessment Tips

- Are your students using the text clues to form logical predictions about the reading?

Minilesson: Pick a Question

Description and Comprehension Strategies
Students select one of three kinds of questions about the text to ask group members.

Materials
- One copy per student of a fiction or nonfiction text that has a table of contents
- Three colors of index cards or sticky notes (one of each color per student)
- Can or paper bag

Teacher Modeling
1. Model and review how to ask three kinds of questions—wonders, quiz questions, and thinking questions—that start with "Why do you think…?" Choose a particular color of index card or sticky note for each type of question. Mix up cards or notes and put in a can or bag. Select and write a question on that card depending on the color.

2. Read aloud a portion of text, pause, and then ask one of the three types of questions. Read more text and ask another type of question. Continue until you've modeled all three types of questions.

Student Participation
1. There are a couple of variations on this lesson:
   - Pass out to each student three cards or sticky notes in different colors and have them write each type of question on a different color. Students ask their group members their questions and post on a chart or file folder. Or, they can put their questions in a bag for others to take turns drawing and answering.
   - Put blank cards or sticky notes in three different colors in a bag for each student to pick one and then pass the bag around the circle, so each student can take a turn selecting a card or sticky note. Students write a question depending on the color they drew and then pose it to the group to discuss.

2. Have your students discuss the questions: Which were some of their favorites? Why?

Assessment Tips
- Can your students ask all three types of questions? Ask the literature circle members to reflect on questioning. If any students are having difficulty, organize a small group of them to meet with and model this questioning lesson using material that they have already read.

Minilesson: Clarify It: Picture It!

Description and Comprehension Strategies

Students work independently to find a passage to read aloud to the group. While the reader shares the passage, the other students in the group sketch what the reader is reading aloud.

Materials

- One copy of the text
- Paper divided into four to six squares to draw on or a slate
- Pencils, markers, or instruments for drawing and sketching

Teacher Modeling

1. Tell students that one way good readers clarify is by visualizing, or making pictures in their heads. If a reader is not making pictures, he or she is losing meaning and needs to reread until a picture forms.
2. Read aloud a passage from the text and then sketch what you visualized.
3. Invite students to sketch along with you.

Student Participation

1. Students select a descriptive passage and take turns reading aloud to team members. Students discuss what they are visualizing from the reading.
2. You also can have students fold their papers into boxes. Each time a team member reads aloud a description, the other students sketch a drawing. Students can also include page numbers from the readings on their drawings.
3. Groups can vote on the most powerful descriptions and discuss.

Assessment Tips

- Ask your students to reflect on the clarifying and visualizing strategies in their literature circles. How does visualizing help them read?

Minilesson: Limited-Word Summary Challenge!

Description and Comprehension Strategies

After reading, students summarize in teams and do so with a limited number of words as designated by the teacher. For example, a team may be required to write a 32-word summary or a 10-word summary. Have groups write summaries and illustrate them to display in the classroom.

Materials

- One copy of the text for each student
- One overhead transparency per literature circle, transparency pens, and overhead projector; or paper, pens, and document camera; or large poster paper or construction paper and markers

Teacher Modeling

1. Choose a text that is familiar to the class. Model writing a summary using a designated number of words on the overhead projector or document camera and decorate it with a few illustrations. Tell students, "Today we are writing a summary using only _____ words." (You determine how many words each lesson or let students suggest a limit.)

2. Ask the class to name the steps involved in writing a clear, concise summary. Model how to select just the main ideas and key vocabulary.

Student Participation

1. Have your students work in literature circles to create limited-word summaries of the text that they have read. Students may write summaries on large poster paper or construction paper, sign their names, and decorate the summary with illustrations. Or, students can use an overhead projector and transparency. Make sure that they include the text's title and author on the transparency.

2. Ask the literature circles to share their summaries with the entire class.

3. Ask students to reflect on what makes a good summary for fiction and nonfiction. How are they similar and different?

Assessment Tips

- Can students work in a group to write an effective summary that includes important events in order?
- Ask students to reflect on how summarizing helps them comprehend what they read. Provide extra support for students who are struggling by working with a small group to create a clear summary.

CHAPTER SUMMARY

- The cooperative nature of reciprocal teaching, along with the built-in scaffolded support, makes it a natural match for student-led literature circles.

- Reciprocal teaching literature circles and other literature circle models can be used in the same classroom. For example, some teachers use the reciprocal teaching model for nonfiction texts and another model (e.g., Daniels, 1994) for fiction texts.

- Students must be trained in three main areas before they embark on reciprocal teaching literature circles: the four strategies, small-group social skills, and literature circle procedures.

- Training for reciprocal teaching literature circles may involve working with reciprocal teaching strategies and role sheets during teacher-led guided reading groups or whole-class lessons with teacher direction.

- Modeling reciprocal teaching literature circles with a peer group or fishbowl (Kagan, 1989) in front of the class is a helpful technique for training students.

- Selecting a "social skill of the day" and a "focus strategy of the day" affords the teacher opportunities and a routine for reinforcing essential social skills and modeling the reciprocal teaching strategies.

- Other important comprehension strategies that are not included in the four reciprocal teaching strategies can be incorporated into literature circles by designating a discussion director.

- Assessment routines for literature circles include teacher observations, modeling with groups, peer evaluation, filling in forms for individual accountability, and student self-evaluations.

CONCLUSION

After I completed a series of demonstration lessons in one inner-city school, a fifth-grade teacher commented, "Reciprocal teaching is one of the very most important and valuable strategies I've learned to teach reading. I am going to use it every day now!" When teachers tell me that their main concern is that their students are not thinking about or understanding what they read, I know I have a proven, research-based set of lessons that I can share with them. One third-grade teacher told me that she feels that "reciprocal teaching takes the mystery out of teaching reading." In my opinion, her words are accurate, because I believe that reciprocal teaching makes reading comprehension strategies more tangible for teachers and students. The reciprocal teaching strategies of predicting, questioning, clarifying, and summarizing have become the essential tools that I use to teach children to read. Of course, we need to add graphic organizers and the other important good reader strategies (McLaughlin & Allen, 2002) for a truly comprehensive reading comprehension program, but the Fab Four reciprocal teaching strategies continue to make an enormous difference in comprehension instruction.

There are so many convincing reciprocal teaching success stories. For instance, consider the struggling fourth graders in Berkeley, California, whose reading levels jumped from a second-grade to a fourth-grade level in the first three months of using reciprocal teaching in an intervention group. Or, consider Ebony, a fifth-grade struggling reader who, in addition to participating in reciprocal teaching in her classroom, also used the strategies to work with her cross-age buddy, a first grader. Ebony's achievement accelerated one grade level, and a year later she had maintained the growth. We celebrate the reading growth of the first graders who read nonfiction several times per week and employed the Fab Four as part of their guided reading lessons. Then, there are the struggling fourth graders who participated in small-group guided reading sessions for three months and successfully introduced reciprocal teaching strategies to their entire class in literature circles.

After just a few weeks of reciprocal teaching instruction, you will begin to notice subtle differences in your students' behaviors, achievements, and attitudes. Struggling readers raise their hands more often to contribute to discussions and appear more confident when reading. Proficient readers engage even more efficiently with grade-level and more challenging texts. As you use reciprocal teaching with your students, you surely will experience your own set of success stories.

Common Questions About Reciprocal Teaching

This section contains a series of questions and answers whose purpose is to review the content of the book and to provide information that you may need as you teach your students reciprocal teaching strategies.

1. What are the four reciprocal teaching strategies? Where did they originate?

The four strategies—predict, question, clarify, and summarize—were originally studied by Palincsar and Brown (1984, 1986) in the early 1980s. The researchers first used the strategies in a paragraph-by-paragraph scaffolded approach with struggling middle school students. Palincsar and Brown and others expanded the research into and use of the strategies and discovered that reciprocal teaching strategies were beneficial to students in a variety of grade levels and settings, including peer groups and interventions (Carter, 1997; Palincsar et al., 1989; Palincsar & Klenk, 1991, 1992). Other researchers and curriculum developers (Cooper et al., 1999; Lubliner, 2001) have created lessons for reciprocal teaching, but they have carefully maintained the integrity and intent of its original design.

2. What results might I expect if I use reciprocal teaching consistently with my students?

I am always amazed at how quickly I begin to see results with reciprocal teaching. The research verifies that reciprocal teaching can yield results in a relatively short amount of time: Palincsar and Brown (1984) found that students who scored around 30% on a comprehension assessment scored 70–80% after just 15–20 days of instruction using reciprocal teaching. After one year, the students maintained the growth (Palincsar & Klenk, 1991). In the schools where I work, which are diverse ethnically and geographically, the students' reading levels rise one half to one full grade level in just 18–20 reciprocal teaching sessions (usually two to three per week).

Even though positive growth may be measured in such a short period of time, I recommend continuing the reciprocal teaching instruction for approximately 76 lessons, or most of the school year, because researchers report even more dramatic results or measurable gains in reading level after an average of this many lessons (Cooper et al., 2000). In one of the inner-city schools where I work, struggling readers experienced rapid growth of one to two years in reading level after just three months. By the end of the school year, three months later, more students reached the target level, and some students advanced an additional grade level in reading ability as measured by the district's assessment measures and the Developmental Reading Assessment (2001).

3. Should I use reciprocal teaching with my struggling readers?

Absolutely. I began by using reciprocal teaching with struggling readers, and it is the number one intervention strategy that I recommend for grades 3–12. Cooper and his teacher-researcher colleagues (2000) decided that they wanted to develop an intervention for struggling readers, and they incorporated reciprocal teaching with some other proven components, such as rereading, graphic organizers, and written responses to literature, to create a research-based intervention plan. Their research findings were positive enough to convince me to try reciprocal teaching as an intervention. Every time I consistently use their plan (Cooper et al., 1999), the students experience one half to one full year's growth after three months of lessons given at least twice a week and anywhere from one to two year's growth after six months. I especially love to witness the improved confidence that these readers almost immediately experience with reciprocal teaching. See Chapter 1 for information on using reciprocal teaching as an RTI strategy.

4. What about the rest of my students? Do they really need reciprocal teaching?

All students can benefit from reciprocal teaching, because it is a useful comprehension strategy that students can use throughout their school careers, including into college. Reciprocal teaching is a reliable and proven guided reading lesson plan for all reading levels. When students read using reciprocal teaching, they not only improve in their reading levels but also in their ability to recall the content (Reutzel et al., 2005).

5. Don't I use these four strategies already? How is reciprocal teaching different from what I am already doing with these strategies?

Most likely, you already teach your students to predict, question, clarify, and summarize. Reading programs and school-district objectives often include these strategies. However, the difference with reciprocal teaching is that the strategies are delivered as a multiple-strategy package used in concert with one another rather than as separate strategies to master one at a time. The aim of reciprocal teaching is for good readers to cycle through the four strategies—not necessarily in order—to make sense of a text. Research (NICHD, 2000) suggests using cooperative learning with multiple strategies, and reciprocal teaching is highly recommended as an effective teaching practice that improves reading comprehension.

6. I am so busy that I can barely teach what I have on my agenda now. How can I fit reciprocal teaching strategies into what I am doing already?

You do not have to overhaul your curriculum to fit reciprocal teaching strategies into your schedule. After introducing the four strategies to your students, you can incorporate the strategies easily into lessons using the district-adopted texts for reading, social studies, and science. Some teachers even ask students to use predicting, questioning, clarifying, and summarizing during math lessons. Reciprocal teaching can be incorporated easily into your school day.

7. How can I fit reciprocal teaching into my district's core reading program?

Reciprocal teaching is a flexible tool that you can use to strengthen and differentiate the comprehension instruction in any core reading program or curriculum model. Whether your district uses a commercial program or you are working from a mix of trade and leveled texts, reciprocal teaching is a research-based technique that can complement and enhance any reading instruction. To yield results, however, you will need to deliver reciprocal teaching lessons at least twice a week. There isn't one "right" way to incorporate the Fab Four. Decide what is best for your grade level and students. Table 17 provides some easy suggestions to help guide you.

Table 17
Suggestions for Incorporating Reciprocal Teaching Into Your Core Reading Program

Core Reading Program	Suggestions for Incorporating Reciprocal Teaching
Basal Reading Program (anthologies)	• Teach the basal stories in whole class and cooperative group lessons using reciprocal teaching. Incorporate the Four Door Chart (see page 110), Fast Fab Four lessons (see page 174), and guided practice at table groups. • Teach the basal comprehension lessons to cover single-focus, in-depth lessons on predicting, questioning, clarifying, and summarizing as well as the other important strategies, including connecting, synthesizing, and inferring. • Or, reserve reciprocal teaching for small-group guided reading, read-alouds, or literature circles. Partners may work during independent work time to discuss the text using the Fab Four. • Use reciprocal teaching with content area reading and your science and social studies materials.
Balanced Literacy Model • Read-aloud • Shared reading • Guided reading • Independent reading	• Incorporate a variety of lessons from this book and guide students in reciprocal teaching lessons during any of the balanced literacy components, including during read-alouds, shared reading, guided reading, and independent reading. • Or, select a consistent time such as during guided reading for delivering reciprocal teaching lessons. • Use reciprocal teaching with content area reading and your science and social studies materials.
Readers' Workshop Model • Minilesson/teacher modeling • Active engagement/partnerships • Small groups, individual coaching • Wrap-up	• Teach reciprocal teaching strategies during minilessons. • Compare and contrast the use of strategies in different genres. • During active engagement and partnerships, encourage students to run through the Fab Four. • When reading independently, students mark their strategy use with sticky notes to discuss later with peers. • Conference with students during independent reading time and ask students to share their strategy use. Coach students and be sure to model one on one some of the strategies. • During lesson wrap-ups, discuss how the Fab Four will help students comprehend the genre they are reading now.

8. What is your best advice for using reciprocal teaching?

Be consistent. If you really want results with struggling readers, use the strategies at least twice a week in an intervention group, and with the rest of the class, use reciprocal teaching two to three times per week in either whole-class, guided reading, or literature circle settings. Using the strategies once a week or just a few times per month may help students somewhat, but students need consistent exposure to the strategies to benefit greatly from them.

9. What foundations must be in place to achieve the maximum results with reciprocal teaching?

Whether using reciprocal teaching in whole-class sessions, guided reading groups, or literature circles, there are some foundations that make the instruction more effective. These essentials are scaffolding, thinking aloud, using cooperative learning, and facilitating metacognition. Scaffolding is the umbrella for the other three foundations, and it simply means good teaching through teacher modeling that usually consists of a think-aloud and student participation with feedback from the teacher or peers. A scaffolded lesson also allows time for metacognition or reflection on the use of the strategies and how their use helped the reader understand the text. When these components are in place, reciprocal teaching lessons may yield better results than if the foundations are not addressed.

10. If reciprocal teaching is so effective, why can't I just teach reading with the four strategies—predict, question, clarify, and summarize?

Reciprocal teaching strategies do work, but they do not stand alone. Throughout this book, I have emphasized the need for a more complete set of reading strategies to teach comprehension effectively. The expanded list of key research-based comprehension strategies comprises previewing, activating prior knowledge, predicting, self-questioning, making connections, visualizing, knowing how words work, monitoring, summarizing, and evaluating (McLaughlin & Allen, 2002; Oczkus, 2004).

11. What is the best way to get started with reciprocal teaching?

No one best way to begin using reciprocal teaching in your classroom exists. The key is to regularly model and practice the strategies with your students. You might begin with whole-class or guided reading lessons depending on your grade level and needs. Upper grades may expand into literature circles with roles for the strategies. See Chapter 2 for lessons to use as you introduce reciprocal teaching to your students.

- Whole Class—Literature Circles—Whole Class

  - You may wish to train your entire class using cooperative pairs or tables before moving into literature circles.

  - It is helpful when introducing your class to the Fab Four to continue modeling reciprocal teaching strategies, using below-grade-level materials at first and eventually progressing to grade-level reading materials.

  - After the class is comfortable with the strategies, introduce them to literature circles by modeling literature circle procedures in front of the class with a group.

  - Finally, return to a whole-class setting and take time to reflect on the strategies in a discussion or to teach a minilesson on social skills or one of the strategies.

- Intervention Group—Whole Class—Literature Circles

  - This plan is the most innovative teaching model that I have used so far.

  - In some classrooms, the classroom teacher and I spend several months working with the struggling students in an intervention group. During those months, we tell the struggling students that they will need to become experts in the four reciprocal teaching strategies, so they can introduce them to the rest of the class.

  - After about three months, the intervention students assist their classroom teacher in modeling the four strategies for the class. The intervention group serves as the fishbowl group. (See the Fishbowl: It's Your Role! lesson, page 206)

  - Then, the class is divided into literature circles, and the reciprocal teaching experts from the intervention group are dispersed among the groups to lead them. I have witnessed struggling readers beam as they teach their class reciprocal teaching strategies.

  - Even after this stage, however, the intervention group continues to meet to ensure the struggling students' progress.

- Guided Reading Groups—Whole Class—Guided Reading Groups
    - I have used this model in grades 1–3 when students may need more time and a small-group format to catch on to reciprocal teaching strategies.
    - Meet with the students in their guided reading groups to model and teach guided reading lessons using reciprocal teaching strategies.
    - After several months, use the strategies in a whole-class setting with shared reading materials, such as Big Books and the district-adopted reading anthology.
    - Use the Fab Four Bookmark (see page 74) for each student to consult throughout the day as you weave the four strategies into your lessons.
    - Continue to meet with guided reading groups and employ reciprocal teaching strategies.

12. How can I use reciprocal teaching with literature circles?

Literature circles are natural places to use reciprocal teaching, because the four strategies can become the roles of predictor, questioner, clarifier, and summarizer. I have found that including the fifth role of discussion director is helpful for discussing other reading comprehension strategies, such as making connections, activating prior knowledge, and inferring. There are many effective ways to incorporate reciprocal teaching strategies into literature circles at every grade level and with any kind of text.

13. What if I already have in place procedures and roles for literature circles that differ from reciprocal teaching?

If you already have literature circles in place, your students have been trained in the basic social skills of group work. Now, all you need to do is decide how to model for them the process of using the four strategies as roles (see Chapter 5, especially Lessons 1 and 2, pages 206 and 217).

Some intermediate teachers who already have in place literature circles using other models (for example, see Daniels, 1994) may opt to designate nonfiction texts and textbooks for use with reciprocal teaching strategies and roles while maintaining another model for fiction texts. Another suggestion is to use reciprocal teaching with the reading anthology and use other literature circle models with novels or core literature. Keep in mind that reciprocal teaching works well with fiction or nonfiction texts.

14. How can I use reciprocal teaching in primary grades?

Primary-grade teachers often prefer the simplicity of using just four roles with reciprocal teaching, and they often use reciprocal teaching during read-aloud lessons or shared reading with Big Books. Using props for each strategy, or even characters or puppets, are extremely effective ways to reach young students using the reciprocal teaching strategies (see www.primaryconcepts.com/rdgcomp/Comprehension-Puppets.asp, for my reading comprehension puppets kit). When I incorporate props into my lessons, I use a crystal ball and pretend I am a fortuneteller when we make predictions. During questioning, young children especially love the use of a microphone. When we clarify words and difficult concepts in the text, we use a pair of oversized glasses. Summarizing is more fun when we pretend to be cowboys and cowgirls and "rope" the main ideas using yarn. Guided reading lessons are especially effective with reciprocal teaching and young children. The built-in format of predict, clarify, question, and summarize is what we do naturally as we process our way through a text. Try making a Fab Four Dial (see page 177) to use during your lessons so students will know which strategy you are working on throughout the lesson.

15. How can I use reciprocal teaching with my guided reading groups?

Guided reading is a great setting for using reciprocal teaching strategies with your students. The small-group atmosphere encourages participation from all students and allows you to assess their progress easily. You can use any reading materials that you already have to conduct reciprocal teaching lessons with guided reading groups. Organize groups flexibly—that is, change them depending on the needs or interests of the students.

Lead a guided reading group through reciprocal teaching strategies by taking turns with the students as they work their way through the strategies and the reading. First, discuss illustrations and headings, and take turns making predictions. Then, instruct your students to read silently or with partners while you quietly coach individual students. After reading, take turns again, asking questions about the text, summarizing, and discussing points or words that your students need to clarify. Throughout the lesson, you may opt to fill in a guided reading chart that fits the text and lesson (see Chapter 4).

I have found that the guided reading setting offers an effective training ground for literature circles. After all the groups have worked with me to learn the four strategies and group procedures, I begin to introduce them to reciprocal teaching literature circles. After I start working with the students in literature circles, I do not discontinue the guided reading groups. I meet with the groups for reciprocal teaching lessons, because students continue to benefit from the small-group format.

16. Are there any common problems that students experience with reciprocal teaching?

Some students may experience difficulty when first learning reciprocal teaching strategies. Their problems may include the following:

- *Predicting*—Students may not make logical predictions based on clues from the text or their experiences.

- *Questioning*—Students may generate only literal questions and may need more modeling in or guidance toward asking inferential or main idea questions.

- *Clarifying*—Students may initially clarify only difficult, new, or confusing words, because students rarely recognize that they are having trouble with an idea in the text.

- *Summarizing*—Students may miss the main points of a given selection, or they may supply a summary that is too long, too short, or a word-by-word rendition from the text.

To avoid these common problems, I recommend teaching the minilessons at the end of each chapter that focus on a particular strategy that is causing your students difficulty. Also, daily teacher modeling and peer practice help students catch on to the strategies.

17. With reciprocal teaching, how can I foster higher order reading skills such as making inferences and evaluating?

Inferring and other higher order reading skills are already embedded in the reciprocal teaching strategies. For example, when students predict, they engage in making a type of inference. Inferring involves drawing a conclusion by gathering clues or evidence from the text and one's own background knowledge. During questioning, encourage your students to ask inferential and evaluative questions. As your students summarize, ask them to think about the selection's theme or the author's message. When they clarify ideas in a text, your students may link points of confusion in the text with higher order questions that they have about the text's content, metaphors and other literary devices, or the author's intent. As you can see, there are many opportunities to include higher order reading skills during reciprocal teaching lessons.

18. How do I help my students become more independent, so they will use the strategies on their own as they read?

Because reciprocal teaching is an interactive exchange and dialogue, your students will naturally begin to use the strategies in their own reading. I like to also use the bookmark, posters, props, and other visual tools to help students internalize the strategies. This method also has built-in supports, such as constant teacher modeling and practice with peers, that offer you many opportunities to let students grow to independence. The release of responsibility is gradual, but we also pull students back to model for them frequently.

Reciprocal teaching is set up to promote independence in students, because it has metacognition and cooperative learning built in, so students practice and rehearse the steps to effective strategy use every time we teach. Table 18 provides some suggestions to help you promote student independence as you use reciprocal teaching in a variety of settings.

Improve Your Students' Reading Comprehension With Reciprocal Teaching

I hope you are enjoying this second edition on reciprocal teaching. My goal is for this book to serve as a handy desktop reference that you will return to time and time again as you implement reciprocal teaching in your own classroom. Whether you read this book from cover to cover or simply skip around and try various lessons, I hope you are motivated to continue using the Fab Four with your students. If you are new to reciprocal teaching, this book contains a wealth of resources to get you started and keep you going. If you already teach with the Fab Four reciprocal teaching strategies, this book offers many effective and innovative ways to enhance your use of reciprocal teaching. It is my goal that you will try reciprocal teaching strategies with your students and witness for yourself the difference this proven set of reading strategies can make in the reading comprehension skills of all students.

Table 18
Suggestions for Promoting Student Independence With Reciprocal Teaching

Setting for Reciprocal Teaching	✓ Ways to Promote Student Independence in Strategy Use

Whole-class lessons	• Alternate between teacher modeling and asking students to try each strategy with partners. Do so often throughout the lesson.
	• Teach the Which One Do We Need? Name That Strategy! lesson often, so students can learn when and how to apply strategies on their own (see page 113).
	• As students work in teams and at tables, gradually decrease modeling in front of the group and allow time for cooperative practice. Circulate to assist students.
	• Also encourage students to demonstrate their strategy use by
	  • Using hand motions for each strategy (see page 54)
	  • Using class reference tools/strategy posters (see Appendix E)
	  • Using independent reference tools such as the Fab Four Bookmark (see page 74)

Guided reading small-group lessons	• Model the strategies one at a time for students. Alternate modeling with partner practice throughout the lesson. • Allow for silent reading and encourage strategy use during that time. Coach individuals (see Table 11, pages 142–143, for coaching suggestions). • Use the Reciprocal Teaching Spinner (see page 230) to promote use of the strategies in any order. • Have students show which strategy is needed during reading by using hand motions or by marking their texts with sticky notes. • Teach the Watch Your Qs and Cs During Reading! lesson often (see page 169). • Assign roles to students during teacher led guided reading groups (see pages 211–216).
Literature circle lessons	• Guide students first using any of the lessons in Chapter 5 (see pages 203–238). • Use fishbowl observations often to model behaviors (see Chapter 5). • Circulate to groups to help scaffold. • Display posters and use bookmarks to guide strategy use. • Videotape groups and show to the class. Discuss points of good strategy use and independence.
Independent Reading (Sustained Silent Reading, Readers' Workshop, etc.)	• Have students place a sticky note next to a portion of text where they used one of the strategies. • Provide students with the Fab Four Bookmark during independent reading. • Ask students to share how they used strategies during independent reading.

Informal
ASSESSMENTS

Rubric for the Reciprocal Teaching Strategies

Strategy	Exemplary (4)	Proficient (3)	Developing (2)	Beginning (1)
Predict	• Uses text features and clues to make logical predictions. • Uses background knowledge to make predictions. • Consistently uses the language of predicting. • Gives solid reasons for predictions. • Discusses predictions with detail after reading to change or confirm.	• Provides predictions that make sense. • Makes predictions based on text clues, background information. • Confirms and changes predictions throughout reading, usually gives reasons for predictions. • Checks predictions after reading. • Uses the language of predicting most of the time.	• Makes some simple, sensible predictions. • Sometimes uses text clues and background to make predictions. • Makes some predictions that are not sensible. • Sometimes gives reasons for predictions. • Begins to use the language of predicting such as, "I think...will happen, because...."	• Predictions don't always make sense. • Does not use text clues such as illustrations, headings, to make logical predictions. • Predictions are wild and not text based. • Experiences difficulty even when prompted in giving reasons for predictions.
Question	• Consistently asks a mix of well-crafted questions including recall questions that go with the events and ideas of the text; inferential questions; and critical thinking questions that take the discussion beyond the text such as "Why [How] do you think...?" or "How does...compare to...?" • Asks questions about the theme and deeper meanings of the text.	• Asks several levels of questions including a mix of literal recall questions about the main ideas of the text, literal recall about important details of the text, and inferential questions. • Wonders about the text and beyond. • Sometimes asks questions of the author. • Asks critical thinking questions, such as "Why do you think...?"	• Asks simple recall questions that go with the text and begin with *who, what, when, where, why, how,* and *what if.* • Asks simple "I wonder..." questions that relate to the text. • Sometimes asks inferential questions. • Sometimes asks main idea questions.	• Experiences difficulty formulating even simple literal recall questions that begin with question words. • Asks questions about details in the text rather than important ideas. • Asks questions that do not correspond with the text.
Clarify	• Identifies words and ideas that are unclear. • Consistently identifies and uses a rich variety of strategies for figuring out difficult words and ideas and portions of text (e.g, reread, read on, sound out). • Identifies and clarifies high-level ideas such as idioms, metaphors, and symbolism.	• Identifies words to clarify. • Sometimes identifies ideas and portions of text to clarify. • Consistently uses more than one strategy for clarifying words and ideas (e.g., reread, read on, sound out).	• Identifies words to clarify. • Identifies ideas and portions of text to clarify when prompted. • Uses the same one or two strategies to figure out words and ideas. • Sometimes does not realize that meaning has been lost. • Begins to use language of clarifying such as "I didn't get..., so I...."	• Does not stop to try to figure out words. • Identifies words to clarify when prompted. • Identifies ideas to clarify when prompted. • Uses only one strategy to figure out words or ideas and needs to be reminded of others. • Does not realize when he or she is stuck.
Summarize	• Retells in own words using some of the new vocabulary. • Gives only most important events, points, and key details. • Summarizes, giving points in order. • Uses text structure to organize summary. • Uses rereading and text supports such as illustrations and headings to summarize.	• Leaves out unimportant details. • Usually retells in own words using a vocabulary word or two from the text. • Gives most of the points in correct order. • Usually draws from text structure to summarize. • Rereads and uses clues from the text.	• Finds it difficult to separate main ideas from unimportant details. • Includes some of the events in order but may give some out of order. • Leaves out some of the important events and ideas. • Needs prompting to reread or use text clues.	• Does not remember much of the reading. • Recalls random ideas or events from the text. • Includes unimportant details. • Needs heavy prompting to respond. • Does not reread or use text clues as tools for summarizing.

Reciprocal Teaching at Work: Powerful Strategies and Lessons for Improving Reading Comprehension (second edition) by Lori D. Oczkus. © 2010. Newark, DE: International Reading Association. May be copied for classroom use.

Predicting

When predicting with fiction, students

• Preview the front and back covers, illustrations, and headings before reading
• Predict what is likely to happen next based on clues from the text or illustrations
• Use what they know (from text and prior knowledge)
• Stop to predict during reading
• Continue to make logical predictions based on clues from the text

When predicting with nonfiction, students

• Preview the front and back covers, illustrations, and headings before reading
• Predict what is likely to be learned based on clues from the text or illustrations
• Apply what they already know to help make a prediction
• Stop to predict during reading
• Continue to make logical predictions based on clues from the text

When using metacognition with either fiction or nonfiction, students tell how predicting helps them understand the text.

The language of prediction that students use[a] may include the following phrases:

• I think…because….
• I'll bet…because….
• I wonder if…because….
• I imagine…because….
• I suppose…because….
• I predict….because….

Questioning

When questioning with fiction, students

• Ask questions based on the text (that is, the answers are in the text)
• Ask questions that are based on the main idea or question of the story
• Ask some detail-oriented questions
• Ask some inferential questions

When questioning with nonfiction, students

• Ask questions based on the text (that is, the answers are in the text)
• Ask questions that are based on the main idea of the reading
• Ask some detail-oriented questions
• Ask questions based on nonfiction text features, such as maps, captions, and diagrams
• Ask some inferential questions

When using metacognition for either fiction or nonfiction, students can tell how asking questions helps them to understand the text.

The language of questioning that students use may include the following words:

• Who
• What
• When
• Where
• Why
• How
• What if

Clarifying

When clarifying with fiction, students
• Express confusion with specific portions of text, such as ideas or events, that are difficult to understand
• Identify words that are difficult to pronounce or understand

When clarifying with nonfiction, students
• Point out confusing ideas related to the content of the reading
• Point out confusing portions of text, such as sentences, paragraphs, and pages
• Identify words that are difficult to pronounce or understand

When using metacognition for either fiction or nonfiction, students
• Give strategies for clarifying words
• Tell strategies for clarifying ideas
• Tell how clarifying helps them understand text

The language of clarifying that students use may include the following phrases:
• I didn't understand the part about…, so I [see list below]
• This doesn't make sense, so I [see list below]
• I can't figure out…, so I [see list below]

So I…
• Reread
• Read on for clues
• Reread the sentence to see if it made sense

• Checked the parts of the word I knew
• Blended the sounds of the word
• Tried another word

Summarizing

When summarizing fiction, students
• Retell the story in their own words and include the setting, characters, problem, key events, and resolution

Or, they
• Give only key points in a short one- or two-sentence summary
• Summarize in a logical order
• Reread to remember main ideas
• Refer to illustrations to retell or summarize the text

When summarizing nonfiction, students
• Retell the key points or ideas
• Leave out unnecessary details
• Summarize in a logical order
• Reread to remember main ideas
• Refer to illustrations, headings, and other text features to retell or summarize the text

When using metacognition for either fiction or nonfiction, students tell how summarizing helps them understand the text.

The language of summarizing that students use may include the following words or phrases:
• First,….
• Next,….
• Then,….
• Finally,….

• The most important ideas in this text are….
• The story takes place….
• The main characters are….
• A problem occurs when….

• A key event is when….
• This part is about….
• This book is about….

Using the Reciprocal Teaching Team When I Read

(Please check off your answers.)

How am I predicting?

Before reading

____ I preview the front and back cover.

____ I study the illustrations and headings.

____ I make predictions using clues from the text.

During reading

____ I stop and use clues from the reading to make more predictions or to change my predictions.

After reading

____ I check my predictions to see if they came about in the text.

Predicting helps me read, because _____

_____

_____

_____

_____

How am I questioning?

Before reading

____ After previewing the cover, illustrations, and headings, I ask questions about the reading. What do I wonder or want to know?

During reading

____ I watch for answers to my questions.

____ I watch for places where a teacher could ask a question.

After reading

____ I check to see if I answered my questions.

____ I have questions that start with *who, when, where, what, why, how,* or *what if.*

Questioning helps me read because _____

_____

_____

_____

_____

How am I clarifying?

Before reading

____ I can tell what might look confusing about the reading.

____ I see some words when I am previewing the text that might be difficult or confusing.

During reading

____ I stop and think about words that are difficult.

____ I try chunking, sounding out, and rereading words.

____ I stop to clarify confusing ideas by rereading, reading on, or asking a friend.

After reading

____ I think about confusing or difficult words and ideas. I go back and figure them out by rereading or talking with a friend.

Clarifying helps me read, because _____

_____

_____

How am I summarizing?

Before reading

____ I think about how the text is organized.

During reading

____ I stop to think about what has happened so far in the reading.

After reading

____ I reread and review the illustrations to keep the reading fresh in my mind.

____ I choose only the main ideas to summarize.

____ I tell the main events in order.

Summarizing helps me read, because _____

_____

_____

_____

_____

_____

_____

Strengthening

COMPREHENSION WITH CROSS-AGE TUTORS

and the Fab Four

Background and Description

Mr. Metzer's fifth graders and Miss Clark's first graders met in cross-age pairs to focus on summarizing, and all the pairs had copies of *Ira Sleeps Over* by Bernard Waber. Mr. Metzer wanted his fifth graders to feel very confident in their summaries, so the class has practiced summarizing prior to the lesson with their little buddies. The little buddies also have been practicing how to summarize with their grade-level anthology and are ready to share brief summaries of the most recently read selection with their big buddies.

The little buddies streamed into the fifth-grade classroom and awaited the usual cross-age buddy read-aloud. This time, each big buddy asked the little buddy if he or she knew how to summarize. The little buddies eagerly shared the summaries that they created for the selection from the anthology. Then, the big buddies began reading *Ira Sleeps Over*, and after they read a page, the cross-age pairs stopped to take turns summarizing what had happened on the page. After reading the whole book, the cross-age pairs constructed brief, written summaries of it and created drawings to accompany their summaries.

Next, each cross-age pair joined with another pair in a cross-age literature circle. The pairs took turns in the circles to share their summaries and drawings for *Ira Sleeps Over*. Then, they took turns asking questions and clarifying words and confusing parts of the book. When both buddy classes are engaged in instruction with reciprocal teaching strategies, the cross-age buddy sessions become a perfect opportunity to reinforce the strategies.

Similar to the above example, this lesson has suggestions for strengthening your students' use of reciprocal teaching strategies during cross-age buddy sessions.

This lesson requires detailed descriptions of the steps for using each strategy. Also, continue discussing read-aloud techniques for big buddies. Explain that to keep the little buddies' attention, big buddies may wish to try engaging in a picture preview before reading, predicting periodically while reading, and allowing the buddies to ask questions during and after reading.

Materials

- Fab Four Bookmark (see page 74) for each student
- Focused Strategy Lessons to Use With Your Little Buddy (see page 264)
- Copies of texts with which to model reciprocal teaching strategies (one per cross-age pair)
- Copies of texts for your students to read to and with their buddies (one per cross-age pair)

Teacher Modeling

1. Before meeting as cross-age buddies, the students from both grade levels should work on reciprocal teaching strategies in their own classes with grade-appropriate lessons. Both teachers will want to familiarize their classes with the Fab Four Bookmark (see page 74).

2. The big buddies' teacher should ask his or her students how their little buddies are doing with reciprocal teaching strategies and discuss the little buddies' progress. Identify which strategies the little buddies need to practice.

3. Ask the big buddies class to vote on a focus strategy for the day that is based on what they think their little buddies need to practice. Remind the big buddies that they will ask their little buddies to try all four reciprocal teaching strategies, but that they will spend more time modeling the focus strategy for their little buddies.

    As an option, choose a piece of literature to have the entire class of big buddies read as practice for the cross-age buddy session. If you do not have multiple copies of picture books available, then you might borrow the little buddies' reading series anthology for the big buddies to read aloud. Or, have the big buddies work with the focus strategy in any book that they select.

4. Invite a student volunteer from the class of big buddies to role-play as a little buddy. Using a picture book, demonstrate how to model a prediction, question, point or word to clarify, or summary for the little buddy. Then, invite a big buddy to do the same for each strategy. Model how to compliment the efforts of and support a struggling little buddy.

5. Model the focus strategy of the day. Show the big buddies how they can focus on the strategy of the day by having their little buddies stop to either draw or write about that strategy.

Student Participation

1. After observing the model lesson that uses the focus strategy, the big buddies should list the steps of that strategy on a class chart on chart paper or a whiteboard to help their little buddies.

2. Instruct the big buddies to try the focus strategy first with a peer partner. They should elicit a written response or drawing from their partner to save for the class debriefing.

3. Have the big buddies try the focus strategy lesson with their little buddies, and ask them to bring the little buddies' written responses or drawings back to your classroom for the debriefing.

4. Instruct each cross-age pair to join another cross-age pair to form a literature circle, so they can share responses to the focus strategy of the day and take turns with other reciprocal teaching strategies.

5. Ask the big buddies to report to their class on their little buddies' progress with the focus strategy. Encourage the big buddies to give specific examples of how their little buddies used the focus strategy and share the written responses and drawings. Plan a follow-up lesson together for the next cross-age buddy session.

6. Ask the big buddies to be prepared to give examples of how they used the focus strategy in their own reading. They may want to share their reflections with their peers and their little buddies in the next cross-age buddy session.

Assessment Tips

This lesson requires the big buddies to assess how their little buddies are doing with the four reciprocal teaching strategies. The goal is for the big buddies to become even more reflective in their own strategy use.

- Observe the big and little buddies during a minilesson as they work with their peers. Collect their writings and drawings and evaluate them to see who needs help.

- Observe all the students during cross-age buddy interactions. Watch for good examples to point out in debriefings and for students who are having trouble modeling or coaching the focus strategy.

- Encourage the big buddies to use the Assessment Tool to Assess How Your Little Buddy Is Doing (see page 263). Once the big buddy has determined which reciprocal teaching strategy needs reinforcement, he or she can choose a lesson from Focused Strategy Lessons to Use With Your Little Buddy (see page 264).

- Have the big buddies share the writings and drawings from their cross-age buddy sessions. Ask them to plan another lesson that will help correct any problems that their little buddies are having with their reciprocal teaching focus strategy use.

Assessment Tool to Assess
How Your Little Buddy Is Doing

Predicting

The buddy can predict well if he or she

- Looks at the cover and illustrations for clues to make predictions and
- Gives predictions that make sense

The buddy is having trouble predicting if he or she

- Does not look at the cover or illustrations for clues to make predictions or
- Makes predictions that do not make sense

Questioning

The buddy can ask questions well if he or she

- Can ask a question
- Knows what a question is
- Asks questions that make sense and have answers in the text

The buddy is having trouble questioning if he or she

- Cannot make up a question
- Does not know what a question is and gives a statement instead
- Makes up questions that do not have answers in the text

Clarifying

The buddy can clarify well if he or she

- Knows more than one way to figure out a word, including looking for parts that he or she knows, blending sounds together, rereading, and reading on for clues
- Knows how to figure out a difficult idea or part
- Rereads

The buddy is having trouble clarifying if he or she

- Cannot use strategies to figure out words
- Does not know when he or she is stuck
- Does not reread

Summarizing

The buddy can summarize well if he or she

- Can retell the reading in his or her own words
- Leaves out details that do not matter
- Tells only the most important ideas

The buddy is having trouble summarizing if he or she

- Cannot remember the reading
- Tells details that do not matter
- Gets mixed up and summarizes out of order
- Leaves out important parts

Focused Strategy Lessons
to Use With Your Little Buddy

When your buddy needs extra work on predicting

- Show your buddy how to look at the cover and make predictions based on visual clues. Say, "I predict..., because...," and then let your buddy try doing the same.
- Model how to look at the illustrations and tell what the book will be about.
- While reading, stop and show your buddy how to use clues from the words and pictures to predict what will happen next. Say, "I see... in the book, so I think... will happen next, because...." Let your buddy try to do the same.
- Draw or write your predictions with your buddy.

When your buddy needs extra work on questioning

- Choose a page from the book and read it for your buddy. Demonstrate how to make up a question and answer based on what you just read. Show your buddy how to create questions that start with *who, what, when, where, why, how,* and *what if.*
- Ask your buddy to try making up a question about a part of the book.
- Draw or write about your questions with your buddy.

When your buddy needs extra work on clarifying

- Choose a long or difficult word from the reading and show your buddy how to figure it out. Give at least two ways to figure out the word (use the Clarifying Words Bookmark).
- Try looking for word parts and chunks that you know, sounding out the word, and rereading or reading on to see if it makes sense.
- Let your buddy try to clarify with another word.
- Choose a confusing idea or part from the reading and demonstrate how you figured it out. Choose from
    - Rereading,
    - Reading on for clues,
    - Using what you know,
    - Letting your buddy try with another part
    - Drawing or writing about clarifying either a word or confusing part of the reading.

When your buddy needs extra work on summarizing

- Choose one page from the reading and reread it aloud. Tell the buddy that you are going to summarize and tell only the important points. Summarize the page, then let your buddy try to summarize the next page.

- Next, show your buddy how to summarize an entire book. For fiction, say
    - "This story takes place...."
    - "The main characters are...."
    - "A problem is...."
    - "A key event is...."
    - "Finally, the problem is solved when...."
  For nonfiction, say
    - "This book is about...."
    - "The most important points are...."

- Let your buddy try summarizing a book.

- Draw or write a summary with your buddy.

LESSON PLANNING

With the Fab Four Menu

The Fab Four Lesson Plan Menu arms you with a list of the minilessons from this book along with additional ideas noted throughout the book that you can use to create new ways to engage students in the four strategies. I enjoy designing lessons by choosing (or allowing students to choose) one menu item from each of the strategies that will help my students better understand the text we are reading.

Keep in mind the following important points when using the Fab Four Lesson Plan Menu:

- *Don't turn the Fab Four into assignments; allow for student choice.* After the students are familiar with some of the menu items, you can promote independence and metacognition by allowing students to select items off the menu. For example, if a student is in charge of summarizing, he or she can decide whether the group will put together a limited-word summary or participate in a drawing or drama activity.

- *Limit writing.* You do not have to incorporate writing, because it will slow down the lesson. The discussions with peers and the teacher are central to the lessons and to improvements in comprehension. When a menu item includes making a written record of some sort, it is usually done quickly and on the spot on a sticky note, with the purpose of enhancing the discussions.

- *Keep up the foundations of an effective lesson.* It is also important to continue incorporating teacher think-alouds, cooperative learning opportunities, scaffolding supports, and ways for students to express their knowledge of the strategies, or metacognition. (See Chapter 1 for a review of the essential lesson foundations.)

The key is to keep students engaged and to fit in all four of the strategies in one sitting or lesson. The Fab Four Lesson Plan Menu makes a handy desk reference as you plan your lessons.

Fab Four Lesson Plan Menu

Directions: Select one menu item from each box (or allow students to choose) for students to complete as they work in pairs or groups to discuss a portion of text. Although students participate in all Fab Four strategies, select at least one of the strategies to model in a teacher think-aloud.

Predict

- **Hand signal for predict** (see page 55)
- **Strategy starters for predict** (see page 268)
- **Roll Your Prediction!** (see page 84)
  Students roll dice and use prediction starters.
- **Prediction Stroll Line** (see page 124)
  Students line up in two lines to share predictions.
- **Word Pop Prediction** (see page 178)
  Students skim the text for important vocabulary prior to reading.
- **I Predict That I Will Learn...** (see page 235)
  Students practice making sensible predictions using nonfiction text

Question

- **Hand signal for question** (Chapter 2, page 55)
- **Strategy starters for question** (Chapter 1, page 268)
- **Pop the Questions** (see page 85)
  Students use a microphone to ask one another questions about the text.
- **Post Your Question** (see page 125)
  Students select or draw a question starter from a bag or envelope and make up a question about the text.
- **Question Starters** (see page 180)
  The teacher provides a prompt or two-to three-word question starter such as, "How many...?" or "Why did...?"
- **Pick a Question** (see page 236)
  Students select one of three kinds of questions about the text to ask group members.

Clarify

- **Hand signal for clarify** (see page 55)
- **Strategy starters for clarify** (see page 268)
- **Pause and Clarify It!** (see page 87)
  Students pause to clarify a word, sentence, part, etc.
- **Clarify and Underline a Word or Idea** (see page 126)
  Students share examples of words and entire sentences to clarify by pointing to them or underlining on a copy of the text.
- **Clarify Bookmark** (see page 181)
  Students identify words and ideas to clarify using the bookmarks.
- **Clarify It: Picture It!** (see page 237)
  Students find descriptive passages to read aloud to the group, with an option for group sketches.

Summarize

- **Hand signal for summarize** (see page 55)
- **Strategy starters for summarize** (see page 268)
- **A "Clear" Summary** (see page 89)
  Students cooperatively sketch/write brief summaries to share on the overhead or document camera.
- **Cooperative Group Summaries** (see page 128)
  Students each take a portion of the text and organize by beginning, middle, end.
- **Draw or Dramatize Summaries** (see page 184)
  Students choose something from the text to quickly draw/dramatize; group guesses at what it is.
- **Limited-Word Summary Challenge!** (see page 238)
  Using a limited number of words students construct brief summaries.

Fab Four Strategy Starters

Suggestions for use:

• Keep next to your desk to use during lessons.

• Cut apart for students to use in discussions.

Predict

I think...

I'll bet...

I wonder if...

I imagine...

I suppose...

I predict...

I think I will learn...because....

I think...will happen because....

Question

I wonder....

Who...?

What...?

When...?

Where...?

Why...?

How...?

What if...?

Why do you think...?

How do you think...?

Clarify

I didn't get the [word, idea, part] so I [reread, read on, sounded it out, etc.].

I didn't understand the part where....

This doesn't make sense.

This is a tricky word because....

I can [reread, read on, think of another word, talk to a friend].

I look for word parts that I know.

I sound out and blend the sounds together.

Summarize

The most important ideas are....

This part was mostly about....

This book was about....

[First, next, then, finally], ...

The story takes place....

The main characters are....

A problem occurs when....

In the [beginning, middle, end], ...

Using
RECIPROCAL
TEACHING
With the Internet

In these fast-paced days of technology, many of our students are more comfortable interacting with technology than we are. They live on the Internet for school projects and entertainment, on their phones for texting, and on social networking sites. Unfortunately, school is typically the only place they encounter "book" print. The good news is that we can find new ways to capitalize on students' love of technology to help us teach literacy. Reciprocal teaching is a perfect strategy to use when teaching students to navigate their way around the Internet. I have found the work of Leu (n.d.) to be especially helpful. He has wonderful insights on using reciprocal teaching with technology or, as he refers to it, Internet reciprocal teaching (IRT). The IRT model includes three phases to help scaffold instruction for students: (1) direct instruction of Internet usage, (2) guided practice of Internet strategy usage in whole class or small groups, and (3) independent inquiry using the Internet strategies. You might model the Fab Four on an interactive whiteboard or on a computer in a small guided group. Students work in small groups using a computer and taking turns, as the leader first initiates each strategy and then invites each group member to contribute. Students might discuss on a class blog their responses to the reading and their ideas for using the Fab Four. In what follows, you will find some suggestions for using the Fab Four with the Internet.

Suggestions for Using the Fab Four With the Internet

Remind students that the Fab Four are helpful in all reading contexts including reading online.

- *Predict*—Teach students to avoid blindly choosing the first reference they find on a search engine. Instead, model for students how to skim and predict which site will be most helpful. Then have them select the site and begin skimming again to critically evaluate the material and predict if it will be useful and keep reading, or to move on. Select a particular site and also model how to predict how it is organized by previewing the illustrations, icons, and links, and skimming the text.

- *Clarify*—Point out words, images, audio clips, illustrations, and such that are confusing. Model for students how to clarify by rereading, reading on, thinking about the context of the material, and using fix-up strategies such as sounding out words.

- *Question*—Have students write wonders before reading the online material. During their reading, ask them to brainstorm more wonders as well as questions to help them recall the material. Have students share thinking or discussion questions.

- *Summarize*—Have students use illustrations and headings to summarize what they learned. Also, have students evaluate and summarize for others their thoughts about the usefulness of the website.

Ask students to reflect on the four strategies and how they helped during the lesson.

Reciprocal Teaching and Social Bookmarking Networks

Adolescent students love conversing with one another on social networking websites or through text messages. Sixth-grade teacher William Ferriter (2010) says he thinks social bookmarking is changing the way students approach the entire reading experience and suggests that teachers in grades 6–12 consider using a social bookmarking application such as the free Diigo (www.diigo.com) where students read text online and highlight or mark comments that are able to be read by others in the class. The teacher creates a secure account seen only by those in the classroom. Students may mark the text with their reciprocal teaching strategies as they read and converse online with one another. The teacher provides frequent models and teaches proper social skills. Ferriter suggests teaching the difference between online communications and face-to-face communication. The site includes training pieces, so you can provide demonstrations for your class.

Icon and Strategy
POSTERS

Predict

Question

Clarify

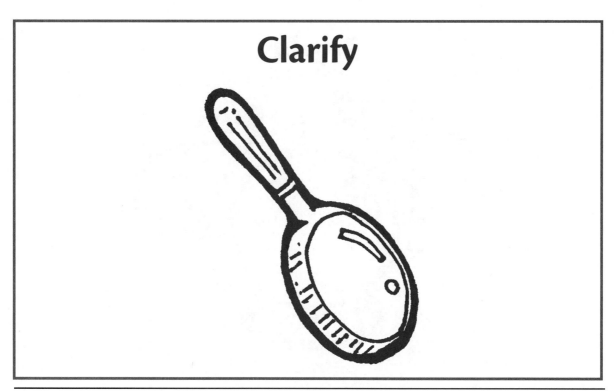

Summarize

Predict

I think....

I'll bet....

I wonder if....

I imagine....

I suppose....

I predict....

I think I will learn...because....

I think...will happen because....

Question

I wonder…?

Who…?

What…?

When…?

Where…?

Why…?

How…?

What if…?

Why do you think…?

How do you think…?

Clarify

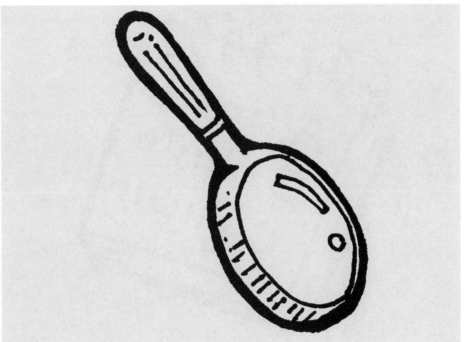

I didn't get the [word, idea, part] so I [reread, read on, sounded it out, etc.].

I didn't understand the part where....

This doesn't make sense.

This is a tricky word because....

To clarify, I can
- **Reread**
- **Read on**
- **Sound out**
- **Look for parts I know**
- **Blend the sounds together**
- **Think of another word**
- **Make a picture in my head**
- **Talk to a friend**

Summarize

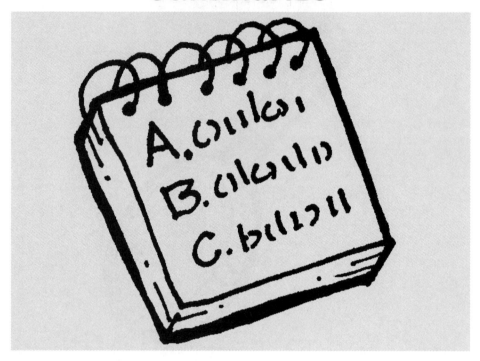

The most important ideas are....

This part was mostly about....

This [book, chapter, part, article] was about....

[First, Next, Then, Finally], ...

The story takes place....

The main characters are....

A problem occurs when....

In the [beginning, middle, end], ...

REFERENCES

Allington, R.L. (2001). *What really matters for struggling readers: Designing research-based programs*. Columbus, OH: Allyn & Bacon.

Allington, R.L. (2009). *What really matters in Response to Intervention: Research-based designs*. Columbus, OH: Allyn & Bacon.

Armbruster, B.B., Lehr, F., & Osborn, J. (2001). *Put reading first: The research building blocks for teaching children to read, kindergarten through grade 3*. Washington, DC: Partnership for Reading.

Aronson, E., Blaney, N., Stephin, C., Sikes, J., & Snapp, M. (1978). *The jigsaw classroom*. Beverly Hills, CA: Sage.

Bender, W.N., & Shores, C. (2007). *Response to intervention: A practical guide for every teacher*. Arlington, VA: Council for Exceptional Children; Thousand Oaks, CA: Corwin.

Bennett, B., & Rolheiser, C. (2001). *Beyond Monet: The artful science of instructional integration*. Toronto, ON: Barrie Bennett.

Block, C.C., Parris, S.R., & Whiteley, C.S. (2008). CPMs: A kinesthetic comprehension strategy. *The Reading Teacher, 61*(6), 460–470. doi:10.1598/RT.61.6.3

Boushey, G., & Moser, J. (2006). *The daily 5: Fostering literacy independence in the elementary grades*. Portland, ME: Stenhouse.

Carter, C.J. (1997). Why reciprocal teaching? *Educational Leadership, 54*(6), 64–68.

Cassidy, J., & Cassidy, D. (2010). What's hot for 2010. *Reading Today, 27*(3), 8–9. Newark, DE: International Reading Association.

Clay, M.M. (1985). *The early detection of reading difficulties* (3rd ed.). Portsmouth, NH: Heinemann.

Clay, M.M. (1993). *Reading Recovery: A guidebook for teachers in training*. Portsmouth, NH: Heinemann.

Coley, J.D., DePinto, T., Craig, S., & Gardner, R. (1993). From college to classroom: Three teachers' accounts of their adaptations of reciprocal teaching. *The Elementary School Journal, 94*(2), 255–266. doi:10.1086/461765

Cooper, J.D. (1993). *Literacy: Helping children construct meaning* (2nd ed.). Boston: Houghton Mifflin.

Cooper, J.D., Boschken, I., McWilliams, J., & Pistochini, L. (2000). A study of the effectiveness of an intervention program designed to accelerate reading for struggling readers in the upper grades. In T. Shanahan & F.V. Rodriguez-Brown (Eds.), *49th yearbook of the National Reading Conference* (pp. 477–486). Chicago: National Reading Conference.

Cooper, J.D., Boschken, I., McWilliams, J., & Pistochini, L. (2001). *Soar to Success: The intermediate intervention program*. Boston: Houghton Mifflin.

Cooper, J.D., Kiger, N.D., & Robinson, M.D. (2011). *Success with RTI: Research-based strategies for managing RTI and core instruction in your classroom*. New York: Scholastic.

Cunningham, P.M., & Cunningham, J.W. (1992). Making words: Enhancing the invented spelling–decoding connection. *The Reading Teacher, 46*(2), 106–115.

Daniels, H. (1994). *Literature circles: Voice and choice in the student-centered classroom*. York, ME: Stenhouse.

Daniels, H. (2002). *Literature circles: Voice and choice in book clubs and reading groups*. Portland, ME: Stenhouse.

Diller, D. (2005). *Practice with purpose: Literacy work stations for grades 3–6*. Portland, ME: Stenhouse.

Duke, N.K., & Pearson, P.D. (2002). Effective practices for developing reading comprehension. In A.E. Farstrup & S.J. Samuels (Eds.), *What research has to say about reading instruction* (3rd ed., pp. 205–242). Newark, DE: International Reading Association.

Eggleton, J. (2007). *Connectors: Teachers' resource book*. Huntington Beach, CA: Pacific Learning.

Ferriter, W.M. (2010). Can't get kids to read? Make it social. *Educational Leadership*, *67*(6), 87–88.

Fielding, L.G., Anderson, R.C., & Pearson, P.D. (1990). *How discussion questions influence children's story understanding* (Tech. Rep. No. 490). Urbana: Center for the Study of Reading, University of Illinois.

Fountas, I.C., & Pinnell, G.S. (1996). *Guided reading: Good first teaching for all children*. Portsmouth, NH: Heinemann.

Fountas, I.C., & Pinnell, G.S. (2007a). *Benchmark Assessment System 1: Grades K–2, Levels A–N*. Portsmouth, NH: Heinemann.

Fountas, I.C., & Pinnell, G.S. (2007b). *Benchmark Assessment System 2: Grades 3–8, Levels L–Z*. Portsmouth, NH: Heinemann.

Fuchs, D., Fuchs, L.S., & Vaughn S. (Eds.). (2008). *Response to Intervention: A framework for reading educators*. Newark, DE: International Reading Association.

Gallagher, K. (2004). *Deeper reading: Comprehending challenging texts, 4–12*. Portland, ME: Stenhouse.

Hacker, D.J., & Tenent, A. (2002). Implementing reciprocal teaching in the classroom: Overcoming obstacles and making modifications. *Journal of Educational Psychology*, *94*(4), 699–718. doi:10.1037/0022-0663.94.4.699

Hansen, J. (1981). The effects of inference training and practice on young children's reading comprehension. *Reading Research Quarterly*, *16*(3), 391–417. doi:10.2307/747409

Harvey, S., & Goudvis, A. (2007). *Strategies that work: Teaching comprehension for understanding and engagement* (2nd ed.). Portland, ME: Stenhouse.

Hiebert, E.H., & Taylor, B.M. (Eds.). (1994). *Getting reading right from the start: Effective early literacy interventions*. Boston: Allyn & Bacon.

Hill, B.C., Johnson, N.J., & Noe, K.L.S. (1995). *Literature circles and response*. Norwood, MA: Christopher-Gordon.

Howard, M. (2009). *RTI from all sides: What every teacher needs to know*. Portsmouth, NH: Heinemann.

Hoyt, L. (1999). *Revisit, reflect, retell: Strategies for improving reading comprehension*. Portsmouth, NH: Heinemann.

Kagan, S. (1989). *Cooperative learning resources for teachers*. San Juan Capistrano, CA: Resources for Teachers.

Keene, E.O., & Zimmermann, S. (1997). *Mosaic of thought: Teaching comprehension in a reader's workshop* (2nd ed.). Portsmouth, NH: Heinemann.

Keene, E.O., & Zimmermann, S. (2007). *Mosaic of thought: The power of comprehension strategy instruction*. Portsmouth, NH: Heinemann.

Kelly, M., Moore, D.W., & Tuck, B.F. (1994). Reciprocal teaching in a regular primary classroom. *The Journal of Educational Research, 88*(1), 53–61.

Kincade, K.M, & Beach, S.A. (1996). Improving reading comprehension through strategy instruction. *Reading Psychology, 17*(3), 273–281. doi:10.1080/0270271960170304

Kohn, A. (1996). *Beyond discipline: From compliance to community.* Alexandria, VA: Association for Supervision and Curriculum Development.

Leu, D.J. (n.d.). *Teaching online reading comprehension.* New York: Prentice Hall. Retrieved November 15, 2009, from www.PHLitOnline.com

Lipson, M.W. (1996). *Developing skills and strategies in an integrated literature-based reading program.* Boston: Houghton Mifflin.

Lubliner, S. (2001). *A practical guide to reciprocal teaching.* Bothell, WA: Wright Group.

McLaughlin, M., & Allen, M.B. (2002). *Guided comprehension: A teaching model for grades 3–8.* Newark, DE: International Reading Association.

Mowery, S. (1995). *Reading and writing comprehension strategies.* Harrisburg, PA: Instructional Support Teams.

Myers, P.A. (2005). The princess storyteller, Clara clarifier, Quincy questioner, and the wizard: Reciprocal teaching adapted for kindergarten students. *The Reading Teacher, 59*(4), 314–324. doi:10.1598/RT.59.4.2

National Center for Education Statistics. (2006). *Section I: Participation in education. The condition of education 2006* (NCES No. 2006-071). Washington, DC: National Center for Education Statistics, Institute of Education Sciences, U.S. Department of Education. Retrieved May 9, 2008, from nces.ed.gov/pubsearch/pubsinfo. asp?pubid=2006071

National Center for Education Statistics. (2009). *The nation's report card: Reading 2009* (NCES 2010-458). Washington, DC: Institute of Education Sciences, U.S. Department of Education.

National Institute of Child Health and Human Development. (2000). *Report of the National Reading Panel. Teaching children to read: An evidence-based assessment of the scientific research literature on reading and its implications for reading instruction* (NIH Publication No. 00–4769). Washington, DC: U.S. Government Printing Office.

Oczkus, L.D. (2003). *Reciprocal teaching at work: Strategies for improving reading comprehension.* Newark, DE: International Reading Association.

Oczkus, L.D. (2004). *Super six comprehension strategies: 35 lessons and more for reading success.* Norwood, MA: Christopher Gordon.

Oczkus, L.D. (2006). *Reciprocal teaching strategies at work: Improving reading comprehension, grades 2–6: Video viewing guide and lesson materials.* Newark, DE: International Reading Association.

Oczkus, L.D. (2008). *The fabulous four: Reading comprehension puppets.* Berkeley, CA: Primary Concepts.

Oczkus, L.D. (2009). *Interactive think-aloud lessons: 25 surefire ways to engage students and improve comprehension.* New York: Scholastic; Newark, DE: International Reading Association.

Ogle, D.M. (1986). K-W-L: A teaching model that develops active reading of expository text. *The Reading Teacher, 39*(6), 564–570. doi:10.1598/RT.39.6.11

Opitz, M.F., & Rasinski, T.V. (1998). *Good-bye round robin: 25 effective oral reading strategies.* Portsmouth, NH: Heinemann.

Palincsar, A.S., & Brown, A.L. (1984). Reciprocal teaching of comprehension-fostering and comprehension-monitoring activities. *Cognition and Instruction, 1*(2), 117–175.

Palincsar, A.S., & Brown, A.L. (1986). Interactive teaching to promote independent learning from text. *The Reading Teacher, 39*(8), 771–777.

Palincsar, A.S., Brown, A.L., & Campione, J. (1989, March). *Structured dialogues among communities of first-grade learners.* Paper presented at the annual meeting of the American Educational Research Association, San Francisco, California.

Palincsar, A.S., Brown, A.L., & Martin, S.M. (1987). Peer interaction in reading comprehension instruction. *Educational Psychologist, 22*(3/4), 231–253. doi:10.1207/s15326985ep2203&4_3

Palincsar, A.S., & Klenk, L.J. (1991). *Learning dialogues to promote text comprehension* (PHS Grant 059). Washington, DC: U.S. Department of Education; Bethesda, MD: National Institute of Child Health and Human Development.

Palincsar, A.S., & Klenk, L. (1992). Fostering literacy learning in supportive contexts. *Journal of Learning Disabilities, 25*(4), 211–225. doi:10.1177/002221949202500402

Paris, S.G., Wasik, B.A., & Turner, J.C. (1991). The development of strategic readers. In R. Barr, M.L. Kamil, P. Mosenthal, & P.D. Pearson (Eds.), *Handbook of reading research* (Vol. 2, pp. 609–640). White Plains, NY: Longman.

Pearson, P.D., & Duke, N.K. (2002). Comprehension instruction in the primary grades. In C.C. Block & M. Pressley (Eds.), *Comprehension instruction: Research-based best practices* (pp. 247–258). New York: Guilford.

Pearson, P.D., & Fielding, L. (1991). Comprehension instruction. In R. Barr, M.L. Kamil, P. Mosenthal, & P.D. Pearson (Eds.), *Handbook of reading research* (Vol. 2, pp. 815–860). White Plains, NY: Erlbaum.

Pearson, P.D., & Gallagher, M.C. (1983). The instruction of reading comprehension. *Contemporary Educational Psychology, 8*(3), 317–344. doi:10.1016/0361-476X(83)90019-X

Pearson, P.D., Roehler, L.R., Dole, J.A., & Duffy, G.G. (1992). Developing expertise in reading comprehension. In S.J. Samuels & A.E. Farstrup (Eds.), *What research has to say about reading instruction* (2nd ed., pp. 145–199). Newark, DE: International Reading Association.

Peterson, B. (1991). Selecting books for beginning readers. In D.E. DeFord, C.A. Lyons, & G.S. Pinnell (Eds.), *Bridges to literacy: Learning from Reading Recovery* (pp. 119–147). Portsmouth, NH: Heinemann.

Pikulski, J.J. (1994). Preventing reading failure: A review of five effective programs. *The Reading Teacher, 48*(1), 30–39.

Plummer, S. (2009, September 21). Kinetic English. *Tulsa World,* pp. A1, A4.

Pressley, M. (2002). Comprehension strategies instruction: A turn-of-the-century status report. In C.C. Block & M. Pressley (Eds.), *Comprehension instruction: Research-based best practices* (pp. 11–27). New York: Guilford.

Pressley, M. (2006). *Reading instruction that works: The case for balanced teaching* (3rd ed.). New York: Guilford.

Reutzel, D.R., Smith, J.A., & Fawson, P.C. (2005). An evaluation of two approaches for teaching reading comprehension strategies in the primary years using science information texts. *Early Childhood Research Quarterly, 20*(3), 276–305. doi:10.1016/j.ecresq.2005.07.002

Rinehart, S.D., Stahl, S.A., & Erickson, L.G. (1986). Some effects of summarization training on reading and studying. *Reading Research Quarterly, 21*(4), 422–438. doi:10.2307/747614

Rosenblatt, L.C. (1978). *The reader, the text, the poem: The transactional theory of the literary work*. Carbondale: Southern Illinois University Press.

Rosenshine, B., & Meister, C. (1994). Reciprocal teaching: A review of the research. *Review of Educational Research, 64*(4), 479–530.

Routman, R. (1999). *Conversations: Strategies for teaching, learning, and evaluating*. Portsmouth, NH: Heinemann.

Routman, R. (2003). *Reading essentials: The specifics you need to teach reading well*. Portsmouth, NH: Heinemann.

Samuels, S.J. (1979). The method of repeated readings. *The Reading Teacher, 32*(4), 403–408.

Samway, K.D., & Whang, G. (1995). *Literature study circles in a multicultural classroom*. York, ME: Stenhouse.

Schulman, M.B., & Payne, C.D. (2000). *Guided reading: Making it work*. New York: Scholastic.

Slavin, R.E. (1987). Ability grouping and student achievement in elementary schools: A best-evidence synthesis. *Review of Educational Research, 57*(3), 293–336.

Sweet, A.P. (1993). *State of the art: Transforming ideas for teaching and learning to read*. Washington, DC: Office of Educational Research and Improvement, U.S. Department of Education.

Taylor, B.M. (1982). Text structure and children's comprehension and memory for expository material. *Journal of Educational Psychology, 74*(3), 323–340. doi:10.1037/0022-0663.74.3.323

Taylor, B. (2008). Tier 1: Effective classroom reading instruction in the elementary grades. In D. Fuchs, L.S. Fuchs, & S. Vaughn (Eds.), *Response to Intervention: A framework for reading educators* (pp. 5–25). Newark, DE: International Reading Association.

Vygotsky, L.S. (1978). *Mind in society: The development of higher psychological processes* (M. Cole, V. John-Steiner, S. Scribner, & E. Souberman, Eds. & Trans.). Cambridge, MA: Harvard University Press. (Original work published 1934)

Wormeli, R. (2009). *Metaphors and analogies: Power tools for teaching any subject*. Portland, ME: Stenhouse.

LITERATURE CITED

Clark, C. (2008, November 3). From stray dog to movie star. *People, 70*(18), 76. Retrieved May 18, 2010, from www.people.com/people/archive/article/0,,20238231,00.html

Ford, J. (2009). *Hotel on the corner of Bitter and Sweet*. New York: Ballantine.

Hale, B. (2001). *The big nap*. Orlando, FL: Harcourt.

Marriott, J., & Keylock, A. (2008). *Fly facts*. Huntington Beach, CA: Pacific Learning.

Scott, J., & Scott, A. (2005). *Antarctica: Land of the penguins*. Glasgow, Scotland: Collins Educational.

INDEX

NOTE: Page numbers followed by *f* and *t* indicate figures or tables, respectively.

A

Abercrombie, Barbara, 52*t,* 109
Adamson, S.C., 197
Allen, M.B., 2, 4, 17, 70, 81, 196, 240, 245
Allington, R.L., 41, 93, 131, 147
Anderson, R.C., 19
Animals Nobody Loves (Simon), 52*t*
Antarctica (Scott), 81–82
Are You Smarter Than a 5th Grader? (TV show), 19
Armbruster, B.B., 19, 33
Aronson, E., 192
assessment options: Assessment Tool to Assess How Your Little Buddy Is Doing, 262, 263*f;* for guided reading groups, 141–145; for literature circles, 201–202; Literature Discussion Sheet for Reciprocal Teaching, 101; Rubric for the Reciprocal Teaching Strategies, 43, 49, 100, 254*f*–257*f;* Self-Assessment Form for Reciprocal Teaching Literature Circles, 204*f;* student use of RT strategies, 60; for whole-class sessions, 100–101
Assessment Tool to Assess How Your Little Buddy Is Doing, 262, 263*f*

B

Bailey, Cathy, 106
Ballard, Robert, 176
Barker, Mary Jo, 47, 119
Basic Comprehension Chart for Guided Reading Groups, 149, 153*f*
Be the Teacher strategies, 16
Beach, S.A., 1
Because of Winn-Dixie (DiCamillo), 172
Benchmark Assessment System, 41
Bender, W., 36

Bennett, B., 119
Beverly Hills Chihuahua (film), 97
Beyond Monet (Bennett and Rolheiser), 119
Birmingham, John, 67
Bishop, Nic, 171
Blaney, N., 192
Block, C.C., 1, 5, 52
Blume, Judy, 187
bookmarks: Clarify Bookmark minilesson, 181–182, 182*f;* lesson using, 70–74; as print supports, 56–57. *See also* Fab Four Bookmark
Boschken, I., 2, 36, 38
Boushey, G., 146
Bridge to Terabithia (Paterson), 187
Brown, A.L., 2, 3, 7, 19, 78, 133, 190, 225, 241
Bunting, Eve, 52*t*
Burton, Martin Nelson, 121
Buscheck, Sandy, 89

C

Caldera, Cheryl, 106
Call of the Wild (London), 122
Campione, J., 7, 241
Canfield, Jack, 76
Carter, C.J., 3, 7, 241
Cassidy, D., 1
Cassidy, J., 1
Charlie Anderson (Abercrombie), 52*t,* 109
Chen, Glorianna, 93, 140, 141*f*
Chet Gecko Mystery series (Hale), 52*t,* 221
Chicken Soup for the Teenage Soul (Canfield et al.), 76
Chiola-Nakai, D., 197
Clara the Clarifier character: introducing RT strategies, 49, 77, 79, 80*f;* nonfiction text, 82–83

clarifying strategy: about, 20–22; Clara the Clarifier character, 49, 77, 79, 80f; Clarify and Underline a Word or Idea minilesson, 126–127; Clarify It: Picture It! minilesson, 237; coaching prompts, 143t; common problems, 249; examples, 16; Fab Four Bookmark, 74, 159; Fab Four Lesson Plan Menu, 267f, 268f; Fishbowl lesson, 213f; Four Door lesson, 106–109; generic plan for fiction/nonfiction lesson, 150–152; graphic organizers lesson, 159; hand gesture for, 54t, 55, 87; icon and strategy posters, 275f; mentor texts, 52t; metacognition and, 169–172, 173f; nonfiction text, 82–83; overcoming difficulties with, 26t; Pause and Clarify It! minilesson, 87–88; RTI and, 38; Rubric for the Reciprocal Teaching Strategies, 256f, 257f; sample prompts for, 21; Which One Do We Need? Name That Strategy! lesson, 114–115

Clark, C., 97

Clay, M.M., 132, 178

Cloud Forest (Bishop), 171

coaching prompts: coaching lesson, 164–167, 168f; guided reading groups, 142t–143t, 159; Reciprocal Teaching Observation Chart, 165, 166, 168f

Coley, J.D., 3

comprehension charts: Basic Comprehension Chart for Guided Reading Groups, 149, 153f; generic plan for fiction/nonfiction lesson, 148–149; graphic organizers lesson, 155–159, 160f–163f

Cooper, J.D., 2, 3, 7, 8, 19, 36, 37, 38, 59, 103, 133, 134, 136, 137, 241, 242

cooperative learning: about, 28, 33–34, 34t; classroom example, 35; Cooperative Group Summaries minilesson, 128–129; cooperative table groups lesson, 102–105; generic plan for fiction/nonfiction lesson, 149; Prediction Stroll Line

minilesson, 124; RTI and, 41; during whole-class lessons, 99

Craig, S., 3

cross-age tutors: Assessment Tool to Assess How Your Little Buddy Is Doing, 262, 263f; Focused Strategy Lessons to Use With Your Little Buddy, 262, 264f; strengthening comprehension with, 258–262

Cunningham, J.W., 147

Cunningham, P.M., 147

D

The Daily 5 (Boushey and Moser), 145

Daniels, H., 188, 190, 196, 247

Deeper Reading (Gallagher), 146

DePinto, T., 3

Developmental Reading Assessment (DRA), 37, 242

DiCamillo, Kate, 172

Diller, D., 146

discussion director: Fab Four Free-for-All! lesson, 232–233; Fishbowl lesson, 209, 215f–216f; literature circles and, 197–198

Dole, J.A., 2

DRA (Developmental Reading Assessment), 37, 242

"Drop It While It's Hot" (Snoop Dogg), 116

dry-erase boards, 57

Duffy, G.G., 2, 5

Duke, N.K., 1, 2, 5, 22

E

Eggleton, J., 2, 16, 36, 92

ELLs (English-language learners): clarifying strategy and, 21; cooperative learning and, 33; Fab Four gestures, 53; print supports and, 56; small-group instruction and, 134

Erickson, L.G., 23

Estes, Eleanor, 117

Extreme Explorer magazine, 109

F

Fab Four Bookmark: about, 56; coaching lesson, 165; cooperative table groups lesson, 102–103; cross-age tutoring example, 260; Do All Four Challenge! lesson, 225–226; Fab Four Free-for-All! lesson, 231–232; Fast Fab Four lesson, 174; generic plan for fiction/nonfiction lesson, 148, 150, 151; graphic organizers lesson, 159; Jigsaw Expert Huddles lesson, 217; lesson using, 70–74, 72*f*; Reciprocal Teaching Spinner lesson, 228; in whole-class lessons, 98

Fab Four characters: introducing RT strategies, 49–50; lesson introducing, 77–79, 80*f*; nonfiction text, 81–83; props for, 50*f*, 51*f*. *See also specific characters*

Fab Four Chart: coaching lesson, 165; generic plan for fiction/nonfiction lesson, 151; graphic organizers lesson, 155–157, 160*f*; guided reading groups and, 132, 151, 155–157, 160*f*; using with reading materials, 62*t*; watching RT strategies lesson, 169.

Fab Four Combo Chart, 156, 162*f*–163*f*

Fab Four Dial: about, 58–59, 59*f*; Fast Fab Four lesson, 174; guided reading groups and, 132

Fab Four Lesson Plan Menu, 265–266, 267*f*, 268*f*

Fab Four Mat: cooperative table groups lesson, 103; engaging students, 92; Pass the Mat lesson, 119–123

Fab Four strategies. *See* RT strategies

Fast Fab Four lesson, 174–176, 177*f*

Fawson, P., 2, 134, 242

Ferriter, W.M., 271

fiction text: discussion director role sheet, 215*f*; Fab Four Combo Chart, 156, 162*f*; generic plan for lesson, 148–154; predicting with, 18*t*

Fielding, L.G., 19, 29, 96

Fishbowl lesson, 191–192, 206–210, 208*f*, 211*f*–216*f*

Fly Facts (Marriott and Keylock), 144

focus strategy of the day, 199–201

Focused Strategy Lessons to Use With Your Little Buddy, 262, 264*f*

Fooling the Tooth Fairy (Burton), 121

Ford, Jaime, 200

Ford, M.P., 146, 147

Fountas, I.C., 39, 41, 131, 132, 147

Four Door Chart: cooperative learning and, 35; cooperative table groups lesson, 102; Fab Four Free-for-All! lesson, 231; guided reading groups and, 111, 137, 141, 144, 146; instructions for making, 110–111; introducing RT strategies, 48–49; Jigsaw Expert Huddles lesson, 217, 218; literature circles and, 202, 207; Pause and Clarify It! minilesson, 87–88; Pop the Questions minilesson, 85–86; RTI and, 41; Rubric for the Reciprocal Teaching Strategies, 49, 108; sample, 48*f*, 112*f*; whole-class lesson, 106–109.

"Frère Jacques" (song), 115

Fuchs, D., 38

Fuchs, L.S., 38

Funky Fish (Eggleton), 16

G

Gallagher, K., 146

Gallagher, M.C., 97

Gardner, R., 3

Gaye, Marvin, 116

Gibbons, Gail, 95

Gleam and Glow (Bunting), 52*t*

Goudvis, A., 2, 4, 5

graphic organizers: guided reading groups and, 155–159, 160*f*–163*f*; literature circles and, 188, 189*f*

Great Hearts (Weber), 219

Grillo, Jennifer, 76

Grimm, Brian, 53

guided reading groups: about, 131–134, 141*f*; assessment options for,

141–145; Basic Comprehension Chart for Guided Reading Groups, 149, 153*f*; Clarify Bookmark minilesson, 181–182, 182*f*; coaching lesson, 164–167, 168*f*; coaching prompts, 142*t*–143*t*, 159; common questions, 248–249; content area textbooks and, 140–141; Draw or Dramatize Summaries minilesson, 184; Fab Four Chart and, 132, 151, 155–157, 160*f*; Fab Four Combo Chart, 156, 162*f*–163*f*; Fab Four Dial and, 132; Fast Fab Four lesson, 174–176, 177*f*; Four Door Chart and, 111, 137, 141, 144, 146; generic plan for fiction/nonfiction lesson, 148–154; getting started, 247; goals of, 135; graphic organizers lesson, 155–159, 160*f*–163*f*; intermediate-grade students and, 133–134; literature circles and, 145; Literature Discussion Sheet for Reciprocal Teaching, 136, 139*t*, 144, 152; organizing, 136–141, 139*t*; power of, 134–135; professional resources for, 146; Project Success Model, 134; promoting independence with, 250, 251*t*; Question Starters minilesson, 180–181; Reciprocal Teaching Guided Reading Lesson Plan Guide, 149, 154*f*; reciprocal teaching in, 10, 11*t*, 46; Reciprocal Teaching Observation Chart, 151, 165, 166, 168*f*; recommendations, 147; RT strategies and, 140–141, 169–172, 173*f*; Rubric for the Reciprocal Teaching Strategies, 139*t*, 141–142; Story Map Prediction Chart, 156, 161*f*; struggling readers and, 95, 137, 139*t*; Watch Your Q's and C's Record Sheet, 169, 171, 173*f*; watching strategies lesson, 169–172, 173*f*; what to do with rest of class, 145–147; Word Pop Prediction minilesson, 178–179

H

Hacker, D.J., 219

Hale, Bruce, 52*t*, 221

hand motion/gesture: with clarifying strategy, 54*t*, 55, 87; Fab Four Free-for-All! lesson, 232; for predicting strategy, 54*t*, 55; for questioning strategy, 54*t*, 55; for summarizing strategy, 54*t*, 55–56; supports and practical tools, 52–62, 54*t*

Hansen, J., 19

Hanson, Mark Victor, 76

Harvey, S., 2, 4, 5

Hatchet (Paulsen), 233

Heffernan, L., 197

Henson, Matthew, 109

Hiebert, E.H., 132

Hill, B.C., 190, 196, 197

The Hotel on the Corner of Bitter and Sweet (Ford), 200

Howard, M., 36

Hoyt, L., 5, 146, 222

The Hundred Dresses (Estes), 117

I

"I Heard It Through the Grapevine" (Marvin Gaye), 116

icons: for dry-erase boards, 57; generic plan for fiction/nonfiction lesson, 148; for posters, 57

ideas: Clarify and Underline a Word or Idea minilesson, 126–127; Clarify Bookmark minilesson, 181–182, 182*f*; clarifying, 22

instructional foundations, 26–29. *See also* cooperative learning; metacognition; scaffolding; think-alouds

Internet Reciprocal Teaching (IRT), 269–271

The Invisible Man (Wells), 172

Ira Sleeps Over (Waber), 259

IRT (Internet Reciprocal Teaching), 269–271

J

Jenkens, Steve, 52*t*

Jigsaw Expert Huddle lesson, 192–194, 193f, 217–219
Johnson, N.J., 190, 197

K

K-W-L charts, 95–96
Kagan, S., 34, 206
Keene, E.O., 2, 4, 5, 19, 35, 70, 81
Kelly, M., 3
Keylock, Andy, 144
Kiger, N.D., 37
Kincade, K.M., 1
Kirberger, Kimberly, 76
Klenk, L.J., 3, 7, 241
Kohn, A., 93

L

"La Bamba" (Soto), 68, 122
Langham, Kathy, 6, 56, 134
Lee, Harper, 53, 93
Lehr, F., 19, 33
Leu, D.J, 270
Lipson, M.W., 22
Listen to the Wind (Mortenson and Roth), 52t
literature circles: about, 187–189; assessment options for, 201–202; Clarify It: Picture It! minilesson, 237; common questions, 247–248; discussion director, 197–198; Do All Four Challenge! lesson, 225–226; Fab Four Free-for-All! lesson, 231–234; Fishbowl lesson, 191–192, 206–210, 208f, 211f–216f; focus strategy of the day, 199–201; Four Door Chart, 202, 207; with Four Door Chart, 110; getting started, 194, 195t–196t, 246; goals of, 189–190; guided reading groups and, 145; I Predict That I Will Learn... minilesson, 235; incorporating other strategies, 196–201; introducing to students, 190–196; Jigsaw Expert Huddle lesson, 192–194, 193f, 217–219; Limited-Word Summary Challenge! minilesson, 238; Literature Discussion Sheet for Reciprocal Teaching, 202, 205f,

207; Pick a Question minilesson, 236; Post Your Question minilesson, 125; practicing strategies lesson, 227–229, 230f; promoting independence with, 250, 251t; reciprocal teaching in, 10, 11t, 46; Reciprocal Teaching Observation Sheet, 199, 203f, 207, 209; Reciprocal Teaching Spinner, 230f; Rotating Roles lesson, 207, 220–221; RTI and, 41; Rubric for the Reciprocal Teaching Strategies, 201, 229; Self-Assessment Form for Reciprocal Teaching Literature Circles, 202, 204f, 219; training for, 194, 194t, 198–199; What I Know strips, 222–224, 223f; What I Wonder strips, 222–224, 223f
Literature Discussion Sheet for Reciprocal Teaching: cooperative table groups lesson, 102–103; Fishbowl lesson, 211f; guided reading groups and, 136, 139t, 144, 152; Jigsaw Expert Huddles lesson, 217, 218; literature circles and, 202, 205f, 207; whole-class sessions and, 101
"The Little Blue Engine" (Silverstein), 47
London, Jack, 122
Lubliner, S., 2, 3, 19, 36, 241

M

Mancini, Henry, 76
March of the Penguins (film), 82
Marriott, D., 197
Marriott, Janice, 144
Martin, S.M., 190
McLaughlin, M., 2, 4, 5, 17, 70, 81, 196, 240, 245
McWilliams, J., 2, 36, 38
Meddaugh, Susan, 52t
Meister, C., 3
mentor texts: recommended titles, 52t; RT strategies and, 51–52
metacognition: about, 28, 32–33; classroom example, 33; Fab Four Dial and, 58, 59f; RT strategies

lesson, 169–172, 173*f*; RTI and, 41; during whole-class lessons, 98–99
Miller, D., 5
Moore, D.W., 3
Morgan, Michaela, 176
Morris, B., 197
Mortenson, Greg, 52*t*
Moser, J., 146
Mowery, S., 18, 255
Mr Grumpy's Outing (Birmingham), 67
Muise, M.R., 197
Mummies (Wilcox), 144
Muth, Jon J., 52*t*
Myers, P.A., 3

N

National Center for Education Statistics, 1, 53
National Geographic, 109
National Institute of Child Health and Human Development, 2, 38, 39, 46, 90, 243
National Reading Panel, 38
The Night Owl (Eggleton), 92
Noe, K.S., 190, 197
nonfiction text: discussion director role sheet, 216*f*; Fab Four characters, 81–83; Fab Four Combo Chart, 156, 163*f*; generic plan for lesson, 148–154; guided reading groups and, 140; predicting with, 18*t*

O

Oczkus, L.D., 2, 4, 5, 6, 11, 18, 23, 25, 27, 30, 31, 34, 36, 40, 48, 49, 50, 51, 52, 53, 54, 57, 59, 62, 72, 74, 76, 80, 82, 107, 110, 111, 112, 116, 123, 139, 143, 146, 147, 153, 154, 158, 160, 161, 162, 163, 168, 173, 177, 178, 183, 189, 193, 194, 196, 197, 200, 203, 204, 205, 206, 208, 211, 212, 213, 214, 215, 216, 221, 223, 230, 244, 245, 251, 255, 256, 257, 263, 264, 267, 268, 273, 274, 275, 276
Ogle, D., 95, 222

Opitz, M.F., 146, 147, 151
Osborn, J., 19, 33
Owl Moon (Yolen), 52*t*

P

Page, Robin, 52*t*
Page, Susan, 145
Palincsar, A.S., 2, 3, 7, 19, 78, 133, 190, 225, 241
Paris, S.G., 55
Parris, S.R., 1, 5
Paterson, Katherine, 187
Patty Reed's Doll, 233
Paulsen, Gary, 233
Payne, C.D., 131, 147
Pearson, P.D., 1, 2, 5, 19, 22, 29, 70, 81, 96, 97
People magazine, 97
Perenfein, D., 197
Peter the Predictor character. *See* Powerful Predictor character
Peterson, B., 132, 138
Pikulski, J.J., 132, 136
Pinnell, G.S., 39, 41, 131, 132, 147
Pistochini, L., 2, 36, 38
Platnick, Norman, 132
Plummer, S., 53
poetry, shared reading of, 47–48
posters: icons for, 57, 273*f*–276*f*; as print supports, 56, 57*f*
Powerful Predictor character: introducing RT strategies, 49, 77, 79, 80*f*; nonfiction text, 81–82
predicting strategy: about, 17–19; coaching prompts, 143*t*; common problems, 249; examples, 16; Fab Four Bookmark, 74; Fab Four Lesson Plan Menu, 267*f,* 268*f*; with fiction, 18*t*; Fishbowl lesson, 211*f*; Four Door lesson, 106–109; generic plan for fiction/nonfiction lesson, 151–152; hand gesture for, 54*t,* 55; I Predict That I Will Learn... minilesson, 235; icon and strategy posters, 273*f*; mentor texts, 52*t*; with nonfiction, 18*t*; nonfiction text, 81–82; overcoming difficulties with, 26*t*; Powerful Predictor

character, 49, 77, 79, 80*f,* 81–82; Prediction Stroll Line minilesson, 124; Roll Your Prediction! minilesson, 84; RTI and, 38; Rubric for the Reciprocal Teaching Strategies, 255*f,* 257*f;* Which One Do We Need? Name That Strategy! lesson, 114; Word Pop Prediction minilesson, 178–179

Pressley, M., 2, 5, 39

print supports: bookmarks, 56–57; Fab Four Dial, 58, 59*f;* posters, 56, 57*f;* strategy dice, 58

Project Success Model, 134

Q

QRI (Qualitative Reading Inventory), 37

Qualitative Reading Inventory (QRI), 37

questioning strategy: about, 19–20; coaching prompts, 143*t;* common problems, 249; examples, 16; Fab Four Bookmark, 74; Fab Four Lesson Plan Menu, 267*f,* 268*f;* Fishbowl lesson, 208, 208*f,* 212*f;* Four Door lesson, 106–109; generic plan for fiction/nonfiction lesson, 150–152; hand gesture for, 54*t,* 55; icon and strategy posters, 274*f;* mentor texts, 52*t;* metacognition and, 169–172, 173*f;* nonfiction text, 82; overcoming difficulties with, 26*t;* Pick a Question minilesson, 236; Pop the Questions minilesson, 85–86; Post Your Question minilesson, 125; Question Starters minilesson, 180–181; Quincy the Questioner character, 49, 77, 79, 80*f;* RTI and, 38; Rubric for the Reciprocal Teaching Strategies, 255*f,* 257*f;* Which One Do We Need? Name That Strategy! lesson, 114

Quincy the Questioner character: introducing RT strategies, 49, 77, 79, 80*f;* nonfiction text, 82

R

Rasinski, T., 151

read-aloud lessons: cooperative table groups and, 102–105; introducing RT strategies, 47, 64–69; reinforcing RT strategies, 64–69; whole-group instruction and, 95

reading comprehension: additional resources, 4, 5*t;* improving, 250, 251*t;* RT strategies and, 17

Reading Recovery level, 138

reciprocal teaching (RT): additional resources, 36*t;* assessment options, 43; in classroom settings, 10, 11*t;* common questions, 241–250; fitting into reading programs, 4–6; goals of, 2–3; incorporating, 244*t;* instructional foundations, 26–35, 26*t*–27*t;* Internet and, 269–271; introducing, 46–52; limitations of, 35–36; next steps, 63; overcoming obstacles, 23–24, 24*t*–25*t;* personal experiences with, 6–8; promoting independence with, 250, 251*t;* reading programs and, 4–6; research on, 3–4; RTI and, 36–43, 39*t*–40*t;* strategies for, 1–2, 16–23; support tools for, 52–62, 54*t.* *See also* guided reading groups; literature circles; think-alouds; whole-class sessions

Reciprocal Teaching Guided Reading Lesson Plan Guide, 149, 154*f*

Reciprocal Teaching Observation Chart: coaching lesson, 165, 166, 168*f;* guided reading groups and, 151, 165, 166, 168*f;* for variety of reading materials, 62*t;* watching RT strategies lesson, 169

Reciprocal Teaching Observation Sheet, 199, 203*f,* 207, 209

Reciprocal Teaching Spinner: Do All Four Challenge! lesson, 225–226; Fab Four Dial and, 58, 59*f;* generic plan for fiction/nonfiction lesson, 148; practicing strategies lesson, 227–229, 230*f*

recorders, role of, 103

Response to Intervention. *See* RTI (Response to Intervention)

Reutzel, D.R., 2, 46, 90, 134, 242

Rinehart, S.D., 23

Robinson, M.D., 37

Roehler, L.R., 2

role sheets: Fishbowl lesson, 191–192, 206–210, 208*f*, 211*f*–216*f*; Rotating Roles lesson, 207, 220–221; training for students, 210. *See also* Fab Four characters

Rolheiser, C., 119

Rosenblatt, L.C., 36

Rosenshine, B., 3

Rotating Roles lesson, 207, 220–221

Roth, Susan L., 52*t*

Routman, R., 99, 145–146, 189

RT. *See* reciprocal teaching

RT strategies: about, 1–2, 16; Clarify and Underline a Word or Idea minilesson, 126–127; coaching lesson, 164–167, 168*f*; coaching prompts, 142*t*–143*t*; common questions, 241–250; Cooperative Group Summaries minilesson, 128–129; cooperative table groups lesson, 102–105; Do All Four Challenge! lesson, 225–226; Fab Four Free-for-All! lesson, 231–234; Fab Four Lesson Plan Menu, 265–266, 267*f*, 268*f*; Fishbowl lesson, 211*f*–216*f*; focus strategy of the day, 199–201; Four Door lesson, 106–109; generic plan for fiction/nonfiction lesson, 148–154; guided reading groups and, 140–141, 169–172, 173*f*; icon and strategy posters, 273*f*–276*f*; introducing, 46–52, 50*f*, 51*f*; lesson introducing, 64–69, 75–83, 80*f*; lesson reinforcing, 64–69; mentor texts and, 51–52; metacognition lesson, 169–172, 173*f*; next steps, 63; Pass the Mat lesson, 119–123; Post Your Question minilesson, 125; practicing strategies lesson, 227–229, 230*f*; Prediction Stroll Line minilesson, 124; reading materials to use with, 59–60, 61*t*–62*t*; Which One Do We Need? Name That Strategy! lesson, 113–118. *See also* clarifying strategy; predicting strategy; questioning strategy; Reciprocal Teaching Spinner; summarizing strategy

RTI (Response to Intervention): about, 36–39; examples, 37–38; tier concept, 36–37, 39*t*–40*t*, 41–43

Rubric for the Reciprocal Teaching Strategies: about, 254*f*–257*f*; as assessment tool, 43; coaching lesson, 166; Four Door Chart and, 49, 108; guided reading groups, 139*t*, 141–142; literature circles and, 201, 229; Reciprocal Teaching Spinner lesson, 229; whole-class sessions, 100, 108, 120

S

Sammy the Summarizer character: introducing RT strategies, 49, 77–78, 79, 80*f*; nonfiction text, 83

Samuels, S.J., 133

Samway, K.D., 190, 196, 197

scaffolding: about, 28, 29, 30*f*; classroom example, 29–30; Four Door lesson, 108; RTI and, 41; in whole-class lessons, 97–98

Schulman, M.B., 131, 147

Scott, Jonathan and Angela, 82

Self-Assessment Form for Reciprocal Teaching Literature Circles, 202, 204*f*, 219

shared reading of poetry, 47–48

Shear, J., 197

Shores, C., 36

Sikes, J., 192

Silverstein, Shel, 47

Simon, Seymour, 52*t*

Slavin, R.E., 136

small-group instruction: alternating with whole-class sessions, 94–96; ELL students and, 134; promoting independence with, 250, 251*t*. *See also* guided reading groups

smart work, defined, 145

Smith, J.A., 2, 134, 242
Snapp, M., 192
Snoop Dogg, 116
"Snow Globe," 146
Soar to Success program, 134
social skills, training students in, 198–199
Soto, Gary, 68, 122
staff development guide, 9–10
Stahl, S.A., 23
Stephin, C., 192
sticky notes, 150, 169–170
Story Map Prediction Chart, 156, 161*f*
The Stranger (Van Allsburg), 52*t*
strategies. *See* RT strategies
strategy dice: about, 58; Roll Your Prediction! minilesson, 84
summarizing strategy: about, 22–23; A Clear Summary minilesson, 89; coaching prompts, 143*t*; common problems, 249; Cooperative Group Summaries minilesson, 128–129; Draw or Dramatize Summaries minilesson, 184; examples, 16; Fab Four Bookmark, 74; Fab Four Lesson Plan Menu, 267*f*, 268*f*; Fishbowl lesson, 214*f*; Four Door lesson, 106–109; generic plan for fiction/nonfiction lesson, 151–152; hand gesture for, 54*t*, 55–56; icon and strategy posters, 276*f*; Limited-Word Summary Challenge! minilesson, 238; mentor texts, 52*t*; nonfiction text, 83; overcoming difficulties with, 26*t*; RTI and, 38; Rubric for the Reciprocal Teaching Strategies, 256*f*, 257*f*; Sammy the Summarizer character, 49, 77–78, 79, 80*f*; sample prompts for, 23; Which One Do We Need? Name That Strategy! lesson, 115
Sunken Treasures (Gibbons), 95
supports and practical tools: hand gestures/motions, 52–62, 54*t*; print supports, 56–59
Survivor (TV show), 233–234
Sweet, A.P., 133

T
table runners, role of, 103
Tales of a Fourth Grade Nothing (Blume), 187
Tarantulas Are Spiders (Platnick), 132
Taylor, B.M., 23, 38, 132
Tenent, A., 219
textbooks, guided reading and, 140–141
think-alouds: about, 28, 30–31; classroom example, 31–32; cooperative learning and, 34; Fab Four characters and, 49, 77–79, 80*f*; Four Door lesson, 108; RTI and, 41; during whole-class lessons, 98; whole-group instruction and, 95
"This Old Man" (song), 116
The Three Questions (Muth), 52*t*
Tiger's Tale (Morgan), 176
Time for Kids magazine, 94
Titanic (Ballard), 176
To Kill a Mockingbird (Lee), 53, 93
Tree of Birds (Meddaugh), 52*t*
Tuck, B.F., 3
Turner, J.C., 55

V
Van Allsburg, Chris, 52*t*
Vasquez, V., 197
Vaughn S., 38
Vogt, M.E., 5
Vygotsky, L.S., 187

W
Waber, Bernard, 259
Wasik, B.A., 55
Watch Your Q's and C's Record Sheet, 169, 171, 173*f*
Weber, Rebecca, 219
Wells, H.G., 172
Whang, G., 190, 196, 197
What Do You Do With a Tail Like This? (Jenkens and Page), 52*t*
What I Know strips, 222–224, 223*f*
What I Wonder strips, 222–224, 223*f*
Whiteley, C.S., 1
whole-class sessions: alternating with small-group instruction, 94–96;

assessment options, 100–101; Clarify and Underline a Word or Idea minilesson, 126–127; common pitfalls, 100; Cooperative Group Summaries minilesson, 128–129; cooperative table groups lesson, 102–105; engaging students in, 92–94; essential foundations for, 97–99; with Four Door Chart, 106–109, 110; getting started, 246–247; goals of, 96; Pass the Mat lesson, 119–123; Post Your Question minilesson, 125; Prediction Stroll Line minilesson, 124; promoting independence with, 250, 251t; reciprocal teaching in, 10, 11t, 46; recommendations for, 99–100; Rubric for the Reciprocal Teaching Strategies, 100, 108, 120; Which One Do We Need? Name That Strategy! lesson, 113–118

Wilcox, Charlotte, 144

Wise, Julie, 76

words: Clarify and Underline a Word or Idea minilesson, 126–127; Clarify Bookmark minilesson, 181–182, 182f; clarifying, 22; Limited-Word Summary Challenge! minilesson, 238; Word Pop Prediction minilesson, 178–179

Wormeli, R., 49

Y

Yolen, Jane, 52t

Z

Zimmermann, S., 2, 4, 5, 19, 35, 70, 81